Herman Melville.
813.009

Arvin,

D0215760

DATE DUE

813.009   18095
Mel

Herman Melville

The American Men of Letters Series

The American Men of Letters Series

Herman Melville

Herman Melville

Newton Arvin

The American Men of Letters Series

GREENWOOD PRESS, PUBLISHERS
WESTPORT, CONNECTICUT

Library of Congress Cataloging in Publication Data

Arvin, Newton, 1900-1963.
    Herman Melville.

    Original ed. issued in series: The American men of
letters series.
    Bibliography: p.
    1. Melville, Herman, 1819-1891. I. Series: The
American men of letters series.
PS2386.A7 1972   813'.3   72-7818
ISBN 0-8371-6524-5

Typography and format designed by

LEONARD W. BLIZARD

Copyright, 1950, by William Sloane Associates, Inc.

Originally published in 1950 by William Sloane Associates,
New York

Reprinted with the permission of William Morrow & Cor
Inc.

Reprinted by Greenwood Press, Inc.

First Greenwood reprinting   1972
Second Greenwood reprinting   1975
Third Greenwood reprinting   1977

Library of Congress catalog card number 72-7818

ISBN 0-8371-6524-5

Printed in the United States of America

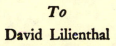

To
David Lilienthal

Contents

Acknowledgments

I N THE WRITING of this book I have incurred even more obligations than one usually does in such cases. My indebtedness to other writers, both critics and scholars, is so heavy that I have long since ceased to be certain about all of its items. The Bibliographical Note is an attempt to discharge some of these, but it is a very incomplete one, and I must hereby make general acknowledgment to two or three score of writers about Melville, without whose work a book of this sort could not be written.

Like everyone whose interest in Melville has carried him very far, I am deeply indebted to Eleanor Melville Metcalf, his granddaughter, whose kindness to me, as to so many others, has been unlimited.

The heaviest of my obligations to other scholars is that to Professor William H. Gilman, of the University of Rochester, who has allowed me to make use of his unpublished doctoral dissertation (Yale, 1947) on "Melville's Early Life and *Redburn*." Mr. Gilman's treatment of the subject is so painstaking that it amounts to a rewriting of the early chapters of Melville's biography, and in giving an account of Melville's early years in Albany, in Lansingburgh, and on the *St. Lawrence*, I could not have dispensed with his work. Mr. Gilman now has a volume of his own in preparation, and when this appears it will be evident how much I owe to his generosity.

Professor Harrison Hayford and Professor Merrell R. Davis very kindly allowed me to make use of an unpublished article by them on "Herman Melville as Office-Seeker," which has since appeared in the *Modern Language Quarterly*. Mr. Jay Leyda has been unfailingly generous in giving me the benefit of his inspired researches into Melville's biography.

In writing of Melville's life in the South Seas I have felt myself on firmer ground than I should otherwise have done, as a result not only of consulting the published writings of Professor Ralph Linton, of Yale University, but of personal talks with Professor Linton about Polynesian life and culture, and particularly about the Marquesans, on whom he is our leading authority.

Mrs. John Hall Wheelock has courteously permitted me to quote from a manuscript essay (and probably an unpublished one) by her father, Charles DeKay, on "The Birth of the Authors' Club."

For permission to quote from unpublished letters and other papers and to refer to annotations in Melville's own books, all at the Houghton Library, I am under obligation to the Committee on Higher Degrees in the History of American Civilization at Harvard University. Mr. Robert W. Hill, Keeper of Manuscripts at the New York Public Library, has been extremely helpful in allowing me to use the papers in the Gansevoort-Lansing Collection there; and Mr. Paul North Rice, Chief of the Reference Department at the same library, has answered fully and patiently more than one question I have put to him. I am also indebted for much valuable assistance to Miss Margaret L. Johnson, Librarian of the Smith College Library. Mr. F. B. Laughlin, Assistant Collector in the Bureau of Customs, New York, has put me in his debt by answering at length some of my queries to him.

To my colleague and friend, Professor Daniel Aaron, I am particularly grateful for his patient reading of the whole book in manuscript and for making many helpful suggestions.

I should perhaps say that this book was finished too early for me to avail myself of either the information or the insights in Professor Howard P. Vincent's book on *The Trying-Out of Moby Dick* or in Professor Richard Chase's *Herman Melville.*

Herman Melville

Loomings

THE ECCENTRIC physician, Thomas Low Nichols, once well known for his views on dietary reform and hydrotherapy, dropped in, one day in the middle 'forties, at the Wall Street law-office of his young friends, the brothers Gansevoort and Allan Melville. Gansevoort, the elder of the two, had recently taken part on the Democratic side in the campaign of 1844, and had just received his reward for these services by being made secretary of the American legation in London. He was to be congratulated of course, but Nichols felt, as Melville himself doubtless did, that he was to be condoled with, too; he was a poor man, and his salary at the legation would scarcely be enough to pay for his gloves and his cab hire. They spoke of these gloomy matters, and then a little later, when the subject had been changed, the other Melville, Allan, remarked that the two of them had a third brother, a brother whom Nichols had never seen. He had been "a little wild," said Allan, and while still hardly more than a boy had run away to sea, sailing first to England and then, after a year or so, joining the crew of a New Bedford whaler and voyaging in the South Pacific. "He got home a few months ago," added Allan Melville, "and has been writing something about his adventures among the cannibals. Would you like to look at it?"

As it happened, Dr. Nichols, who had a couple of hours to spare, did have a curiosity to see it. He sat down immediately, he later said, and opened the package of "the sailor boy's" manuscript. It was a book entitled *Typee,* and the brother of his friends was of course Herman Melville. Nichols read through the manuscript, he tells us, at one sitting, was convinced at once that it would be a great success, and advised Gansevoort Melville to take a copy with him to London and arrange for its publication there. The English reviews, he felt sure, would be eulogistic, and this would guarantee the success of the book in the United States; Nichols was by no means certain that the process could be reversed.

The opinionated doctor proved to be a shrewder judge of these matters than he was of a meat diet. Gansevoort Melville did take the manuscript of *Typee* to England with him; without much difficulty he persuaded John Murray to accept it, and late the next winter the young author's book was published simultaneously in London and New York. Its American title was *Typee: A Peep at Polynesian Life,* and as Nichols had predicted, it was a sensational success. Everybody read it; everybody felt that he had to read it and express an opinion about it; everybody felt that he had to take sides about the book pro or con. There were those who alleged that hardly a word of it was to be accepted without scrutiny. There were others who found it as easy to believe as any travel book of its sort, and easier than many. Still others were outraged by *Typee* on moral grounds, and in a manner that only heightened its appeal for the majority: it was "profligate," "voluptuous," "perverse." It was written, protested a church review, to delight the voluptuaries of a corrupt London society, and had no place in a library of American books. But these cries of indignation, and of course the whispers of skepticism, were pretty well drowned out by the general din of enthusiasm. *Typee* "made the multitude crazy with delight," said a magazine writer two or three years later, and all voices, said another, "are unanimous in laudation of

its interest and pleasantness." The "vivacity," the "animation" of *Typee*, its "easy, gossiping style"—these and a dozen
other qualities of charm and liveliness were not to be resisted; and Herman Melville, so recently a penniless seaman,
had emerged almost explosively on the social and literary
scene as a celebrity of something like the first rank. Living
with his mother in an up-state town the following summer,
Melville came in one day from hoeing in the garden to find a
request, one of many, for his autograph. In supplying it he
remarked to his correspondent: "You remember someone
woke one morning and found himself famous." He himself
had tasted a little of Byron's sudden glory.

Meanwhile *Typee* had been reviewed in two particularly
interesting quarters. A few weeks after Walt Whitman had
become editor of the Brooklyn *Eagle*, and was certainly writing most of its book notices, that journal, reviewing Melville's volume, described it as "a strange, graceful, most read-
able book," and added: "As a book to hold in one's hand and
pore dreamily over of a summer's day, it is unsurpassed." The
early Whitman manner, the ruminative Whitman manner,
seems almost unmistakable; but whoever the reviewer in the
Eagle was there is no doubt that the critic of the Salem
Advertiser, in Massachusetts, was Nathaniel Hawthorne. To
Hawthorne, who had just moved back to Salem, Herman
Melville was as unknown personally as he was to Whitman,
but he could hold out against the spell of *Typee* as little as
any man. The book, he said, was lightly but vigorously
written, and he confessed to knowing no work that gave a
freer and more effective picture of primitive life. There were
scenes in the book, doubtless, that were not for the eyes of
the very young, the very chaste, or the very easily inflamed;
but how were these to be avoided in a faithful account of
Polynesian life and manners? The subject clearly demanded
a certain voluptuousness of coloring. The author "has that
freedom of view—it would be too harsh to call it laxity of
principle—which renders him tolerant of codes of morals that

may be little in accordance with our own; a spirit proper enough," added Hawthorne indulgently, "to a young and adventurous sailor, and which makes his book the more wholesome to our staid landsmen."

With such a send-off from the press as a whole, and particularly—though he could not have realized this at the moment —from two fellow-writers of genius, Gansevoort Melville's wild young brother was launched on his literary career.

At the time when *Typee* was being welcomed with so much enthusiasm, Herman Melville was a young man of just twenty-six—younger, for such fame, than any other American writer of his stature ever was. If he had been and perhaps still was a little wayward, there were plenty of things in his own history and in his family's to account for this. He was a man of genius, but he was not an inexplicable freak, and he came by even his wildness naturally enough. There was a strain of wildness, or at least of oddness and irregularity, in the family entourage, and no one could have been more aware of this than Melville himself. No one could have been more responsive, in his youth at least, to family consciousness and family pressure generally, and if he was an Ishmael, as of course he was, he was an Ishmael who dwelt always "in the presence of all his brethren."

His brethren were a strongly characterized group, on both sides of the house, but it strikes us very quickly as we look at what is known about them that they were characterized, on the two sides, in quite different and rather contradictory ways, and that they handed on to Melville a contrarious, unstable, yet very creative sort of heritage. There is a marked contrast, which one can hardly miss, between the Melvilles, his father's family, and his mother's, the Gansevoorts of Albany. The complexity, the contrariety, in his own nature had some of its roots in this ancestral antithesis. From the Melvilles, certainly, came the waywardness we have spoken of. So far as one can talk of inheritance at all, it was mainly from them Herman Melville derived what was restless, excitable, mercurial, and experimental in his nature; in short, no doubt, his essential gifts as a writer. Fortunately for his capacity to put those gifts to use, there was the other strain, the Dutch, the Hudson River, the Gansevoort strain; the strain of solidity, of toughness, of constitutional soundness and sanity, of a certain healthy and preservative dullness and phlegm, imperturbable, unexcited, and inert. By no means an unexampled union of opposites in family histories, but one that in this case is far more striking and proved to be far more fruitful than in most.

It was from his Albany forebears, from his mother's relatives, those corpulent and massive worthies who seem to have stepped straight out of *Knickerbocker's History*, that Melville inherited the bodily vigor, the reserve of stamina and even stolidity, that saw him through so much heavy stress, both physical and psychological; and he knew it. "A thoroughly developed gentleman is always robust and healthy," he says in *Pierre;* and in this sense he was glad to be regarded as a genuine offshoot of the Gansevoorts. Master-brewers when they had settled in Albany in the seventeenth century, the family had rapidly made their way upward toward the condition of landed gentry and even patroons. Large grants of land had come to an early ancestor for his exploits in an Indian war, and in the eighteenth century his descendants had proceeded to marry their sons and daughters into several of the great Hudson River families; Melville's ancestral line on this side reads a little like Irving's mock-heroic roll-call of the warriors who fought under Peter the Headstrong: "There were the Van Wycks, and the Van Dycks, and the Ten Eycks —the Van Nesses, the Van Tassels, the Van Grolls. . . ." There were at any rate, literally, the Ten Eycks, the Van Rensselaers, the Van Schaicks, and others; and then, in the epoch of the Revolution, the Gansevoorts had produced their Ajax in the person of General Peter Gansevoort, the hero of Fort Stanwix.

This grandfather had died five or six years before Herman was born, but his memory had by no means died with him in family circles, and his reliquiae lay all about Melville in his boyhood. He is the heroic old general in *Pierre*, of course, the hero's grandfather, "grand old Pierre," and the younger man's ancestor-worship in the novel is not far from pure autobiography on Melville's part. There is a portrait of General Glendinning in *Pierre* which inspires in his grandson a longing to behold the original in life; and in reality there is a portrait of General Gansevoort by Gilbert Stuart which Melville knew well in his childhood. As represented there, Peter Gansevoort is a soldierly, middle-aged man in regimentals, with epaulettes and an order, cutting very much the same sort of figure as, say, General Henry Knox or General Horatio Gates; stout and even heavy, broad-shouldered, full-cheeked, blue-eyed, and florid, with a look of uncomplicated candor and untroubled exteriority. "Unruffledness" is the word Melville uses for the look of the fictional General, and the real General Gansevoort can rarely have been flustered or shaken. His one great characteristic action had been a feat of tenacity. Everyone in New York state once knew that Peter Gansevoort had held Fort Stanwix, where the city of Rome now is, against the attacks of the British and their Indian allies marching down the Mohawk Valley to join forces with Burgoyne as he moved southward from Canada. Certainly Herman Melville knew all this, as he knew the large kettledrum his grandfather had captured from the British, and the silver-tipped ceremonial staff he had wielded in military reviews. What wonder if the contemplation of these facts and these relics in boyhood inspired in him, as they did in Pierre, "a little twinge or two of what one might call family pride"?

For his grandfather had been only the most eminent and prosperous of a generally eminent and prosperous clan. Their public distinction and worldly well-being had been a fixed point of reference for Herman Melville throughout his boyhood and youth. When the boy Wellingborough Redburn, in Melville's fourth book, boasts, in his forlornness and penury, of having had a great-uncle who had been a member of Congress in the days of the old Constitution, and "used him upon all emergencies, like the knight in the game of chess," he was departing only a little from the actualities. Melville's great-uncle, Leonard Gansevoort, had not been a member of Congress, to be sure, but he had been a leader in the old Provincial Congress of New York during the Revolutionary years and afterward a state senator at Albany. Closer to the boy Melville, solidifying and aggrandizing half the immediate scene of family life, were his uncle Leonard Herman Gansevoort (another general and the uncle after whom he was named) and Leonard Herman's brother, Peter Gansevoort, who had been private secretary to DeWitt Clinton, and was later a judge of the Court of Common Pleas; one of the principal gentlemen, as they would have said at the time, of his city and his state.

It was into this notable clan that Melville's father, Allan Melville, had married, four or five years before Herman was born. His own family of Boston merchants were only a shade or two less notable than his wife's connections; they had indeed not very remote relations among the Scots peerage, a fact of which they were very conscious; but in any case they were a good many shades more vivid and even volatile than the Gansevoorts. A glance at the portrait of Allan Melville's father, at the long, narrow, osseous face, the high-arched nose, the salient cheekbones, the heavy-lidded, cogitative eyes, and the tense mouth, would be enough to tell one that. If General Gansevoort's countenance is that of a Dutch brewer refined and ennobled, Major Melville's is that of a Scots Covenanter only a little mollified by prosperity and Boston. And indeed he had acted, during the revolutionary struggle, in the truculent, uncompromising spirit of his Presbyterian ancestors in Glasgow and St. Andrew's. Conservative though he was by temper and association, he was a Boston merchant on whom the restrictive acts of Parliament no doubt bore heavily, and at an early hour he had allied himself with the disaffected elements; he had been one of the famous band of "Mohawks" who had boarded the ships of the East India Company in Boston Harbor, one night in 1773, and dumped the offending cargo into the water. His descendants were to preserve for many years a vial of tea leaves that had been gathered from his boots on that memorable night.

Major Melville's later life had been respectable and meritorious rather than dramatic. He was for many years surveyor and inspector of the port of Boston—a post to which Washington had appointed him—and then naval officer of the port— a post from which Andrew Jackson had removed him; but there are reported traits, even in the older man, which point to the strain in him of something ever so slightly unstable, capricious, and off-center. One of these was his passion for attending fires—he was one of the fire-wards of Boston—a passion which is said to have grown upon him "like gambling," and at last to have brought on his death from exposure and fatigue at the age of more than eighty. Psychiatry today would no doubt have its commentary on this curious trait, with its suggestion of strong, deflected sexuality; and psychiatry might also have its commentary on the engaging eccentricity which led the old gentleman, to the end of his career, to go about the streets of Boston in the cocked hat and knee breeches which had been the fashion in his youth. It is only too well-known that old Major Melville was the inspiration for Oliver Wendell Holmes's pleasant piece of light verse, "The Last Leaf."

The most remarkable of Major Melville's sons was not Herman's father but his uncle, the second Thomas Melville, who became in fact the second Major Melville also. Of this almost fictive uncle Herman Melville was to see much, especially in his teens, when the Major was living, an aging man in his sixties, on a farm near the town of Pittsfield in the Berkshires; and for none of his aunts and uncles did he probably have a tenderer feeling. As a young man in the last decade of the eighteenth century, Thomas Melville had betaken himself to revolutionary Paris, where he had had a somewhat legendary career as a banker, had once been acting American consul in Paris, and had been a familiar of such early republican notables as Joel Barlow and James Monroe. In the late days of the Consulate he had alarmed his relatives in Boston by marrying a French wife, the adopted niece of Mme. Récamier's husband, and in spite of what would seem to have been powerful connections, Thomas Melville, with his "enterprising and sanguine temperament," was ruined in business toward the end of the Empire, and came home to Boston with empty pockets, a pretty French wife, and two small children. A few months later the War of 1812 broke out, and Thomas Melville, who had renounced the family Federalism and turned Jeffersonian, had enlisted in the army and been sent to Pittsfield as a commissary with the rank of major. There he was to live for the next twenty-five years. When the War of 1812 was over, he had acquired a farm south of the village, moved into the spacious mansion which a Tory from Albany had built on it, and set himself up as a kind of gentleman farmer.

For such a role, oddly enough, he appears to have had some talent; he was once described as the best farmer in Berkshire County. But he seems not to have been destined for material success; his years at Pittsfield were an alternating series of hopeful expansions and gloomy retreats, and they ended, the year Herman Melville was eighteen, in the elderly Major's renunciation of his Pittsfield estate and his departure for the prairies of Illinois. Ardent, high-tempered, generous, romantic, and impractical, Uncle Thomas must have been a singular foil to Uncle Peter Gansevoort. At any rate, his nephew's memories of him were tinged everywhere by the sense of his charm and pathos. Melville had known him best as a grayhaired but unwrinkled man in his sixties, hardly at all bowed by age, still preserving the traces of the good looks of his

youth, and in the midst of plain Berkshire farmers and vil-
lagers retaining the mildness and urbanity of his manners,
"with a faded brocade," as Melville said, "of old French
breeding." Years after his uncle had died, Melville remembered how he had often raked with him in the hayfields near
Pittsfield, and how at the end of a swath the Major would
pause at times in the sun, lean on his rake, and taking out his
satin-wood snuffbox, help himself to a pinch of snuff—quite
naturally and yet with a look which, as Melville recalled it,
gave him the air of some shadowy refugee from the court of
Louis XVI, "reduced to humble employment in a region far
from the gilded Versailles." A stately and unbroken exile,
an urbane failure—this was the personal image that hovered,
perhaps more engagingly than any other, before the eyes of
the young Melville.

Such was the lively and fertile mixture of elements in
Melville's ancestry. In all the circumstances of his early life
and nurture, too, there was the most risky but creative
mingling of the fortunate and the injurious. If he was destined to be the kind of writer he was, then it is easy to see,
given the kind of hindsight we have, how all the forces, both
happy and unhappy, of his childhood and youth were working to that end. Much has been made, and has to be made, of
the things that hurt and handicapped Melville; he himself
furnished a hundred pointers in that direction. In his old age
he once marked these lines in a poem of James Thomson's:

> Pondering a dolorous series of defeats
> And black disasters from life's opening day.

And certainly the defeats and disasters were anything but
imaginary. In fact there was the most delicate and precarious
interplay in Melville's early life between the forces making
for high expectation, emotional security, and a basic confidence, and the forces making for disappointment, insecurity,
and distrust. The special product of this interplay, given the

always inexplicable genius, was the mind of Melville the writer. But it is a mistake to forget that the light spaces are as real a part of the true picture as the shadows.

He was fortunate, for one thing, in the scene and the moment. Born in New York in 1819, in the same year as Whitman and at only a few miles' distance, Melville was old enough, or young enough, to grow up and to come of age in the most bracing air the American mind was to know for several generations. What made it so would take long to describe, and besides it would be largely a matter of intangibles; but can we doubt, when we look at the results, that there was something peculiarly invigorating, for a writer-to-be, in that highly oxygenated atmosphere of the American states in the 'twenties, the 'thirties, the 'forties? That there was something menacing in it too, something equivocal, something that might prove hurtful, we know well enough; and we should not expect Melville to be untouched by it. Of the tonicity, however, there can be no question—the tonicity, for that matter, of the intellectual air of the whole Western world in those decades: no impressionable young American could fail to feel the lift and swell of Europe at his back in the days of Byron and Goethe, of Heine and Victor Hugo and Carlyle. But the vitalities at home were unmistakable too; southward and westward, in the energies released by Jefferson and Jackson, expressing themselves in the work of Poe and Simms and the pages of the *Southern Literary Messenger;* in New England, in the fresh animation that was breaking through the ice-crust of Federalist Unitarianism, and burgeoning in Transcendentalism, in Prescott, in Dana, in Hawthorne; in New York itself, even earlier, in a score of infectious ways.

No doubt it strikes us as belonging to an age of almost primeval innocence, the "old" New York of Melville's childhood; no doubt the little Knickerbocker city of the 'twenties may seem to us to have sounded the notes of urban genteelism and ingenuous sophistication rather than of intellectual ardor, seriousness, or profundity. It was certainly no Weimar, no Edinburgh, the New York in which Melville grew up; the New York of John Jacob Astor and Henry Brevoort, John Beekman and Philip Hone, of the New Park Theatre and Peale's Museum and Niblo's Garden; the New York where Cooper was starting the Bread and Cheese Club and Woodworth was producing *The Forest Rose* and the representative wits were J. K. Paulding, George P. Morris, and Fitz-Greene Halleck. Certainly no one can pretend that, even at its most intense, the intellectual life of the town was Athenian. It was very far, nevertheless, from being empty or arid.

It was in just the years of Melville's childhood that Fenimore Cooper, virtually a New Yorker, was publishing *The Spy* and all his other early novels—novels which, as Melville later said, produced in his boyhood a vivid and awakening power on his mind. Another New Yorker, Washington Irving, though living abroad, was writing things like "Rip Van Winkle," "Dolph Heyliger," and *The Conquest of Granada*. It is true that, compared with Hawthorne, Irving was later to seem a mere "grasshopper" to Melville, but his feeling for so attractive a writer, and one so close to his childhood ambience, was a tender one nevertheless, and in his old age he was to dedicate a little fantasy in prose and verse ("Rip Van Winkle's Lilac") to the "happy shade" of Washington Irving. Meanwhile, in the 'twenties, William Cullen Bryant had moved to New York, where he was editing the *Post* and lecturing on poetry at the new Athenaeum and defending the still-unaccepted romantic writers. S. F. B. Morse was lecturing at the Athenaeum also, on the fine arts; and in general the air was alive with talk of new writers and new books, of new plays and "native" operas, of new schools of historical and landscape painting.

Not only so, but Melville's own family, if it was not at the very center of all this, was by no means on its fringes; and one can be sure that family conversation abounded in these references. Except that Allan Melville was a New Englander, the Melvilles were quite a typically "good" New York family of the decade, prosperous, cultivated, traveled, genteel. Melville's uncle, Peter Gansevoort, thought that his sister Maria, Melville's mother, read too many "foolish and nonsensical novels," as perhaps she did. In any case, Allan Melville himself, with his highly literate Scots Presbyterian and Boston Unitarian background, was both a man of the world and a man of taste, like his more eminent contemporary, Philip Hone. In his youth he had been capable of turning out quite decent heroic couplets, for the eyes of his friends, and his letters betray everywhere a love, a very Early American love, of swelling periods and a noble diction. An importing merchant who dealt mostly in French dry-goods—silks, taffetas, ribbons, Leghorn hats, gloves—he had crossed the Atlantic half a dozen times, had traveled much in England and France, had in fact lived in Paris for months, and is said to have spoken French like a native. Not infrequently he entertained at his dinner table mercantile and other visitors from abroad, and like any man of taste he had brought home with him from Europe various *objets d'art* and pieces of furniture, as well as fine books, paintings and engravings, and "two large green French portfolios of colored prints," one of which (one of the prints, that is) represented a great whale stuck full of harpoons and pursued by three dashing whaleboats.

In such comfortable surroundings Herman Melville spent his first ten years of life. Just how solidly practical a business man Allan Melville was is a difficult question; but he was well connected, he was almost unquenchably sanguine by temperament, he was affable and probably charming, and for him, as for New York merchants generally, the 'twenties, with some ups and downs, was a prosperous decade. "My sales continue rapid & advantageous," he writes to his brother-in-law midway through the decade, and in fact their various removals from house to house seem always to have signified a steady rise in the world. They were living far down on the still genteel Pearl Street when Herman was born; five years later they moved up town to a new brick house, "replete with conveniences" such as marble mantelpieces and grates for Lehigh coal, on Bleecker Street; and in 1828 they moved again, this time around the corner to a fashionable neighborhood on Broadway and a house that, along with other advantages, had a large room in its center with what Maria Melville called "a handsome Cornish" running around it. There was a family governess, as well as a French manservant who, for the boy's incredulous interest, had been born in Paris; there were dancing schools and children's parties and long vacation visits with the relatives in Albany, in Boston, in Pittsfield; and educationally speaking, there was the New York Male High School, a private academy. "Black disasters" must have seemed very remote indeed.

For of course the felicity of Melville's early childhood by no means depended wholly on the family well-being; in a much truer sense it was the product of what seems to us to have been an exceptionally tender and affectionate spirit in all the family relationships, especially in the immediate circle. Allan Melville may have been, indeed he was, conventional, sententious, a little pompous, with a touch of Elijah Pogram or Aristabulus Bragg in his makeup; no doubt his conversation was freely sprinkled with "Sir's"; he makes on one indeed a final impression of weakness rather than power; but all this did not keep him from being a man of real sensibility and a particularly warm and loving father. There is a great deal more than mere stilted formulism in his family letters; they make it quite clear that Maria and the children had genuinely engrossed his emotional life. "Adieu and love me always," he writes to Maria in the tones of a young lover on the eve of sailing to Europe again after several years of marriage; and more than once he protests, with unambiguous sincerity, that when his wife and children are away from him his life is reduced to "mere vegetation." To young Herman he was as much attached as to any of them. "My beloved son Herman" and "our dear Boy" he calls him in one letter, and writing to his own father, when Herman was a boy of ten, he confesses that although the youngster is not a bright scholar nor much inclined to study, he is a most amiable and innocent child none the less, and "I cannot find it in my heart to coerce him."

We have glimpses in *Redburn* of visits to the riverside wharves and docks, and other little excursions, which the solicitous father and the small boy must often have made together; and the result of all this was inescapable. Young Herman idolized his father. The boy may have been, as he seems to have been, a rather stolid and sedate youngster outwardly, "backward in speech and somewhat slow of comprehension," less buoyant, as his father thought, than the gifted Gansevoort; but it goes without saying that his nature was warmly affectionate, eager to love and quickly responsive to being loved; and Allan Melville's paternal protectiveness was repaid with a passionate filial devotion. There is no reason to question the truthfulness of *Pierre* on this head, or to doubt that when Melville says in *Redburn*, in his half-fictional role, "I always thought him a marvellous being, infinitely purer and greater than I was," he is speaking not only for Wellingborough Redburn and his father but for himself and Allan Melville. To him as to Redburn the memory of his father was a sacred memory.

With his mother, Herman's relations in his early childhood may have been more complex; they were later to be very complex indeed; and certainly Maria Melville impresses one as a far stronger and more positive character than her accomplished husband. Limited she may have been intellectually; she was certainly, in a guileless way, ambitious socially. She does not fail to note in a letter that they have moved to the "Fashionable side" of Broadway, or in another letter that some oysters she has pickled are not only excellent in flavor but "the same which some of our Stylish Neighbours in Bond Street gave at a large Party of Fashionables." Life in Albany in her girlhood had accustomed Maria Melville to taking for granted the most distinguished associations within reach, and the more metropolitan, more cosmopolitan New York of the 'twenties may have caused her some throes of disappointment, even of hurt pride. "Fashionables I am affraid have no hearts," she remarks, and the phrase suggests in its context a mixture of kind-hearted indignation and some personal resentment. Doubtless she preferred the more brilliantly promising boy Gansevoort to his less taking younger brother, and we can identify her, not of course literally but in a poetic sense, with the mother of Timophanes and Timoleon to whom Melville, in a late poem, attributes these sentiments:

> When boys they were I helped the bent;
> I made the junior feel his place,
> Subserve the senior, love him, too;
> And sooth he does, and that's his saving grace.
> But me the meek one never can serve,
> Not he, he lacks the quality keen
> To make the mother through the son
> An envied dame of power, a social queen.

In the long run the ambitious and commanding side of Maria Melville's nature was to gain the upper hand, and to wreak injury on the emotional career of her "meek" second son. Meanwhile, however, and so long as one speaks of the earliest years, there is no reason to doubt that Maria Melville was warmly maternal, simple, robust, and affectionately devoted to her husband and her brood. Six months after Allan's death, as she entered his father's house in Boston, she broke into a fit of hysterical weeping; and when, at the end of his teens, Herman himself was on the verge of going to sea for the first time, she wrote that she had put together everything she could afford that would make him comfortable, and said of his departure: "I can hardly believe it & cannot realize the truth of his going." Young Redburn, again, alludes to "my best friends, that is to say, my mother and sisters," and declares that at the time of his first voyage, "the name of mother was the centre of all my heart's finest feelings." If this is not literal autobiography, it is not easily distinguishable from it. And if there was anything amiss emotionally in the Melville household, it was not that their affections ran too shallow but that they ran too deep and were, if anything, too intense. The "world" was to give the lie very brutally to some of Herman Melville's earliest and most natural expectations.

When the first bolt struck, it struck with sudden and scarifying violence at the cheerful family circle in the new house on Broadway. Allan Melville, some time in the late 'twenties, had invested several thousand dollars in a firm of which he was a silent partner. In the summer of 1830 this business failed and was dissolved, and in the space almost of a few days the proprietor of the elegant merchandising establishment on Pine Street was wiped out. Allan Melville was a bankrupt and a ruin. Every effort to retrieve his position proved miserably futile; lawsuits were instituted against him, writs were served on him, and some weeks later the family removed not only from Broadway but from New York itself and took refuge, in chagrin and confusion, with the generous but no doubt dismayed relatives in Albany. It was not many weeks before Allan Melville was writing to his father in Boston for the loan of $500 with which to discharge some urgent debts and "provide necessaries for my Family."

One October night in 1830, in the midst of a violent storm, a middle-aged man and a boy of eleven, Allan Melville and his son Herman, sat waiting all night at the Cortlandt Street dock for the belated boat to Albany. It was not the first and of course it was not the last of Herman Melville's many embarkations; but there is something in this image—the tempestuous night and the defeated man, with his small son, waiting through the tedious hours for a boat that could only carry them to a painful destination—something touchingly premonitory of much of Melville's life, and especially of his

ensuing decade, the vital decade of his teens. After promising
him so much, and promising it so benignly, experience was
now to administer a series of bitter and sometimes benumb-
ing shocks and disappointments. The wonderful security,
material, social, emotional, of his infancy and childhood had
collapsed abruptly, and what was now in store for him, as for
his family, was a chronic insecurity: anxiety, renewed hopes,
humiliation, the beginnings of restoration, and then repeated
disasters and repeated falls. He was to learn prematurely that
in this world, as Ishmael says in *Moby Dick*, "head winds are
far more prevalent than winds from astern," and this precocious knowledge was to make him very largely the man and the
writer he was.

The adversity of Melville's early years has several dimensions, and one of them is impersonal and historical. However
inept Allan Melville may really have been as a merchant,
there was something representative and even rather fine in
his failure. The fact was that he belonged to a class, the class
of importers and commission merchants, which had already
had its *aetatem auream* and was about to pass from the scene,
or at any rate from the forestage of that scene. Allan Melville's grandfather had made a sizable fortune as a merchant
in eighteenth-century Boston; his father had carried on the
business and at least maintained the fortune; but comparable
fortunes, implying comparable social and political influence,
were not much longer to be made after 1830. The economic
center of gravity was shifting to the newer class of mill-
owners, ironmasters, and transportation magnates; and the
Melvilles were unwittingly carried under by the decline of
at least a modest patriciate and the rise of a new and more
powerful plebs. So indeed, in the long run, less sensationally,
were the Gansevoorts, whose status was not that of the seaport
merchants but of the Hudson Valley landlords and patroons;
yet for them too the waxing nineteenth century was to spell a
quiet, inconspicuous ebbing of the social and economic tide;
and although a man of real strength, like Peter Gansevoort,

could turn to some account the conditions of the new age, the Gansevoorts in the end sank out of sight quite as mournfully as the Melvilles. When, as an obscure man of fifty, Melville himself one day, out of curiosity, dropped in at the Gansevoort Hotel in New York, on the corner of West Street and Little West Twelfth, bought a package of tobacco, and inquired what the word Gansevoort meant, he was solemnly informed that it was the name of "a very rich family who in old times owned a great deal of property hereabouts." After listening to this piece of pompous misinformation, Melville walked round the corner to his office in the Customs on Gansevoort Street, where he meditated, as he wrote his mother, on the instability of human glory and "the evanescence of—many other things."

With Melville then, as with Kleist or Leopardi, one has to reckon with the psychology, the tormented psychology, of the decayed patrician. Of all that, however, anxious as their situation was, none of them could have been much aware in the autumn of 1830 when they were making the unhappy move to Albany. And for the moment the outlook was not hopelessly bleak. Albany after all was almost as much their home as New York—for Maria even more her home—and what James was to call "the sweet taste of Albany" cannot have been wholly embittered for them by their reverses. Even for the boy Henry James, a decade and more later, the little city was still to preserve much of its Fenimore Cooper charm, and though already in Melville's boyhood it was ceasing to be the old colony town of the Van Rensselaers and the Van Vechtens, and becoming the more democratic, more "common," more Jacksonian city of Martin Van Buren and the Albany Regency, it must still have retained a spell for imaginative boyhood—with its fine prospect up and down the Hudson, its steep cobbled streets, its Greek Revival state house on the hill, and its Dutch mansions on Market Street and Pearl Street, with the pinkish red bricks, the stepped gables embellished with wrought-iron dates or initials, and the white stone steps leading up to doors with fanlights above them. That, at any rate, was the note of Albany as James was to remember it, and it cannot have been very different in the early 'thirties.

For a few weeks the plight of the Melville family was a serious one, but before long a temporary modus vivendi was reached. Allan and Maria took a house a few doors below Grandmother Gansevoort's great old house on Market Street; Allan entered the employ of a dealer in furs; and late the next spring, with his temperamental buoyancy, he was writing to his father that Albany, thanks largely to the Canal, had wonderfully improved of late, and that it contained a busy and thriving population of "nearly 30,000 Inhabitants." Meanwhile, the boys had promptly been put in school, and for a year or two Herman was a pupil, in the same "department" with two of the elder Henry James's brothers, at the excellent Albany Academy on the hill near the state house. For a year or two, strict and even stern though the discipline at the Academy was, life must have been outwardly cheerful enough for young Gansevoort, Herman, and their sisters, with young people's parties at their more fortunate cousins', with coasting on the steep hills during the winter days, swimming and boating on the Hudson in warm weather, and doubtless forays to the north of the city where lay the terminus of the Erie Canal and the piers and wharves that swarmed with "canallers" and their laden barges.

But the relative well-being of that year and a half was far shakier than what had preceded it, and it ended in misery and terror in the dark hours of mid-January, 1832. Smile as he might, optimistically, to keep up his courage, Allan Melville had lost his bearings in the commercial world once for all, and, burdened with debts and hopeless responsibilities, he collapsed at last, physically and mentally, and took to his bed in final despair. The days that followed were days that Herman Melville can never have forgotten; they brought his childhood to a piteous end. The strain of nervous instability that may always have lain behind Allan's gentlemanly exterior now asserted itself, and after several days of mental excitement and sleeplessness, he suddenly became actually deranged, and Peter Gansevoort sent in haste and distress for Thomas Melville at Pittsfield. "I found him *very sick*," wrote Thomas to their father—"under great mental excitement—at times fierce, even *maniacal*." Less than a fortnight later, a fortnight of a grimness that one can only imagine, Allan Melville was dead.

His death was the direst and the most decisive event emotionally of Herman Melville's early life. Deprived of an idolized father on the very verge of adolescence, the boy Melville underwent—can there be any doubt?—an emotional crisis from whose effects he was never to be wholly free. In the midst of a general insecurity, the most vital embodiment of security, the security of fatherhood, was forcibly wrested from him, and the frightening sense of abandonment, the reproachful sense of desertion, must equally have been intense and overwhelming. They were to give color and direction to much of his succeeding life. "Where is the foundling's father hidden?" he asks in *Moby Dick*, and imaginatively speaking, psychologically speaking, can there be any doubt that Melville identified himself with the by-blow and the orphan? Between the poles of loving remembrance and grief-stricken resentment—"irrational" resentment at being forsaken in this way—his feeling toward his father was henceforth to vibrate. He was to spend much of his life divided between the attempt to retaliate upon his father for this abandonment and the attempt, a still more passionate one, to recover the closeness and the confidence of happy sonhood.

For the family as a whole, for Maria and her eight children, Allan Melville's death was of course a crushing disaster, and for the next eight or nine years, all the years of Herman Melville's adolescence, their history as a family was the not unfamiliar but always bitter history of poor relations; of appeals to relatives, of shifts and stratagems, of brave struggles for rehabilitation, temporary runs of luck, and renewed reverses. As it happened, the loss of means and status was never quite complete or permanent; it might have taken a less painful toll if it had been. Neither settled prosperity nor irrevocable penury, but a demoralizing half-world between the two—such was the lot of Allan Melville's widow and orphans after his death.

Soon after that event, young Gansevoort, a boy of barely sixteen, was taken out of school and put into business on his own as his father's successor at the fur store. His business card was soon to read, very maturely: "G. Melville, Dealer in Furs, and Manufacturer of all Descriptions of Fur, Cloth, Morocco, & Fancy Caps." Touchingly young as he was, Gansevoort had inherited, as it seems, enough of the ancestral vigor to make a success of the business at first, and thanks partly to this and partly to a legacy from Grandmother Gansevoort, there was a brief restoration of the family fortunes. There was even a move to a new and spacious house in a more fashionable neighborhood. But the Arch Principals, as Melville was later to call them, seem not to have included the prosperity of the family among their unsearchable designs. When hard times set in for the country as a whole, as they did catastrophically in the spring of 1837, the Melvilles were among the first to feel the pinch, and within a few months Gansevoort Melville, like his father before him, was swept under and went bankrupt. A few weeks later Maria Melville herself entered bankruptcy, and there followed a dismal series of duns and lawsuits, foreclosed mortgages, and enforced sales even of personal possessions, that ended, so far as it did end, in the abandonment of the new house and withdrawal to a cheaper and much reduced way of life at the little town of Lansingburgh, a few miles up the Hudson beyond Troy. Now at last something like real indigence confronted them, and it is not unlikely that before long Herman's sisters—Helen Maria, Augusta, Catherine—were thrusting down their painful pride and taking in sewing.

For the boy himself those four or five years had naturally meant a dipping and rising of fortune along with the family as a whole. For a time, during the year or two that followed Allan's death, Herman had had some sort of boyish clerical job in the New York State Bank, of which his Uncle Peter was one of the directors; and perhaps he was taken quite out of school at the time. Later, during the brief sunny period of renewed prosperity, though he worked during free hours in Gansevoort's store, he was sent to study at the new Albany Classical School near their house, where one of his masters was later to recall him as strict in his truthfulness and distinguished as a writer of themes. Much of the year when he was fifteen he probably spent at Pittsfield with his uncle Thomas Melville and his family, still living in the great mansion south of town which Melville was always to remember with pleasure—the big handsome eighteenth-century house with its larch-shaded porch looking off under the elms by the roadside across the meadows to South Mountain ("the dark, mysterious mountain," as Longfellow described it) and, within, its ample hall and stairway, its wainscoted parlors, and its solid oaken timbers like the massive gun-deck beams of a line-of-battle ship. Noble though the house itself was, Thomas Melville's affairs were as hand-to-mouth as any struggling farmer's in Berkshire County; there were times, indeed, when he was to be in jail for debt. But to all this sort of thing Herman was becoming seasoned; it brought Thomas Melville closer to the remembered image of the boy's own father, and indeed Thomas and Allan had been such warmly affectionate brothers that the approximation, for Allan's son, was by no means emotionally difficult. In any case his life at the farmhouse and his labors in the meadows and hayfields along the Housatonic seem mainly to have left a genial and pastoral memory behind them.

He was just eighteen the summer of Gansevoort Melville's bankruptcy, and the next three years, in spite of mitigations, were to end, as everyone knows, by implanting "a damp, drizzly November" in his soul and launching him on the search for a substitute for "pistol and ball." He had dreamed as a boy of going to college in time and becoming a great orator like Patrick Henry; what he actually did in the fall of '37 was to take a job as schoolmaster at a remote little district school four or five miles south of Pittsfield village, to board around with the homely, unlettered families of his pupils, and to put down, so it was later said, a rebellion of the bigger boys, his contemporaries, who had banded together to lick him. A dark year with his anxious and embittered mother and sisters at Lansingburgh followed. Somehow it was found possible for him to spend that winter studying surveying and engineering, rather unaccountably, at the Lansingburgh Academy, and at the end to obtain a document that certified his proficiency in these branches. An attempt was made, by the unflaggingly generous Uncle Peter, to get him a job in the state canal system, "any situation, however humble it may be"; but nothing came of this, fortunately; and then, early in the summer of 1839, Melville took at last the step the Arch Principals had most particularly plotted for him, and went to sea.

With what was certainly a "knot intrinsicate" of feelings— eagerness for adventure and shrinking from an unfriendly world, reluctance to leave his mother and sisters and an un-acknowledged but irresistible longing to tear himself from their too intense embrace—Melville betook himself to New York early in June and there signed up as a "boy" on a merchant vessel, the *St. Lawrence*, and a few days later was being carried by it out of New York harbor and across the Atlantic to Liverpool.

Melville's boyhood came to an end on the day the *St. Lawrence* weighed anchor and set sail down the East River. What had his boyhood been like, in the inward and emotional sense? What *he* had been like, more or less on the surface, it is not very difficult to say. We know that, as a little boy, he had struck his father as not very buoyant or brilliant, but sedate, sober, and amiable. As a boy in his teens—blue-eyed, chestnut-haired, fair-complexioned, with a straight nose and a rounded chin—he would have struck most observers, one imagines, as a grave, undemonstrative, self-reliant young fellow, with much firmness beneath his good manners. He seems, at any rate, to have called forth no reproaches.

Yet we need very little evidence to tell us that, behind all that, there was a world of vivid and complicated feeling in his nature. However sedate his boyish exterior may have been, his emotional life was the reverse of phlegmatic. His capacity for love was intense even to a precarious degree. Much of it was directed toward his immediate family, but much too to the companions of his own years. Has any other American writer expressed more eloquently than Melville does in *Pierre* the warmth and vehemence of what he calls "the preliminary love-friendship of boys"?—that boyish passion of affection and devotion that is so normal in a certain phase of growth and that, as Melville says, "sometimes transcends the bounds of mere boyishness, and revels for a while in the empyrean of a love which only comes short, by one degree, of the sweetest sentiment entertained between the sexes." With Pierre as a boy such a romantic friendship had sprung up between himself and his cousin, Glendinning Stanly; and we may speculate, if we wish, on the possibility that one of Melville's own cousins—Stanwix Gansevoort, perhaps, his Uncle Leonard's son, who was only two years his junior—was the object of a similar devotion on his part; it matters very little. In *Redburn* he alludes also to "a fine, generous boy" in his home village, named Tom Legare, "whom I much loved," and adds with curious emphasis of emotion: "But I must not talk about Tom now." For most adolescent youngsters there would have been nothing in the least problematic in all this; for Melville it was to contain the seeds of a permanent difficulty.

It seems extremely likely, moreover, that with all his outward gravity, the child Melville was by no means wholly free from the fears and anxieties of sensitive childhood generally; his psychological balance, like his father's, was delicately and even dangerously poised. One recalls the waking nightmare or childish hallucination he describes so eerily in the fourth chapter of *Moby Dick*. To be sure, it need not have happened precisely so in reality, but that it did essentially happen, we may be reasonably certain. His "stepmother," as he explains, had sent him to bed shortly after midday one sunny day in June, as a punishment for some childish misdeed, and there, after hours of waking misery, he had fallen at last into a troubled nightmare of a doze. From this, after darkness had fallen, he had awakened slowly, and opening his eyes in the darkened room, was transfixed with horror to be aware that some silent form or phantom was seated beside his bed and that, while his arm hung over the counterpane, a supernatural hand seemed placed in his. For hours he lay there, "frozen with the most awful fears," until somehow sleep came again, and then for months afterward he brooded over the terrifying mystery. So early as this did Melville discover that "the invisible spheres were formed in fright"; and, at least for memory, the discovery was associated with his mother. It is curious, too, that the recollection should recur to him as he describes Ishmael's waking up, on a frosty morning in the Spouter-Inn, to find his Polynesian bedfellow's arm thrown over him "in the most loving and affectionate manner." The whole passage is a singular mingling of the elements of fear, resentment, a protective humor, and an obscure, unrecognized sexuality.

Certainly there were many things in Melville's relations with his mother that, especially as his teens wore on, were to enhance the inward stresses, not relieve them. Undoubtedly there grew up between the two, the widowed and deprived woman and the fatherless adolescent, with his excessive need for love, an intense and contrarious relationship, and a far from fortunate one. From a certain point of view the pattern is familiar and even classic. Her husband's death had thrown Maria Melville, a woman quite evidently of strong emotionality, back upon her children for emotional support, and they, on their side, had now to find in her, if they could, not only a mother but a substitute father as well. They were all beset, the whole time, by a hundred painful practical difficulties, and the emotional atmosphere that resulted was inevitably shot through with intensities and perils. It was fortunate, to be sure, that their very numbers distributed and relieved the pressures, and for both his mother and Herman it was by no means as if they were wholly dependent upon each other. It was Gansevoort, after all, who during a certain period was the precocious "man" of the family, and his breakdown and early death, the year *Typee* was published, was the price he paid for playing that premature role. Meanwhile it was pretty certainly to Gansevoort, in fact, that Maria had turned as the favored son and almost as a kind of husband, and Herman, as a result, was doubly deprived. His mother could not or would not shower upon him the affection he craved, and the sense of orphanhood began to grow upon him. There was a period, however, after Gansevoort Melville's bankruptcy, when Herman, having learned to find his account in the other role, was forced in his turn to step into the male headship of the impoverished family. These were the months that just preceded and followed the voyage to England, the difficult months at Lansingburgh, the months when Melville himself had to be both son and "husband."

It was from these demands, and from these unfulfilled needs, that he fled to the *St. Lawrence* and later to the *Acushnet*. For bereavement and poverty, though they had certainly evoked the admirable vein of iron in Maria Melville's nature, had quite failed to sweeten or soften her, and the woman who, under happy circumstances, would doubtless have developed into a bland, florid, indulgent patrician matron, stiffened and hardened herself in her deprivation, and became more and more the exacting, aggressive, overbearing, haughty, and worldly woman whom family tradition preserves for us. There are certainly traits of her in Mrs. Glendinning in *Pierre,* though the relationship between Pierre and his mother, that tender, romantic relationship that makes their daily intercourse a kind of questionable love-making, almost certainly embodied for Melville not a reality but a wish. To his niece, Mrs. Morewood, he once remarked in his old age that his mother "hated him." It is not necessary to suppose that the remark expressed his whole feeling toward Maria in order to believe that it could well have expressed one strand, and a vital one, in that feeling. What it meant, of course, in its hardly disguised way, was that Melville, on one side of his nature, hated his mother; quite transparently he attributed his own sentiment to her. And if he was capable of entertaining such an emotion it can only have been because he loved Maria Melville not with deficient but with excessive love. Impossible to miss the perilous intensity of feeling between the mother and the son, or the depth of the injury it was almost certain to wreak. Beneath Melville's "characteristic gravity and reserve of manner," as Hawthorne later found it, there was a tiger-pit of irritable and contradictory emotionality.

With his mother, too, was inextricably associated what was surely the most decisive intellectual and spiritual influence of his early life, his saturation in orthodox Calvinism. It was not literally true, as he says humorously in *Moby Dick,* that he had been "born and bred in the bosom of the infallible Presbyterian Church." His Melville ancestors, to be sure, had been leaders in the Scots kirk since the days of Andrew Melville ("Scourge of Bishops") and John Knox, but Thomas Melville, his grandfather, had succumbed to the liberalizing influences of late eighteenth-century Boston and turned Unitarian. It was in the spiritual domain of Buckminster and Channing that Allan Melville had been reared, and his own religious outlook, as a result, was a typically Unitarian fusion of reasonableness, optimism, "Arminianism," and trust in the rational beneficence of a paternal deity; a kind of pious

Deism, in short, with belated overtones of the *Essay on Man*. These are the tones one hears when, in a letter to his brother-in-law, Allan speaks of a God "who sees the end from the beginning, & reconciles partial evil with universal good." Perhaps, even in early childhood, Allan's second son might have caught from him something of this liberal and enlightened theological cheerfulness; if so, it would have helped to engender some of the spiritual conflicts from which he was certainly to suffer.

For Unitarianism was, almost by definition, a cool and unaggressive theology, and Allan Melville seems not to have insisted on his own bias in the religious rearing of the children. It was Maria Melville's inherited Calvinism that took the primacy here. It was in a Dutch Reformed Church that perhaps all the children, certainly Herman, were baptized; it was the Broome Street Church (Dutch Reformed) that they all attended during most of their New York years; and in the first melancholy days of her bereavement it was a Reformed church, the ancient North Church in Albany, that Maria took at last the formal step of "joining." It would have been the soundest, most conservative Calvinist orthodoxy that Melville in his teens imbibed from the sermons of the Rev. Mr. Ludlow or the Rev. Mr. Vermilye, successive pastors of that church.

Neither the humanitarian rationalism of the Enlightenment nor the transcendental, romantic ardors of the early nineteenth century had availed in any way to soften or emasculate the austere, earnest, pessimistic orthodoxy of the Reformed Church in America. Still, in Melville's childhood, its standards of doctrine, unweakened since the sixteenth century, continued to be the old Belgic Confession, the Heidelberg Catechism, the famous Canons of the Synod of Dort. Melville need not as a boy have mastered these rigorous formulations of doctrine in order to be deeply affected by the teaching and preaching that flowed from them, to have his sense of man and the universe profoundly, however indirectly, molded by them. The whole tendency of Reformed doctrine, as a writer on the Church once said, was "to exalt God and abase man"; and the future author of *Moby Dick* was not likely to listen light-mindedly to such a gospel. A God whose sovereignty was absolute and whose power was infinite; a just, rigorous, angry, but also merciful God, whose ways were not to be searched or sounded by mortal understanding—such was the deity that, as everyone knows, Calvinism had imagined and evoked from the beginning. A deity, moreover, who had foreknown and forewilled all possible events in universal or human life, and by whom all things were determined. "We believe," says the Belgic Confession, "that the same God, after he created all things, did not forsake them, or give them up to fortune or chance, but that he rules and governs them according to his holy will, so that nothing happens in this world without his appointment." A transcendent Father, in short, whose anger one might well fear but whose goodness and justice, inscrutable though they were, one might not question. A Father whose lineaments might have been descried by the young Melville in the stanzas of an old Reformed hymn, a hymn of the sort he was himself to imitate:

> Can creatures, to perfection, find
> Th'eternal, uncreated mind?
> Or can the largest stretch of thought
> Measure and search his nature out?

> .   .   .

> He frowns, and darkness veils the moon,
> The fainting sun grows dim at noon;
> The pillars of heav'n's starry roof
> Tremble and start at his reproof.

> These are a portion of his ways;
> But who shall dare describe his face?
> Who can endure his light, or stand
> To hear the thunders of his hand?

Of the children of this perfect Father, however—of human-kind—what could be said except that, in Adam, they had one and all sinned against their Father and disobeyed him, and that they were, in consequence, as natural men, sunk in the most wretched condition of utter and absolute depravity? "Therefore all men," read the Canons of the Synod of Dort, "are conceived in sin, and are by nature children of wrath, incapable of any saving good, prone to evil, dead in sin, and in bondage thereto." From within man's own fallen nature, in the darkness of his corrupted will, no hope of salvation can imaginably arise. Such is the somber view of the human condition that would have been inculcated in Melville at home, at church, even at school, in his early years. Such is the view which he himself later described as "that Calvinistic sense of Innate Depravity and Original Sin, from whose visitations, in some shape or other, no deeply thinking mind is always and wholly free." The just penalty for this depravity, as he well knew, was eternal and irretrievable damnation for most of mankind; but he knew too that, according to orthodoxy, God had willed, out of his infinite mercy and inexplicable goodness, to elect a small number of human souls to salvation and eternal beatitude. For this they had to thank, not their own merits, which were nonexistent, but the free grace of God, unmerited but "irresistible." What is mere human goodness or virtue but the "filthy rags" of our righteousnesses? God's arbitrary grace is all; and it was in this spirit that Melville himself was once to allude to "that most true Christian doctrine of the utter nothingness of good works."

Of course one ought not to overstate or falsely simplify. In the prevailingly cheerful, democratic, "progressive" America of the 'twenties and 'thirties, far too many other currents of thought were moving for Melville to be obsessively and inescapably overshadowed by a sixteenth- or even a nineteenth-century Calvinism. Yet the religious tone of his mother's household seems to have become increasingly intense as time passed; one hears of formal family prayers, of the reading of

religious tracts, of a somber observance of the Sabbath. And
Melville's mature mind is incomprehensible save partly
against this dark-hued distance. In some important senses,
given the kind of imaginative writer he was by nature, this
youthful indoctrination was a fortunate and positive thing.
Better that his mind should have been imbrued in the severe
grandeurs of Calvinist pessimism than in the "icehouse" chill
of Unitarian complacency. Against the shock of discovering
what devils his fellow-men could become, of encountering
in his own experience "the mystery of iniquity," Melville
was at least partly braced by the doctrines he had heard ex-
pounded in the North Church. Braced, too, against the discovery of the terrible limits imposed upon human will and
desire by the tough, unmalleable, implacable resistance in
things; by Necessity, if one chooses to call it that, by Fate,
by God's will; in any case, by some force or forces in experience that "determine" or "predestine" what shall befall us,
and not our purposes. Besides, there was always present at
the heart of Calvinist Protestantism, despite its dogmatisms,
that essentially humble and saving sense of something unaccountable, something unanalyzable and incomprehensible,
something mysterious in the scheme of things, in "God's
ways," that was to find so deeply responsive an echo in Melville's own meditations.

Yet the dogmatisms were there too, and they exercised a
dangerous sway over Melville's mind. They led him to believe or to hope that, beyond all the apparent formlessness,
wildness, and anarchy of experience, there was an ultimate
Rationality, an absolute order and purpose, in the knowledge
of which one could reassuringly abide. They led him also to
believe or to hope that, beyond all the moral and physical
evil in human affairs, beyond wickedness and suffering, there
was an absolute Goodness or Justice on which one could un-
questioningly rely. If he had been a thirteenth-century
writer, or a seventeenth-century one, Melville could have and
doubtless would have accepted these absolutes, these finali-

ties, trustfully and without perplexity. In fact, however, he was an American writer of the mid-nineteenth century, biased by both disposition and experience to doubt and anxiety; the time had passed when such a man could accept any truths, however sublime, on the mere strength of revelation and certainly of theological authority; and in the abyss that yawned between his early Calvinist certainties and his acquired uncertainties he came near to foundering.

The Enviable Isles

FOR THE BETTER part of five years, from the day he joined the crew of the *St. Lawrence* to the fall of 1844, Melville was to lead a life of constant movement, strenuous action, and sometimes irresponsible vagabondage. At an age when most young writers in the modern world have devoted themselves to studies, to their own work, to the companionship of their intellectual fellows, Melville was washing down decks, reefing stunsails, standing mastheads, and generally rubbing shoulders with the brutalized, exploited, and mostly illiterate seamen of the merchant vessels, the whalers, and the men-of-war of his time—when he was not rubbing shoulders with nonliterate South Sea islanders. It was half the secret of his felicity as a writer, this substitution of a whaleship (as he said) for Yale and Harvard in his freshest youth; and it was also, but much more obscurely, half the secret of his infelicity. To spend those five years as he did was to follow the deepest grain of his nature, and Melville clearly prospered as a writer because he had done so; in sum, of course, and on a final accounting, he had done well. But he paid a heavy price for doing as he did, and the splendid brevity of his productive career as a writer, the hobgoblins that assailed him, the premature flagging of his literary energies—these things had many causes and conditions, but one of them was this extreme physical mobility of his earliest years and the particular strain it put upon his inner elasticity. When he says in *Moby Dick* that "to insure the greatest efficiency in the dart, the harpooneers of this world must start to their feet from out of idleness, and not from out of toil," he was speaking, as so often, out of deep self-knowledge.

Nevertheless, he had not joined the crew of the *St. Lawrence* out of mere careless desperation, bitter though his general outlook may well have seemed to him to be. There were positive motives too, the simplest of which was the old longing to see the world which men of a certain temper have always felt, and which an imaginative boy, growing up in a seaport, where the masts of the shipping were visible from the streets, and the piers and docks within walking distance, could hardly fail to feel. Melville could not remember the time when he had not fancied what it would be like to board one of the great ships in New York harbor and set sail for "Europe"—or for parts still more remote and romantic. He could not remember the time when his father's house had not abounded in souvenirs of foreign travel; and the result, as he himself said, of "this continual dwelling upon foreign associations" was to breed in him "a vague prophetic thought, that I was fated, one day or other, to be a great voyager." His father had been, if not a great voyager, at least a pretty indefatigable traveler, and no motive now was more powerful for Melville than the drive to follow in Allan Melville's footsteps. Nor had Allan been unique in the family circle; on the contrary, Melville had been beset by globetrotters throughout his boyhood. He himself alludes particularly, though in partly fictional terms, to an uncle on his father's side, Captain John DeWolf II, a sea-captain by calling, who as a young man had sailed to Okhotsk in Siberia and then crossed overland on a dog-sled to St. Petersburg in the company of Langsdorff, the Russian naturalist who had been with Krusenstern on his famous voyage round the world.

The names of the great travelers indeed—Krusenstern, Captain Cook, Vancouver, Ledyard, Mungo Park—had scintillated before him like constellations during his whole boyhood, as the names of great soldiers do before other boys; and one can be sure that there were many moments on that first voyage to England, and some moments even in Liverpool, when young Melville was repaid for a thousand bitternesses by the exhilarating sense of having at last slipped his moorings and launched out upon the highways of the globe. *Redburn*, which records this voyage in imaginative if not in literal terms, is pervaded by the remembered elation of a boy's first days and nights at sea, his first apprehension of the boundlessness and grandeur of the ocean, his first dizzy scramble up the mainmast to loosen a skysail by starlight, his first glimpse of a school of whales. And at the end of this initiatory sail there was Liverpool, with all its squalor and misery, to be sure, but with its fine "foreign" character also; the noble spectacle of its great new granite docks, its rows and rows of vast gloomy warehouses, its handsome public buildings, the Town Hall and the Merchants' Exchange and the Custom House, and then the Lancashire countryside, still so richly English and still so easy for a healthy young man to reach by walking.

It was at any rate a starter for a young voyager—but for this particular young voyager how disenchanting, how anticlimactic, how full of mortifications it was! Travel was one thing for Allan Melville, a well-to-do young merchant and a cabin passenger; it was a comparable thing for young John DeWolf, scion of an old shipping family and the associate of men like Langsdorff; it was another and quite different thing for the empty-pocketed, out-at-elbow young Herman Melville, setting out from the needy household at Lansingburgh and shipping before the mast, not as an able seaman or even an ordinary seaman but in the humblest possible capacity, that of a mere "boy." *Redburn* abounds in subjective reality, we may be quite sure, and nothing is more credible than that

Melville himself, or some friend on his behalf, hinted to the real Captain Brown (as Redburn's friend does to the fictional Captain Riga) something about the distinction of his family connections, only to discover, once the ship had got under weigh, that in Captain Brown's hard eyes he was not the son of a former importing merchant but a shabby, immature greenhorn from an upstate village, and that his first job was to clean out the pigpen and be quick about it. The command, in fact, would not even have come from Captain Brown himself but from some irascible mate, and in general the abrupt transition from his mother's genteel household to the tough, coarsened, misanthropic, often vitiated society of a trading vessel's crew in that era was almost certainly an ordeal by violence and emotional shock. If the sensitively well-bred youth Melville was not made the butt of a hundred boorish jokes and the victim of a hundred sallies of unfeeling persecution, one's sense of the human actualities is badly at fault.

Fortunately there was toughness of a sort in Melville too, and a great fund of healthy humor; he survived the ordeal, but beyond a doubt he was permanently scarred by it. There was, for example, a sailor named Jackson on the *St. Lawrence*, as there is a sailor named Jackson on the *Highlander* in *Redburn;* it is true that he did not die on the voyage home, but one has no difficulty in imagining that the real Jackson was as ferocious a bully, as cruel a misanthrope, and as depraved a character generally as the fictional one. He would not have been an untypical seaman of the period if he had been, and what his abandoned talk and his cynical behavior would have done to Melville's already injured sense of human kindness, it is easy enough to guess. Melville hints, moreover, but only hints, in speaking of the sailors and their profanity, at "another ugly way of talking they had"; he raises the merest corner of a curtain, and drops it at once, when he alludes to the putridity of vice and crime that reeked up from among the pestilent alleys of Liverpool—the alleys that, while the *Highlander* (and surely the *St. Lawrence*) lay anchored in Prince's Dock, the sailors mostly frequented; and certainly, on this "first voyage," which might have been so wholesomely adventurous, there is not much doubt that the impressionable youth was precociously introduced to some of the ugliest possible aspects of human life.

He was pretty certainly introduced also to some of its blackest miseries. The Liverpool of the 'thirties had its genuine points of interest, but it had other sights, and these predominated, that could have inspired in a humane mind only a shuddering skepticism about the whole future of the society that tolerated them. The Liverpool that Melville saw was the Liverpool of the days that followed the hated new Poor Law and preceded the repeal of the Corn Laws; the Liverpool of Chartist agitation; the Liverpool that was not far from or much unlike the "Coketown" that Dickens was to depict in *Hard Times* and the "Darkshire" city of Mrs. Gaskell's *North and South*. Even in the 'fifties, when Hawthorne was living there as American consul, his walks about the poorer quarters of the city, though they fascinated him, appalled him with their revelations of filth, abjectness, and degraded misery. The great port was already in Melville's time "the black spot on the Mersey," and what it had to show him, rather more unforgettably than its Graeco-Roman public buildings, was the heart-sickening squalor of its working-class lanes and courts, its Rotten Rows and Booble Alleys, its cellar-dwellings and spirit-vaults, its beggars, its diseased children, its crimps and land-sharks and whores. Whether he literally saw, as he describes seeing in *Redburn*, the starving woman with the three children, all dying together or already dead, in the squalid sidewalk vault in Lancelott's-Hey, the fact is that he could very well have seen just such sights in the grim Liverpool of 1839. They did not do much to confirm the hopeful views of man and society that his father must once have wished to inculcate in him.

Yet the thought of his father seems never to have been long out of his mind on this English voyage. Again we depend

upon *Redburn* and its imaginative kind of truthfulness, but
nothing could ring truer than Melville's reiteration there of
young Redburn's joyful sense, in the midst of his humiliations, that after all he was taking precisely the voyage his
father had taken more than once, and that Liverpool, when
he reached it, would glow for him with reminders of his
father's visits. The map in the old guidebook to Liverpool
that had come to him from his father had a number of dotted
lines traced on it in ink, and these marked out for him the
older man's excursions about the city: could he not, by following where those lines directed him, in some strange and
secret sense rejoin his father? So strong was this wish, at least,
that as he followed the indicated route down Old Hall Street
and then across Chapel Street, passing under an arch and
emerging into the fine quadrangle of the Merchants' Exchange, the impression of his father's having been there before him was so vivid "that I felt like running on, and overtaking him round the Town Hall adjoining, at the head of
Castle Street." But then, so he says, he checked himself with
the bitter thought that his father "had gone whither no son's
search could find him in this world." Besides, the shabby and
unpresentable youth could hardly expect to have entry where
his father had had it; of this he was reminded at every turn.
And as for the inherited guidebook, it was now thirty years
or more out of date; it misled him more often than it directed
him aright; and in the end he was forced back on the melancholy reflection that "the thing that had guided the father
could not guide the son."

Friendless and hard up in a foreign city, and with only the
riotous seamen of the *St. Lawrence's* crew for companions,
Melville, like young Redburn, must have found his heart
"yearning to throw itself into the unbounded bosom of some
immaculate friend." Did he in actuality strike up a romantic
friendship with a young Englishman, hovering about the
sailors' boardinghouses near the water front, as he represents
himself doing in *Redburn?* There was a person named Henry

Gill who joined the crew of the *St. Lawrence* before it sailed homeward from Liverpool: was he the "original" of Melville's interesting Harry Bolton? Impossible to say, but if Harry is sheer invention, then surely he is a curious phantom for Melville to have conjured up in what was only the second year of his married life, when he wrote *Redburn,* just ten years after Liverpool.

It is at the sign of the Baltimore Clipper, a water-front boardinghouse, that Redburn encounters the rather mysterious young Britisher, Harry Bolton, inquiring of an American sailor about America and the means of getting there. He is a small but perfectly formed youth, with dark curling hair, a brunette complexion, "feminine as a girl's," large, black, womanly eyes, beautiful white hands with long fingers, and a voice that is "as the sound of a harp." Clearly he is the son of a gentleman, and Redburn is so charmed with his appearance, so eager to enjoy the society of someone of his own class, that he boldly introduces himself to the youth, and offers to give him whatever information he may. Harry is at first somewhat disconcerted by Redburn's shabby costume, the old shooting-jacket and the rest, but he seems pleased with the American nevertheless, and the two youths ramble about St. George's Pier together until nearly midnight, exchanging confidences. Almost at once they become fast friends, and Redburn, delighted at the thought of taking Harry back to America with him, introduces him to Captain Riga and gets him a berth on the *Highlander's* crew. Even as a sailor, Harry aims at being a dandy; he equips himself with a becoming outfit, including a striped Guernsey frock which leads Redburn to call him "my zebra"; but the voyage to America proves a miserable one for Harry, as the voyage out had proved for Redburn. The sailors despise him for his effeminacy and naturally persecute him without mercy, and it is only because his singing voice is incomparably melodious, and he can beguile them with his songs, that they tolerate him at all.

Both Redburn and Harry, when they arrive in New York, are unconscionably defrauded of their pay by the knavish Captain Riga. Redburn receives information that requires him to leave New York promptly and return home, and he and the luckless Harry are reluctantly but inescapably separated. After this, Harry disappears from Redburn's unforgetting ken, and it is only some years later, when Redburn, like Melville, is a sailor on a whaling vessel in the Pacific, that he learns from another Englishman how Harry, off the Brazil Banks, had met his fate on *another* whaler. With a touch of either literal or emotional truth that for Melville is full of meaning, he tells us that, while a whale was lashed to the side of the vessel and the cutting-in taking place, Harry had fallen overboard and been crushed to death between the ship and the whale's corpse. In a certain sense this real or imagined friend was another victim of Moby Dick's, and whether he ever "existed" or not, his image hovered before Melville's imagination, as he wrote *Redburn*, with a singular intensity of sentiment and tenderness:

> Poor Harry! a feeling of sadness, never to be comforted, comes over me, even now when I think of you. . . .
> But Harry! you are mixed with a thousand strange forms, the centaurs of fancy; half real and human, half wild and grotesque. Divine imaginings, like gods, come down to the groves of our Thessalies, and there, in the embrace of wild, dryad reminiscences, beget the beings that astonish the world.
> But Harry! though your image now roams in my Thessaly groves, it is the same as of old; and among the droves of mixed beings and centaurs, you show like a zebra, banding with elks.

Was there not, in Melville's or in Redburn's feeling for Harry Bolton, something as irregular, as equivocal, as the hybrid creatures of mythical fancy he evokes in this curious passage? In his copy of Shakespeare's sonnets, Melville once marked with a check the twentieth sonnet, the most frankly epicene of the sequence, though not at all one of the best; the sonnet that begins:

> A woman's face with Nature's own hand painted
> Hast thou, the master-mistress of my passion.

Did he find in this poem an expression of the same ambiguous emotion, the same perplexed attraction, he may once have felt for a young English ne'er-do-well?

Whatever the answer, and whether Henry Gill was the "real" Harry Bolton or not, the *St. Lawrence*, after lying for five or six weeks in Prince's Dock, weighed anchor again and stood out to sea for America. At the end of September, after a crossing probably less eventful than that in *Redburn*, the ship sailed between the Narrows and came to anchor at its pier in the East River. With his four crowded months of excitement, novelty, and some misery behind him, young Melville was soon back at home in Lansingburgh.

"Oh! he who has never been afar," says Melville in *Redburn*, "let him once go from home, to know what home is." And in reality the young Melville, as he journeyed up the Hudson again, must have felt his heart swelling with homesick eagerness to find himself once more in the embraces of his mother and sisters. If he had hoped for a moment, however, that somehow affairs at home had been transformed in his absence and taken a happy turn, he must very soon have been dismally disenchanted. In the year and a half that followed, the family fortunes sank to their very nadir. There was one humiliating October day when Herman, who in Gansevoort's absence was apparently the man of the family, was dispatched to Peter Gansevoort in Albany with an urgent request for a loan of money. In the same month his mother's furniture was advertised for sale. There was nothing for it, in the absence of more inviting prospects, but for Melville to resort again to the drudgery of schoolteaching, and very soon he was walking back and forth, at the beginning and the end of every week, and doing so the winter long, over the thirteen-mile stretch between Lansingburgh and the hamlet of Greenbush, where he had managed to get a job in another school.

The one or two glimpses we have of him in the next twelve months or so are not merely gloomy ones, but, scanty though they are, they help us to understand why he ended by "running away" again to sea. It is rumored that a youthful love affair, which ended badly, was one of the spurs in the sides of his intent. Nothing is more likely, though we know next to nothing about this unlucky romance. Even before Melville sailed for England, he had very modestly begun his literary career by contributing a couple of half-humorous, half-"Oriental," and wholly juvenile essays, the "Fragments from a Writing-Desk," to a Lansingburgh newspaper, and these had borne witness, along with their quite genuine sprightliness of style, to a real preoccupation on his part with the charms of the other sex. It is said that the girl with whom Melville was in love rejected him in favor of another suitor: it may well have been so, and in that case we are at liberty to guess that if Melville was rejected it was partly because, unbeknown even to himself, he wished to be.

There was a demon of restlessness in him anyway, and in the summer of 1840 it drove him, not this time to sea, but overland and westward to visit his Uncle Thomas, now living —though not prospering—near the banks of the Mississippi, at Galena, Illinois. It was a trip that left behind it a deposit of long-remembered impressions. Images of the inland landscape, of farms, of prairies, of rivers, lakes, and forests, were to recur throughout Melville's work as a counterpoint to the dominant imagery of the sea; his memory owed many of them to this youthful journey. In *Moby Dick* he describes himself as having once been a vagabond on the Erie Canal, and no doubt he journeyed westward and perhaps homeward too by that route. It would account, along with some boyhood impressions, for the full-blooded sense of the bold and lawless life of the Canallers that comes out so powerfully in "The Town-Ho's Story." In the same tale the "ocean-like expansiveness" of the Great Lakes, "those grand freshwater seas of ours," is also evoked, and doubtless Melville knew them at first hand as a lake-boat passenger. He surely had seen for himself "the goat-like craggy guns of lofty Mackinaw," and there is something quite authentic in the image, elsewhere in *Moby Dick*, of Michigan oxen dragging the stumps of old oak trees "out of wild wood-lands."

Yet it was not the lakes and the forests of the great west that sank deepest into his memory but the prairies and the Mississippi River. There was something in the almost oceanic vastness and swell of the one and in the wide, slow, watery resistlessness of the other that spoke with peculiar force to an imagination for which both spatial immensity and the element of water were clearly symbolic. It is characteristic that Melville should have used "The Prairie" as the title of the chapter in *Moby Dick* in which he expatiates on "the awful Chaldee of the Sperm Whale's brow" and its almost featureless inscrutability, and that the legendary White Steed of the Prairies, a creature of "that unfallen, western world, which to the eyes of the old trappers and hunters revived the glories" of primeval times, should figure so conspicuously and with so spectral a beauty in the great chapter on "The Whiteness of the Whale." As for the Mississippi, though it cast a less profound spell over Melville than the prairie did, the memory of it was to remain lurking in his imagination, and when he came to write *The Confidence Man* he was to make the great river the setting of his most despairing book.

On other and more purely personal grounds the Illinois excursion must have proved to be a familiar mingling of the adventurous and the anticlimactic. It would have been a pleasure for him, though certainly a touching one, to see Thomas Melville again, for the old man, like a more stately Colonel Sellers, was now characteristically serving as secretary of the Chamber of Commerce in the booming lead-mining town of Galena—Melville was much later to remark in a letter that "all the lead in Galena" could not fashion the plummet that would sound the deepest seas of thought—but the luckless star that had frowned on Uncle Thomas for so long had not yet set, and the family was living in a humble little house and in a hand-to-mouth manner that again suggests the ménage of Mark Twain's Colonel. No doubt it was partly owing to the painfulness of all this, so close to him emotionally, and then no doubt to the renewed painfulness of so much that confronted him when he returned to Lansingburgh—where we lose sight of him for a few months—that Melville ended by finding himself, as he says, "growing grim about the mouth," and realizing that the "hypos" were getting the upper hand of him. Dry land was beginning again to scorch Melville's feet, and it was not long before he was bidding good-bye to Lansingburgh once more and setting off, on a December day, to the greatest of the whaling ports, New Bedford. There, or rather at Fairhaven nearby, he signed up as a foremasthand on the whaler *Acushnet*, which on the third of January, 1841, put out to sea from Buzzard's Bay and set sail for the South Pacific.

Life on the *St. Lawrence* may have been harsh and disillusioning for Melville in many of its aspects, but it had by no means cured him of his deep, irrational, almost mystical longing for the sea—and for the liberation, mingled with dread, that it symbolized for him. On one level, it is true, a prosaic one, there was nothing that calls in the least for explanation in a needy and adventurous young American's going to sea on a whaler in the 'forties. Young Americans did so by the hundreds at the time, and one of Melville's own cousins, an unlucky son of Thomas Melville's, had sailed from Fairhaven itself on a whaler only five or six years earlier. But it goes without saying that the prosaic and even the adventurous motives will carry one only part of the way in understanding

the behavior of a youth like Melville. We must take him at
his word, in every sense but the literal one, when he says that
the chief of his motives was "the overwhelming idea of the
great whale himself." So it surely was; as truly as that the
idea of tiger or elephant or polar bear has drawn other imaginative men after it to the bush, the jungle, the Arctic
waters. The great beasts of both land and sea are images of
power, of hostility, of beauty and use that lie deep and potent
in the primordial memory of mankind: what wonder if the
hugest of all animals, either extant or extinct, should come to
loom in the mind of a young writer as an irrational but irresistible symbol, and draw him like a moving magnet in its
pursuit?

The image of the whale, moreover, would have been particularly real and vivid to the minds of a great many men,
Americans especially, in that heyday of the whaling industry. For many nineteenth-century Americans the whale would
have filled the imagination as the tiger has always filled it for
Asiatics or as the wild boar did for mediaeval Europeans. The
sailors themselves had even given names to individual whales
whom they came to recognize, or thought they recognized,
like the white whale called Old Tom about whom Emerson
once heard a sailor gossiping in the stagecoach. And during
the weeks that just preceded his voyage to Liverpool Melville
might very easily have read in the *Knickerbocker Magazine*
a description by J. N. Reynolds of "an old bull whale, of
prodigious size and strength," who was "white as wool,"
named Mocha Dick or the White Whale of the Pacific. According to Reynolds, it was well known that numerous boats
had been "shattered by his immense flukes, or ground to
pieces in the crush of his powerful jaws." Along with many
another impression this vivid article of Reynolds's must have
taken deep root in Melville's mind; and, in any case, the profoundest truth about his setting off on a whaling voyage was
certainly, as he says it was, that "two and two there floated

into my inmost soul, endless processions of the whale, and midmost of them all, one grand hooded phantom, like a snow hill in the air."

Of the eighteen months Melville spent on the *Acushnet* we know factually almost nothing, and from one point of view it is as well that this is true. The ship doubtless made first for the Azores and the Cape Verde Islands, and then sailed southward to cruise for whales on the Brazil Banks, where Melville's "first lowering" may have taken place. After touching at Rio, as it certainly did, and (if we are to believe *Typee*) beating for forty days about Cape Horn, "that horrid headland," the *Acushnet* put in at Santa on the coast of Peru. The following fall or winter it was cruising on the "Off-Shore Ground" westward from the coasts of Peru and Ecuador, in the vicinity of the Galápagos group. It was now that Melville first saw those desolate, ashen islands, once called the Encantadas, populated by ugly lizards and woebegone tortoises, where "the chief sound of life is a hiss." Whither the *Acushnet* next betook herself has to be guessed; the chances are that she proceeded in the late winter to recruit at the Sandwich Islands, where she might have remained for two or three months, and then sailed southward again to the whaling grounds roundabout the Society and the Marquesas Islands. What we know for certain is that one day at sunset, early in July 1842, Melville saw the blue, jagged contours of the peaks of Nuku-Hiva, one of the Marquesas, rising on the horizon. The next morning, after running with a light breeze all night, the *Acushnet* stood in to the land and dropped anchor in the lovely bay of Tai-o-hae. A few days later, having had as much of life on board a whaler as for the moment he could endure, Melville jumped ship and with one companion fled into the interior of the island.

In one sense there was nothing remarkable in his doing so. At some time during the *Acushnet's* voyage both the first and the third mates, as well as thirteen members of its crew of twenty-three, had escaped from it, either by actually deserting or by having to be put ashore "half dead" with some disease. The first mate had had a fight with Captain Pease and had gone ashore at Payta in Peru. A Negro sailor named Tom Johnson had gone ashore at Maui in the Hawaiian Islands and died at a hospital there. The boatswain had either run away or been killed at Roa-Pua in the Marquesas. And all these incidents were commonplaces of the old whaling industry. The fact is that, along with its elements of adventure, excitement, and (at least for a youth like Melville) "honor and glory," which were wholly real, the life of a foremast-hand on a typical whaler of the time was as nearly unendurable as working life can be and not prove fatal. It is no part of Melville's purpose in *Moby Dick* to represent realistically what existence was like on all its sides for a seaman on a boat like the *Acushnet*, and he does not do so. But we may be sure that he knew, and knew with a bitter knowledge, in his own person. In the early chapters of *Typee* there is a glimpse of what he had gone through; a glimpse that, if we can believe the best writers on whaling, is rather understated than not.

At its worst, says E. P. Hohman in *The American Whaleman*, the life of a whaling seaman represented "perhaps the lowest condition to which free American labor has ever fallen," and he remarks elsewhere that American whaling "had all the essential characteristics of a sweated industry." If Captain Pease's conduct was, as Melville implies in *Typee*, "arbitrary and violent in the extreme"—if his reply to all complaints and remonstrances was "the butt-end of a hand-spike"—it was not because he was a rare case of sadistic cruelty. On the contrary, as S. E. Morison remarks in *The Maritime History of Massachusetts*, "brutality from officers to men was the rule," and many whaling skippers, pious though they might be on shore, were "cold-blooded, heartless fiends" on the quarter-deck. Along with the fearful risks and dangers of the hunt itself, which carried a natural elation with them, there were a thousand things in mere day-to-day life on board a whaler that could only have been galling to a youth like

Melville, and have ended by reducing him to rebellious desperation: the cramped, airless, almost lightless filthiness of the forecastle quarters, the dreariness and monotony of the food, the prospect of drawing some trifling wage or no wage at all at the end of a three or four years' voyage, and the association for the most part with the typically brutalized and degraded members of a whaler's crew ("dastardly and mean-spirited wretches," Melville calls them). There had surely been many moments and even hours during his eighteen months aboard the *Acushnet* that had repaid Melville for some of his sufferings; moments of absorbing, self-forgetful excitement in the actual chase of some great monster of a Sperm Whale, hours of trancelike contemplation as he stood at a masthead gazing out over the infinite Pacific, hours of sociable relief and jollity during a "gam" with some other whaler. But such diversions as these could not compensate indefinitely for the prevailing misery and humiliation, and in the end Melville found these latter unendurable.

The next few weeks of Melville's life, the weeks of his residence in the valley of Taipi-Vai, which he calls Typee, were to be one of its great episodes. Unlike any other American writer of his stature, save perhaps Parkman, Melville was not only to indulge the fantasy of primeval life, the life of the archaic peoples, but actually to dwell in its midst, quite cut off for the moment from any link with Westernism, whiteness, or civilization. The weeks may literally have been very few; certainly they were no more than three or four; and Melville may have been alone among the Taipis for hardly more than a fortnight. In a sense it does not matter; his days in the island valley were long with a length no calendar could measure, and they left a permanent stamp upon his spirit.

He had not been alone when, taking advantage of a day's shore leave with the starboard watch, he had struck out from the little settlement of Tai-o-hae into the thickets and ravines of the interior. His companion was another young sailor, a

black-eyed, curly-haired boy of seventeen named Toby
Greene, for whom he had formed an attachment on the
Acushnet, and who was as bitterly discontented as he. Knowing nothing of the lay of the land, and having provided themselves with only a few ship's biscuits, the two of them spent a
series of miserable days and nights wandering about among
the mountain ridges and ravines of Nuku-Hiva, suffering
from thirst and hunger by day and drenched with rain in
temporary shelters at night, until at last they were driven to
descend into what might be an inhabited valley—inhabited
perhaps, as they feared, by the savage Taipis—and did in fact
find themselves in the midst of those dreaded people. To
their astonishment the Taipis proved to be, at the beginning, friendly, gentle, and hospitable; the two young white
men were at once taken in as guests by the family group they
had first encountered, and after many hours of sleep, and
some prodigal meals of *popoi,* coconut milk, and other delicacies, they were quite restored.

Toby, at any rate, was quite restored. Melville himself had
begun to suffer during their wanderings from a mysteriously
painful and swollen leg, and now, in spite of the violent min-
istrations of a Taipi *tuhunga,* it grew no better. Their hosts,
for all their courtesy and lavishness, proved unaccountably
hostile to the idea that either of them should leave the valley,
but at last they were prevailed upon to allow Toby to find his
way back to Tai-o-hae for the sake of obtaining medicines,
and after one unsuccessful attempt he did manage to make
his return to that settlement, only to be victimized by a rascally beachcomber and shanghaied on board another whaler.
Melville, who learned of Toby's mishaps only some years
afterward, was now left alone, puzzled and apprehensive,
among the amiable but in so many ways unaccountable Taipis. It was to be a fortnight, perhaps three weeks, before he
made his own escape.

During that short period he neither saw nor was seen by
another white man. How literally and trustfully can we take

the account of these days that Melville himself was to put down in *Typee?* Toby Greene later turned up to bear witness to the "entire accuracy" of Melville's story, to the point where the two of them were parted, and other travelers and even anthropologists have testified since that much of *Typee* has the ring of truth. The question of course does not need to be pressed prosaically and beyond a certain point. *Typee* is a work of the imagination, not sober history, and one constantly crosses in it the invisible line between "fact" and the life of the fancy and the memory. Nothing in it does violence to one's sense of the human realities generally, and in that light one prefers to lean toward credulity rather than skepticism.

In any case, if Melville now found himself quite cut off and almost cornered among a tribe of Polynesians, it was by no mere external accident or chance; his situation and even his plight were the expressions of a deep-seated wish. Nor was it a unique or eccentric one. Young as he still was, Melville had already experienced in his own feelings that revulsion from the Western, the modern, the complex, which in one way or another half the imaginative spirits of the nineteenth century underwent, as some of those in the eighteenth and the twentieth had done or were to do. Like most of them he called what revolted him "civilization," but it is not the word that very much matters; it is the emotion animating it. This has been made light of, misapprehended, and caricatured by dull historians and critics, most of whom have ended only by caricaturing themselves. In actuality that emotion, however "mistaken," was a serious, inevitable, deeply authentic one, and again and again it proved highly creative. Given the profound disharmonies that more and more afflicted the developing culture of Europe and America—its material complexities over against its moral crudities and social inequities, its literate rationalism outstripping and losing touch with its emotional and imaginative needs, its surface more and more discordant with its depths—given these things, and along with them the knowledge of simpler, fresher, less harried ways of life, there remains nothing comic or extravagant in the longing felt by so many sensitive men to escape from civilization and take refuge among the happier peoples of an archaic culture who not only had no cities and no machines, but seemed to have no rich and no poor, no abstract ideas, no mental conflicts.

It ought not to be hard to understand why, even at twenty-one, Melville should have wished to flee from a civilization that so largely signified to him the worries and humiliations of poverty, the daily pressure to make money and get ahead, the settled warfare between intellect and feeling, the ever-renewed clash between impulse and conscience. He shared such emotions with two or three generations of European writers and with such other Americans as Cooper, Parkman, and Thoreau; unlike these last, however, he was not strongly drawn to the American Indian and the virile severities of his culture but to the warmer, more epicene, more relaxed and gracious culture of the South Sea islanders. Like everyone, he already had his impressions of the Tahitians, the Hawaiians, and the Marquesans, from his reading; and of the Marquesans, even specifically of the Taipis, he must certainly have heard by word of mouth from his older cousin, Midshipman Thomas Wilson Melville, who had visited Nuku-Hiva and Taipi-Vai as a member of the crew of an American man-of-war, the *Vincennes*, when it touched at the Marquesas in 1829. There was a deep strain of the tropical, the indolent, the sensual and feminine in Melville; and when the word went round on the *Acushnet* that they were shaping their course for the Marquesas, he felt, as he says, a sudden thrill of elation at the thought that he would soon be seeing "those islands which the olden voyagers had so glowingly described."

Now that he was there at last, though in the ambiguous role of a kind of pampered prisoner, there was much that might well have ended by reconciling him to his lot. There was the romantic beauty of the island itself, a literally romantic beauty of mingled ruggedness and luxuriance, wildness and softness, of basaltic cliffs and shattered mountains rising from amidst valleys like that of Taipi, richly carpeted, watered by clear streams through their whole length, and shaded by groves of the coco-palm, the pandanus and hibiscus, and everywhere the elmlike magnificence of the breadfruit tree. As dwellers in these lovely valleys one found a people of such surpassing beauty as to move to extravagance a long series of hard-bitten, unromantic seadogs like their discoverer Mendaña, like Captain Cook and David Porter, to say nothing of later and less impassive characters like Stevenson, who thought the Marquesans perhaps the handsomest race of men extant. And indeed Melville and Stevenson vie with each other in evoking the physical beauty of these people: their large, luminous eyes like those of fine animals, their light olive or golden brown skins, their perfect white teeth; the beauty, as it appears, of the men especially— like Melville's friend, the statuesque Marnoo—tall, strongly muscled, elegantly outlined, "swift in action," as Stevenson says, "graceful in repose."

Later travelers and students have remarked that, like the Greeks, the Marquesans had long made a cult of physical beauty. Melville indeed had already seen that this was true, and tells us how much time and thought both men and women gave to their personal cleanliness, to the care of their fine skins, to the bedecking of themselves with chaplets, earrings of flowers, and garlands about the neck, and to the tasteful arrangement of their mantles and tunics. It was all a revelation and an education of the senses for a young American of the Protestant middle class in the mid-nineteenth century, citizen of a culture that distrusted and belittled physical beauty; but it was an education that was to prove for him in the long run a disturbance and a source of conflict. It was to do so, if we read between the lines, partly because this cult of physical beauty, as one gathers from travelers both earlier and later than Melville, implied inevitably a Greeklike cult of physical love also, a frank and astonishingly free celebration of the power of a Polynesian Eros, an unashamed and sometimes orgiastic sexuality. It was the happy and harmless sensualism of a culture that had not yet undergone the penalties or enjoyed the rewards of social complexity and psychological maturity, and Melville was debarred, as a writer for the general public, from reproducing all that he had certainly observed; he had to content himself with discreet intimations. But later gossip among the beachcombers of the Pacific that he himself had had a child by the original of Fayaway is not in itself hard to credit, and in any event his experience among the Taipis and the Tahitians did much to intensify the emotional perplexities of his later life.

Meanwhile, however, the charm of Taipi-Vai must have been all but overwhelming. For the inhabitants of the valley were not only beautiful physically; on one side they were irresistibly charming as mere human beings, with their natural fine manners, their graciousness and their grace, their love of laughter and play, their impulsive affectionateness and prevailing good temper among themselves. In Melville's picture of the tranquillity that mostly reigned in the valley there is nothing that cannot be confirmed if one turns to other and perhaps more exacting observers. What wonder if he was tempted at moments to abandon for it the world of chronic strife and rude contention he had left behind him? Besides, and quite as important to a born artist like Melville, the people of these islands were perhaps the most accomplished craftsmen in all Polynesia, refined workers in stone and wood and, as tattooers, the human body; whose skilled workmen or *tuhungas* were often deified and worshipped after their deaths. *Typee* makes fully evident how genuine was Melville's interest in the craftsmanship of the Taipis, how closely he followed the processes of tapa-making and tattooing, and what pride he took in his own imitative achievements as a tapa-maker and a wood-carver. It was a release, like his achievements as a seaman, for impulses that had had

little outlet in his education and were to have little, except
in literature, in his mature life.

In these and in similarly recreative ways the weeks in
Taipi-Vai mainly passed. Melville's days were largely a round
of healthy pleasures; swimming in the shaded pools with
Fayaway, Kory-Kory, and their troop of youths and girls; re-
clining on tapa-mats and languidly smoking in the afternoons
at the *tai* or men's house; and, on one occasion, participating,
in "full" Marquesan costume for once, in an orgiastic festival
which Melville calls the Feast of Calabashes and which was
probably a harvest festival of the breadfruit. A delicious
cycle not of Cathay but of Nuku-Hiva might seem to have
stretched out in prospect before his imagination. In fact it
was no such matter, and he does not pretend that it was. The
reality principle, if nothing else, was too strong in Melville
to allow him, probably for more than a few hours on end, to
yield himself heart and soul to the enchantments of primitive
life; probably not a day passed that something in him did not
cry out not only against the crude physical danger but against
the subtle moral menace that it concealed for him. Almost
from the beginning he must have felt, as D. H. Lawrence was
later to feel, that he "couldn't go back" to the primeval, much
as he might long to; that for better or worse he was a man of
the Western nineteenth century and must settle his accounts
with his own age; that civilized man could not live by breadfruit alone, and that only self-destruction could follow from
his attempt to do so. Like Gauguin, too, fifty years later, he
must have discovered before very long that "there is such a
thing as Homesickness." And in fact Melville makes it clear
that, before he finally broke away, he had fallen into a fever
of homesickness from which he was hardly free for two
successive hours.

Some of his reasons for feeling this he himself makes much
of in *Typee;* others, which may also have moved him, we have
to guess at, with the perceptions of other writers to help us.
Melville does not say so explicitly, but he too, like Henry

Adams and others, may have ended by finding the Polynesian, with all his charm and grace, a little tiresome on other levels. It was hard of course to resist his beauty and his childlike, faunlike nature, but gradually it may have come to seem even harder to be patient with his childlike, faunlike mind, or rather with his mindlessness, as from a Western point of view it virtually was. Henry Adams was to find the Samoans the least imaginative people he ever met, essentially practical in their interests and even in their superstitions; and if Henry Adams is thought to be a rather too sour observer, we may remind ourselves that other and more sympathetic visitors have confessed that the typical Polynesian—like the typical Greek, no doubt, for that matter—seems not to have an inner life of any interesting complexity or, in our own sense, any rich development of individuality. It is no real disparagement of the South Sea peoples to say this; their great qualities are their own, and civilized man has lost something irreplaceable in losing them; but the chasm is there, nevertheless, and Melville was obeying a true instinct when he acted as if it could never really be crossed with impunity. A certain deep sense of kinship with Polynesian man was never to leave him, as Queequeg in *Moby Dick* indicates to us, but it was a kinship he wanted to feel on an ideal level, not at the sacrifice of his own wholeness, and both *Typee* and *Omoo* make it clear that, conflicting as his feelings were, the longing to *get back* was the strongest of them.

Meanwhile, in Taipi-Vai, there were cruder reasons than these for Melville's increasing restiveness. Charming as the hospitality of the tribe was, it began to be oppressive so soon as Melville discovered that it was also jealous and prohibitive, and that barriers of a startling ferocity would be placed in the way of any attempt on his part to take his leave. Just why this was true he himself was never quite clear, and it is not easy now to say with any confidence. We know, as Melville did not, that there were not one but three distinct tribes of Taipis in the valley, all habitually in conflict with one an-

other, and that he seems to have found himself a guest of the
tribe that occupied the midmost part of the valley. It is possible that, without his taking in the fact (for he understood
only a few words of their speech), his own Taipis had formally adopted him into their tribe, and that they did not
want him to fall into the hands of the others. Even if this was
true, however, Melville himself had darker fears, and he can
hardly be blamed for having them.

He knew already that all the Marquesans were reputed by
sailors and travelers to be lovers of human flesh; that "long
pig" was one of the greatest of their delicacies. Unlike many
white men's beliefs about "savages," this one was based on
reality, and though the Taipis, like the others, knowing what
horror the thought inspired in Europeans, denied the charge
stoutly, they certainly practised cannibalism then, and not
only cannibalism of the ritualistic sort. It was one of the
fears that had troubled Melville and Toby from the beginning. For many days, and until after Toby's departure, nothing happened to confirm their dread. There came a day,
however, when Melville, returning from the *tai* to the house
of old Marheyo, his host, was speechlessly horrified to discover
that the inmates of the house were examining the contents of
three tapa packages he had often observed hanging from the
ridgepole, and that, though these were now hastily bundled
away, they actually contained three human heads, one of
them a white man's. It was a shocking revelation, and what
wonder if it seemed to Melville to throw a grisly light on his
own possible fate?—especially as, a few days later, after one of
their brief, fierce battles with the Hapas, their enemies of a
neighboring valley, the Taipi warriors returned to the *tai*
with the bodies of three slain foes, and Melville was sternly
hurried away from the scene. What followed he could not
know precisely, and for two days he was forbidden to approach either the *tai* or the tabu groves, but everything, including the steady, thunderous sound of drums beating, suggested to his apprehensive mind that some horrid feast was

in progress. On the third day he was again allowed to visit the *tai,* and there, quite by chance, his eye fell upon a carved vessel of wood, partly covered, which contained, there could be no doubt, the disordered members of a human skeleton, the bones still fresh with moisture.

Melville's determination to escape from the valley was now as fierce as his hosts' was to detain him. Just how this was effected he never makes quite plain, and perhaps it was not really plain to him. What he tells us is that he managed to prevail upon the handsome Marnoo, an ingratiating youth from a nearby tribe who could speak a little English, to help him to escape by any means whatever, and that by some native grapevine Marnoo did succeed in getting word of Melville to the captain of an Australian whaler, who had anchored in Tai-o-hae Bay and was attempting to recruit his depleted crew. Sailing around to Comptroller's Bay, at the foot of Taipi-Vai, this captain hove-to off the mouth of the bay and sent in a whaleboat manned by natives, with articles of exchange for the white man. News of the strangers' arrival spread quickly through the valley, and in the excitement that followed, Melville succeeded, despite his lameness, in making his way down to the sea and putting himself in the protection of the boat's crew. He had not done so without the angriest opposition, and it must be that, as he himself believed, the Taipis were somehow passionately divided among themselves over the wisdom of keeping him, and the protests of the other party thwarted the intentions of his captors. However that may be, he managed, he says, to wade out to the rescuing boat and, after a tender embrace of farewell to Fayaway, who had followed him "speechless with sorrow," he tumbled into the boat and was rowed away. Even then they were all pursued by infuriated Taipis, and an attempt was made to cut them off at a headland across their course, but the attempt was frustrated, and a short time later the exhausted young white man was scrambling aboard the *Lucy Ann,* a whaling bark from Sydney.

The twelve months that followed his escape from Taipi-Vai proved to be the longest period in Melville's life of mere carefree, youthful, irresponsible vagabondage; with the utmost zest he threw himself into the business of making a vice of necessity. It is true that our impressions of those months are based largely on *Omoo*, his second book, and that *Omoo* was written in the happy flush of seeing *Typee* become a popular success; the book may very well add a hue to the rainbow of even a glowing reality. As Lawrence remarks, Melville is at his happiest in *Omoo*, really taking the world as it comes, for once; taking it carelessly, recklessly, even a bit knavishly; but on the whole the book is as close to what must have been the emotional truth as it is known to be to the "facts." One can very easily see why. There was a real strain of the vagabond in Melville, of the gipsy, the beachcomber; there is such a strain, to be sure, in most genuine writers; but it was a more special thing than this in Melville, and now at last it was given really free rein, as it was never to be again. He might try later to recapture the picaresque freedom of those months, but he would not succeed. And even earlier he had not had it; the weeks on the *St. Lawrence* and in Liverpool had hardly been consistently lighthearted weeks; the long months on the *Acushnet* may have been adventurous but they were not free; and in Taipi-Vai, of course, he had been to all intents and purposes a prisoner.

Now he was to be, for a few golden months, really footloose. On the *Lucy Ann*, to be sure, he was not quite that, for naturally he had signed up at once as a member of the crew. But he continued to suffer from the malady in his leg, which meant that his duties had to be light ones, and in any case the cruise of the *Lucy Ann* proved to be mercifully brief. The captain, a cockney named Ventom, who had got command of the ship through some sort of pull, not only was a hopelessly incompetent seaman, but very soon after they left Nuku-Hiva he came down ill, and the real control of the vessel passed into the hands of the jolly, efficient, but drunken mate, James

German. After touching at one or two other islands in the Marquesas, at Tahuata and at Hiva-Oa (where Gauguin was to die), the *Lucy Ann* set its course to the westward, and for two or three weeks cruised about in the mid-Pacific on the lookout, quite ineffectually, for whales. Meanwhile Ventom's illness took a turn for the worse, and though German attempted to persuade the crew to recognize him as captain in case Ventom should die, he failed to win them over, and yielding to circumstances he agreed to point the ship's head for Tahiti. At daybreak a day or two later—it was September 20, 1842—the *Lucy Ann* sighted the peaks of Tahiti standing like blue obelisks against the sky, and before the day was over had come to anchor in the offing outside the harbor of Papeete, the little Tahitian metropolis.

They had arrived at the storied island at a moment of crisis in its sorrowful history. A few days earlier—not the *same* day, as Melville pretends—the French admiral, Dupetit-Thouars, arriving at Papeete in his frigate, the *Reine Blanche*, and alleging some of the pretexts familiar in such cases, had forced the native queen, the famous Pomare IV, to accede to his establishing a protectorate over the island. Pomare's bias was toward the English colony and the Protestant missionaries; she soon slipped away to the neighboring island of Moorea (Melville's "Imeeo"), and the general excitement and confusion that followed were to prove a boon to Melville and his fellow seamen. These latter, infuriated by Captain Ventom's having himself taken ashore but refusing to allow the *Lucy Ann* to be brought into harbor, had broken into open rebellion, and were of course immediately branded as mutineers. Their own view was that, once the Captain himself had abandoned the bark, the cruise was lawfully over, and that they could not be forced to put to sea again under command of the drunken mate. They were all bitterly discontented with affairs on the *Lucy Ann* already, and Melville, after attempting, with his new friend "Long Ghost," the demoted surgeon of the vessel, to talk the men into mod-

erate courses, threw in his lot with the mutineers. It was to be
his one act of literal, though certainly not of spiritual, mutiny.

A pleasant comedy of colonial bluster, martinettishness,
and incompetence now followed. The acting English consul,
a pug-nosed alcoholic named Wilson, having made Ventom's
cause his own, attempted to browbeat the mutineers into putting to sea again, and, when this failed, persuaded the French
commander to throw them into irons in the brig of the *Reine
Blanche*. After a day or two of this, there was a change of plan
somewhere, and before the *Reine Blanche* sailed away, Melville, Long Ghost, and the other sailors were released from
their irons and carried on shore at Papeete. Here they were
bullyingly examined again by Wilson, and then led off, along
the charming Broom Road, about a mile from the town, and
thrown into the easy and indeed comic incarceration of the
"Calabooza Beretanee," the makeshift English prison. Their
jailer was an enormous, easygoing old Tahitian known as
Captain Bob; their chains were of the lightest; they were the
recipients of repeated calls from friendly and even admiring
natives, some of whom adopted certain of the sailors, including Melville, as *taios* or special friends; and Melville and
Long Ghost, as the only educated men among them, were be-
friended markedly and quite irregularly by two French
priests and a cheerful Irish padre named Columban Murphy.
Still another attempt was made by Ventom and Wilson, in
an official hearing, to frighten the men into rejoining the
crew of the *Lucy Ann*; but the case against them, though
legally serious, was shaky on every other ground; the authority of the English officials, under the new French protectorate, was shadowy at best; and in the end, having made up a
new crew from among the beachcombers of Papeete, the
Lucy Ann sailed away, in mid-October, leaving the unre-
pentant mutineers behind.

From now on all pretense of holding them prisoners was
abandoned; the Calabooza became their headquarters rather

than their jail; and they were quite free to roam about the beautiful environs of Papeete at their will. The Tahiti of 1842 was a very different place from Taipi-Vai, and partly for that reason the quality of Melville's response to the Tahitians was at least subtly different from that of his response to the Taipis. In both cases one recognizes the presence of a strain of self-protectiveness; half-consciously, no doubt, Melville was too much aware of his own leanings toward a Polynesian way of life not to adopt a defensive breeziness and even levity in speaking of the Polynesians. But it is quite true that, by the time he reached Tahiti, the natives of that island had lived too long under the pall of European and Christian invasion not to have lost most of the "savage" virtues the Taipis had kept—but without, of course, genuinely acquiring the virtues of civilization. In the two generations since Captain Cook's and Captain Bligh's visits the Tahitians had been pretty thoroughly tamed and dispirited by English naval officers, by American whalers, and perhaps most of all by the courageous but terribly wrong-headed Christian missionaries who had forced them to don the vices of a midway condition when they forced them to don the ugly garments of a half-Europeanized culture. Probably they were not yet the "commonplace, dreary, spiritless" people Henry Adams was to find them, and even in Adams's time his view was doubtless a partial one. But already in the 'forties the essential cords of their existence had been snapped; their cults had been broken up and their idols destroyed; their beautiful crafts had been forbidden or at least discouraged; their games and festivals were all tabu; and as a natural result they were no doubt, to some extent, what Melville makes them seem, a still charming and likable but idle, restless, mercurial, and purposeless people. The Tahitian "characters" he draws—the pilot Jim, Captain Bob, the fickle Kooloo (Melville's temporary *taio*), the insinuating beauty Ideea—are mostly comic ones.

This is partly because the prevailing tone of *Omoo* is gay

and unserious, and yet it is clear enough from the book itself that Melville by no means missed the intense melancholy of the Tahitian fate. He certainly did not miss the responsibility for it of the missionaries, to whom he pays his respects in terms that made him a marked man in certain church quarters. Meanwhile he and Long Ghost had lingered no great while on the island of Tahiti after the *Lucy Ann* sailed away. During all the weeks of their stay they had seen the sun set daily behind the high, fantastic, purple peaks of the little neighboring island of Moorea—the peaks that La Farge later painted so glowingly—and early in November they decided to decamp quietly and seek their fortunes there. They had got wind of two white men, a Yankee named Zeke and a young cockney named Shorty, who had started a kind of tropical truck garden in the valley of Maatea for the raising chiefly of sweet potatoes, and who were looking for a couple of stout hands to assist them. Neither Melville nor Long Ghost had the slightest intention of committing themselves irrevocably to any activity so arduous as farm work, but it was an excuse for slipping away from Papeete and the skeleton of authority there, and for a few days, having reached Moorea by night, they did go through the motions, more or less grudgingly, of toiling in the potato patch with Zeke and Shorty or carrying loads of potatoes down to the beach for transportation to Tahiti.

A few days of this was quite enough for the two leisure-loving beachcombers. Melville was really bent, for the moment, on forgetting all the lessons he might ever have learned from Allan Melville about industry and frugality, and even all the lessons he had ever learned from anyone about sober, dutiful, regular, middle-class behavior; and he and Long Ghost succeeded in persuading Zeke and Shorty to let them break their very oral contract and set out again on their rambles. They had heard of a relatively remote native village named Tamai, on the banks of a beautiful lake on the other side of Moorea, where life was still being led with a primitive simplicity but little corrupted since Captain Cook's time; and thither they betook themselves on foot. On the whole, though the people of Tamai were nominally Christians, they were in fact a much less overshadowed and vitiated community than Tahiti; and the two white youths managed to talk an old chief into arranging for them a performance of one of the forbidden native dances by a group of girls; a performance that took place by moonlight on the fern-carpeted banks of the lake. According to Melville, he and the old chief had much ado to keep Long Ghost in hand during the voluptuous progress of the dance; his own emotions he leaves undescribed.

Tamai, at any rate, they found so enchanting that they might have lingered there indefinitely if the sudden appearance of some strangers, reputed to be missionaries, had not put them to rout. Returning to Zeke and Shorty's to reconnoiter, they decided to make their way over to the western side of Moorea and the bay of Tareu (Melville's "Taloo"), on the shores of which was the village of Papetoai ("Partoo-wye"). Here Pomare had her temporary residence; nearby there was a sugar plantation; a solitary whaler was rumored to be lying in the little-used harbor; and all in all Papetoai seemed to offer opportunities, if it should come to that, for employment—for they had formed the scheme, not perhaps so fanciful as it sounds, of trying to obtain posts for themselves in Pomare's retinue. Early one morning, at any rate, they bade a final farewell to their former employers and set out on foot to make their way along the shore of the island, following, beneath the leaning coco-palms, the quiet lagoon with the coral reef beyond it. A few days later they arrived at Papetoai. The bay of Tareu, with the groves and hills round about, proved to be one of the most beautiful spots Melville had yet come upon; they were the guests during their whole stay of an aristocratic native with the hybrid name of Jeremiah Po-po, who with his wife Arfretee lavished upon them the characteristically simple but prodigal hospitality of ancient Moorea; and they seemed at last to have reached a private little utopia of irresponsible leisure and freedom.

It was what, for a certain interval, Melville wanted and needed, but it was not what he wanted in the deepest sense or for *more* than a golden interval, and he could not make himself over into the thoroughgoing beachcomber that Long Ghost seems to have been. His eyes began to turn more and more consideringly to the *Charles and Henry*, the Nantucket whaler that Melville calls the *Leviathan* and that seems to have been lying then in the harbor. He even made overtures to its crew. At first he got little encouragement, and it was probably with hardly more than the shadow of serious intent, but in a spirit of devil-may-care adventure, that he joined the graceless Long Ghost in an attempt on the favor of Queen Pomare. It was an act, as one cannot help feeling, of very dubious courtesy and taste; perhaps the solitary act of the sort in Melville's life; but in any event, if his own story is to be believed, Melville and his companion made their way through the outer courts and passages of Pomare's "palace"—a cluster of large native houses, of course—and by ingratiating themselves with one of her guards, they did in fact succeed in intruding into the presence of the melancholy queen herself. They found her surrounded by the oddest litter of elegant European gifts, a folio volume of Hogarth among others, and of native articles. One glance at Pomare was all they were to have. Surprised and offended, the Queen issued an angry order and waved the two audacious white men out of her presence.

It was perhaps only a day or two later, probably in mid-January 1843, that Melville succeeded in catching the friendly eye of Captain John Coleman, the skipper of the *Charles and Henry*, whom he describes as a tall, robust Vineyarder. Captain Coleman, if it was he, proved to be insurmountably suspicious of Long Ghost, but he ended by deciding that Melville himself was a safe bet and agreed to add him to his crew. In a very short time, laden now with gifts of tapa and fine matting from the good, motherly Arfretee, Melville had boarded his third whaler and, slipping out of the harbor of Tareu at sunrise, headed again for the wide Pacific.

A few months later, toward the end of April, the *Charles and Henry* came to anchor in the roadstead of Lahaina, a busy port on the island of Maui in the Hawaiian group. The cruise of the *Charles and Henry* had been almost as profitless as that of the *Lucy Ann* had been, and Melville, who had probably signed on only for the cruise, was discharged a few days later. He now put whaling behind him once for all; he was never to join the crew of another whaler, whatever honor and glory might attach to that life. He had had enough at last, in this literal sense, of the cruise and the chase.

The chances are that he had had enough also of the life of an *omoo* or beachcomber, and was now only biding his time until the right means of getting home should present itself. It is true that for three or four months he continued to knock about the "Sandwich" Islands in what must have been a very beachcombing sort of way. He had soon left Lahaina, and before long had found his way to the now still busier port of Honolulu. There is a credible story of his having been observed setting up pins in a bowling-alley in that rather raffish town, where bowling-alleys did in fact abound; and early in the summer he certainly entered into an agreement with a young English storekeeper named Isaac Montgomery to work for him as a bookkeeper and general clerk for twelve months thereafter. But for some reason or other the agreement was broken less than three months later, and Melville had started back to America.

Perhaps, as some writers have suggested, his steps were hastened away from the islands by the appearance in Hawaiian waters that summer of Captain Pease and the *Acushnet*. Certainly an affidavit to his desertion at Nuku-Hiva a year earlier was filed by Captain Pease at Lahaina soon after Melville moved on to Honolulu; and if he knew this, as he

could easily have done, it cannot have enhanced the pleasure
he took in Hawaiian life. Probably his pleasure in it was not
very intense in any case. His few allusions to Hawaii and the
Hawaiians are mostly captious and even contemptuous; he alludes to the king, Kamehameha III, in language of unbridled
and probably unjust disdain; and he seems to have been
shocked by the scenes of public rejoicing and revelry—what
he calls "universal broad-day debauchery"—which took place
when the brief occupation of Hawaii by the English was
formally withdrawn that August. Probably he had quite
ceased, for the time, to take any pleasure whatever in the
spectacle of Polynesian life, at least as he saw it in these
haunts of the invading and despoiling white; probably he was
really weary not only of primitive existence but of his own
placelessness and anonymity, and would have seized upon almost any resource for getting home, short of joining the crew
of another whaler.

He was soon to have his chance. Early in August an American man-of-war, the frigate *United States*—a fine old ship that
belonged to the era of the *Constellation* and the *Constitution;* Decatur had commanded it during the War of 1812—
arrived in the harbor of Honolulu. A week or two later Melville joined the crew of this vessel as an enlisted man, and on
August 20th the *United States* weighed anchor and stood
out to sea. During the next fourteen months Melville was
leading the life of a sailor in the American navy.

He was to have to bide his time with what patience he
could before reaching home, for the frigate, which when he
enlisted was the flagship of the Pacific squadron, was in no
great hurry to return to America. For almost a year, indeed, it
was to remain in the Pacific, where Melville was still to see
much that was new to him as well as to see again some of the
spots he had already visited. The *United States*, for example,
very soon touched at the Marquesas Islands and in fact at
Nuku-Hiva itself, riding at anchor for a day or two in Tai-o-
hae Bay and entertaining ceremonially the young "king" of

the island, Moana, and his consort Vaekehu, she of the celebrated legs and buttocks, great masterpieces of the tattooer's art. But Melville did not set foot again on the island that had been his refuge and his prison. Nor did he probably leave the vessel when, a few days later, it anchored in Matavai Bay at Tahiti, though they remained for a week in that harbor and entertained Pomare's consort on board. Toward the end of October the *United States* set sail for the coast of South America, and Melville had seen the last of his Enviable Isles. During much of the time that remained to him in the South Seas, the frigate was to lie at anchor in the bay of Callao, the station for the American squadron at that period.

From Callao it was but eight miles inland to Lima, and on one occasion at least, when his watch had shore leave, Melville made the journey overland to the old City of the Kings, the city Pizarro had built. If he saw Lima only once, and then only for a day or two, his hours there were clearly among the most densely packed—packed with intense impressions and unfading images—of Melville's life. Ever afterward Lima was to remain one of the cities of his imagination, "the strangest, saddest city thou canst see," as he calls it in a famous passage; a city whose leaning spires and wrenched copestones and tilting crosses he was never to lose from his memory. Beautiful as its environs were, between the sea and the Andes, and beautiful as the city itself was, with its white churches, its white town houses, and its straight white avenues, Lima was a city in whose whiteness and beauty there was a latent horror, too; again and again it had been shattered by earthquakes, and once at least it had been utterly destroyed. It was a city that lived under the constant menace of nature's most tigerish destructiveness; and that also, or so Melville says, enjoyed an evil fame all along the coast for a special inner destructiveness of its own, a special corruption, so that men had made a proverb of the phrase, "Corrupt as Lima." Perhaps it was these things that, along with his sharp, strong visual impressions of the Peruvian city, gradually converted Lima for Melville into a kind of symbol, and made him feel, with Don Pedro in "The Town-Ho's Story," that "the world's one Lima." The city had become not only his Lisbon and his Sybaris but something more than either.

Meanwhile, however, his days and nights on the *United States* were mainly occupied in other ways than in poetic sight-seeing; they were occupied in the hundred and one strenuous and severely disciplined duties of a common seaman in the old navy. When he enlisted, according to his own account, Melville had been assigned to the starboard watch and specifically to the maintopmen, where his own individual station was on the main-royalyard; and much of his time, night and day, was spent aloft with his comrades of the maintop, taking part in the working of the ship. Other hours were spent washing down decks, polishing brass, and at regular intervals participating in the kind of drill known as "general quarters," when all hands were mustered to their stations at the guns and put through the motions of a mock battle at sea. At such times, Melville's own station was at one of the thirty-two-pound guns on the starboard side of the quarter-deck— Gun No. 15, specifically, or Black Bet, as she was known among the gun's crew—and here his particular duty, he says, was to ram and sponge Black Bet as the gun was run in and out of the porthole. Then, on the first Sunday of every month he would take part with the rest of the crew in the "muster round the capstan"; passing in review before the officers, being inspected by them, and listening—Melville, with angry rebellion in his heart—to a reading of the grim Articles of War.

There was rebellion in his heart, if we are to believe *White-Jacket*, during many hours of his fourteen months in a man-of-war, and on this subjective side the book can hardly be a great distortion of the reality. A deep, passionate resistance to all forms of outward coercion had by this time become a fixed aspect of Melville's emotional life. Docile as he had seemed to be as a child, and well-behaved as he presumably was in his teens, the origins of his rebelliousness lay deep in his nature and his experience, and the events of his wander-years had ended by creating in him a settled hatred of exter-nal authority, a lust for personal freedom. He was of course the descendant of rebels and, besides that, he was already in-fected by the famous individualism of his era, its self-trustful defiance of all arbitrary and unspontaneous control. But this was only part of the story, and the less important part; what was more important was something more obscure and more idiosyncratic than that, and something harder to define: the growing and intensifying sense of his own exceptionalness as a person, his possession of only dimly apprehended great gifts, and the ways in which he was more and more deviating from the normal and familiar roads; along with these, the re-sentful sense that circumstance and mankind together had al-ready imposed their will upon him in a series of injurious ways. It is easy to see that, with all his humor and all his adventurousness, Melville was already, at the age of twenty-four, a deeply neurotic person in one of the most creative meanings of the word, and that his hatred of discipline and authority, of the paternal principle in that sense, reasonable though much of it was, was a hatred that had its source in a malady.

As for discipline in the American navy at the time Melville belonged to it, no doubt much of it was as exaggerated and in-sensate as he alleges; there is other evidence than his own that this was true. Certainly, at a hundred points, it must have been peculiarly calculated to rasp the sensibilities of a youth like Melville. If there had been nothing else to outrage him on board the *United States*, there would have been the shock-ing practice of flogging; a practice that still existed, though it was soon to be outlawed by act of Congress. If, only once, he had been forced to look on while another man was stripped to the waist at the gangway, bound to the gratings, lashed by the cat-o'-nine-tails, and ultimately cut down in a bleeding and more or less exhausted state, his emotions would be understandable enough. As it happens, Melville was forced to look on at a scene like this, according to official records, some one hundred and sixty-three times during his months on the *United States*. It is not hard to understand why incidents like these, along with others less painful but exasperating enough, should have inspired in him a lasting detestation of naval discipline that went hand in hand with his detestation of war itself. His animus, however, was not only against irrational and brutal discipline but against any discipline imposed from without.

Inwardly, as a result, his life on a man-of-war must have been filled with dangerous and hurtful tensions; impulses of a destructive sort must more than once have risen in him, only to be precariously repressed. It seems highly unlikely that he had, in literal actuality, the experience he describes in *White-Jacket*—the experience of being himself ordered to be flogged, being rescued from this humiliation at the last moment by the intervention of an officer, and feeling the irresistible impulse meanwhile to fling himself upon the unjust Captain Claret and carry both himself and the other over the bulwarks of the vessel to a death-by-water below it. There is no record of any such incident in the log book of the cruise, and no mention of it in a personal journal kept by one of the other seamen; in short, it was all but certainly an event that never took place in the world of physical action. But this does not mean that it never took place in any sense; as Melville says in *Mardi*, "what are vulgarly called fictions are as much realities as the gross mattock of Dididi"; and this particular fiction did certainly occur in the world of feeling and wish. It speaks to us far more eloquently of its inventor than any "true" narration could have done.

Yet Melville's life on the homeward voyage of the *Neversink*, as he calls the frigate, was not merely an affair of uninterrupted tension and discontent; to represent it as such would be to indulge in biographical melodrama. It was life at sea, after all, and given what the sea meant to Melville, in the profoundest sources of his existence, such a life could never, in these years, have failed of its intense satisfactions. The friendships he formed, moreover, among the crew of the *United States* would themselves have kept these months from being a blank waste. He says that he made little effort to rub acquaintance with any great number of his fellow sailors, but his capacity for friendship, along with his need of it, was very great, and among his comrades of the maintop he struck up several intimacies; with a lean, saturnine, bookish man whom he calls Nord; with a nautical poet he calls Lemsford; with Griffith Williams, a good-humored Yankee from Maine; and above all with "matchless and unmatchable Jack Chase," his idolized captain of the maintop.

With Jack Chase, indeed, Melville formed one of the great friendships of his life, broken off though it was when they reached port at the end of the cruise. Nearly fifty years later he was to dedicate *Billy Budd* to "that great heart," and to model the character of Billy himself, in some sense, on his friend. And indeed John J. Chase, to use his actual name, must have been something like as heroic a figure as Billy. Tall and well-knit, with a clear eye and a great brown beard, Jack Chase, says Melville, was a frank and charming person, whom the seamen loved and the officers admired, and to whom even the Captain spoke with a slight air of respect. An Englishman, and a great stickler for the rights of man, he had in actual fact given evidence of his sway even over the officers by having been reinstated in the navy with only a reprimand after he had deserted his ship to fight for the liberties of Peru. He had been captain of a main-deck gun at the slaughterous Battle of Navarino; he had been at one time a dashing smuggler; but he was somehow a gentleman, nevertheless, whatever his history, with infinite good sense and good feeling, a love of poetry, especially of Camoëns, and a free and noble style in singing chanteys. "My sea-tutor and sire" Melville calls him; he alludes to himself as Jack Chase's pet; and no doubt for a few months Chase did fill the role of the half-paternal, half-brotherly friend for whom Melville was constantly seeking.

For months, off and on, the frigate had lain in port at Callao, but early in July 1844, under a new captain, C. K. Stribling, it got under weigh at last for America. Another wintry rounding of Cape Horn; an anchorage of seven or eight days in the harbor of Rio de Janeiro; a naval race out of that harbor with three other American men-of-war and a French corvette; a sail northward in mostly squally weather through the Atlantic, and then at last, on October 3rd, the *United States* drew near to land, stood in to Boston Harbor, and came to anchor in the Navy Yard at Charlestown. Melville's version of their arrival is a picturesque one; according to this, it was not Boston Harbor but Norfolk, and the ship drew near to land on a starry night; as it did so, the maintopmen were all aloft for the last time, and Jack Chase, pointing shoreward, sang out a fine, port-making passage from the *Lusiads*. In prosaic fact, it was broad daylight, and the sailor-diarist drily remarks that they "furled sails, hoisted out the boats, and sent on shore all men whose time had expired." Melville, as it happened, had enlisted for three years, a period of which almost two-thirds still remained; but Captain Stribling obtained permission from the Secretary of the Navy to release the entire crew, and on October 14th Melville received his discharge. Within a few days no doubt, a sailor's life behind him for good, he was at home again in Lansingburgh with Maria Melville and his sisters.

The Author of *Typee, Omoo,* &c.

MOST MODERN WRITERS have come to the literary career in response to a vocation of which they have been conscious from boyhood on; if they have not lisped in numbers, they have at any rate filled their adolescence with plans for novels, for ambitious poems, for plays. One cannot say flatly that this was not true of Melville; we do not know whether it was or not. But in spite of the "Fragments from a Writing-Desk," one's impression is that Melville came to literature, not after long and conscious preparation, but with a kind of inadvertence. He speaks of having dreamed as a boy of becoming a great traveler and even of becoming a famous orator but never of becoming an author. The need for movement, for flight, for the coarse stuff of experience was stronger in him in his earliest youth than the need for expression. The germ of what was creative in him needed to ripen, not in solitude or in intellectual labor, but in the push and stir of action. In the beginning, for Melville, was decidedly not the word, but the deed. Not until he had to come to terms with the dense material world and the actualities of the human struggle was he prepared to give himself out in language and form. His development, in that sense, as he recognized, had been abnormally postponed, and when it came, it came with a rush and a force that had the menace of quick exhaustion in it. Could it possibly be maintained at that pitch over the span of a long career?

That remained to be seen, but meanwhile, in just this respect, in the postponement of creation to action, Melville makes one think, not of the representative modern man of letters, for whom action has been either secondary or without significance, but of a heterogeneous list of writers, as different from one another as from him in power and in character, writers like Smollett or Stendhal or Fenimore Cooper or Tolstoy, who spent their earliest years, not at their writing desks, but on the deck of a ship or in the train of a marching army. Bookish as Melville had always been and was increasingly to be, he came to the profession of letters as a kind of brilliant amateur, and he was never quite to take on, whether for better or for worse, the mentality of the professional.

This is hardly to say that he was a lesser writer than those who did. Nor certainly is it to say, on a more superficial level, that he was not, once he had found his tongue, almost unaccountably productive. One imagines him writing *Typee* in much the same spirit in which Dana had written *Two Years* or in which the young Englishman Kinglake was writing *Eothen:* because he had seen a bit of the world, because his head was stored with fresh impressions and entertaining circumstances, and because his relatives and friends had drawn him out in conversation in a way that aroused and ignited him. No doubt he wrote *Typee* almost casually; it turned into a great success before his eyes; his powerful literary instincts were fully awakened, and there followed, during the next five or six years, at a breathless pace, four other books— *Omoo, Mardi, Redburn,* and *White-Jacket*—in the composition of which he can hardly have paused or deliberated. Neither Dana nor Kinglake had done anything of the sort, and that is one difference between them and Melville.

This was the school of writing, nevertheless, that furnished Melville his springboard as an artist. It was no mere accident that it did so, but a characteristic fact that holds for no other nineteenth-century writer of his stature. He did not begin at once, like most of them, as a writer of tales, sketches, or novels for the periodicals or the booksellers' libraries of the era; he did not begin as a successor of Sterne or Godwin or Scott, of Mrs. Radcliffe or Hoffmann. He began as one more writer of travel narrative, and the books from which he took off were not *Tristram Shandy* or *Waverly* but Mungo Park's *Travels in the Interior of Africa*, the Rev. C. S. Stewart's *Visit to the South Seas*, and of course the book he called "my friend Dana's unmatchable *Two Years Before the Mast*." Saying this is something like saying that George Eliot began as a writer of critical and philosophical articles for the *Westminster Review*; no other writer of just that sort has gone on to write books like *Middlemarch*, and none of the other writers of "travels" or "journals" or "narratives" went on to write books like *Moby Dick*. But George Eliot's whole work is pervaded by the attitudes of the moralist and critic, and Melville, for his part, was always to be an imaginative writer for whom the facts of movement through space, of change of site, of physical unrestingness and the forward push were basic. The voyage or quest was not simply a subject or an occasion for him; it was an archetypal pattern of experience to which his whole nature instinctively turned, and he was to lose half his strength not when he lost contact with the earth but when he stood still upon it.

Typee and *Omoo*, to be sure, were books that he wrote, if not off the top of his mind, at any rate off its less profound levels, and it is idle to look for great depths or difficulties in them; to do so would be to miss their special quality of spontaneity and youthfulness. Yet there are intimations of complexity in them, and in a purely literary sense, easy though they seem, they are curiously many-faceted. They owe something, in a general way, to the whole tradition of travel literature since the modern age of discovery began, and particularly to the voyages of the eighteenth century, to the writers of the age of Cook and Carteret and Bougainville, whose aim was always to be lucid, impersonal, informative; to suppress *themselves* and to convey the facts, however novel or strange, with the most reasonable and enlightened objectivity. A love of information for its own sake was one of the aspects of Melville's complex mind, as every reader of *Moby Dick* knows; and when, in *Typee*, he describes the process of making tapa or the operations of the system of tabu, or when, in *Omoo*, he dilates on the botany and the economy of the coco-palm, his tone and manner are not easily distinguishable from those in which Captain Cook or Bougainville or Langsdorff had expatiated on exactly similar subjects. Melville's first two books have been quoted by anthropologists since his time, by Sir James Frazer for example, as having at least some claim to trustworthiness, despite Melville's very small comprehension of the language of Taipi or Tahiti. The fact is that, whenever his imagination was at work most freely and naturally, it sought for and found the factual, prosaic counterpoise to the inwardness and ideality that were its essential expression; and *Typee* and *Omoo* owe much of their vitality to their apparently unpoetic ballast of facts.

A transformation, however, had taken place in the literature of travel since the eighteenth century, just as it had done in literature generally, and such books could no longer be written sustainedly in the old manner, any more than novels could be written in the manner of Diderot or Smollett. The dry, clear, sober impersonality of the older writers had given place to a more and more frankly personal and subjective style, whimsical, humorous, lyrical, sentimental, or poetic; Melville began writing in a period that had formed its taste on such lighthearted and charming books as Heine's *Pictures of Travel*, Irving's *Alhambra*, Kinglake's *Eothen*, and Gautier's *Travels in Spain*. Information of a kind does indeed appear in books like these, but what really counts in them is not that but feeling, fancy, atmosphere, and the effort to evoke as many and as brilliant pictures as possible. The sense of the painterly has usurped the place of the older interest in fact.

Even in a writer like Mungo Park, at the turn of the nineteenth century, one detects already a strain of personal feeling and even a sense of the pictorial that is by no means merely "eighteenth century"; and Mungo Park was almost certainly one of Melville's literary masters. There are deeply moving passages in Park's *Travels,* but what happened to travel writing after his time becomes evident when one turns to Melville abruptly from a writer of his sort. Here is a passage, quite typical of Park's ordinary narrative style, from his account of a night spent at an African town in the kingdom of Kajaaga:

> I found a great crowd surrounding a party who were dancing by the light of some large fires, to the music of four drums, which were beat with great exactness and uniformity. The dances, however, consisted more in wanton gestures than in muscular exertion or graceful attitudes. The ladies vied with each other in displaying the most voluptuous movements imaginable.

Compare with this—in its quiet, taciturn failure to realize a potentially quite wonderful picture—compare with it Melville's description in *Omoo* of the dancing girls at Tamai or, better yet, this description in *Typee* of a fishing party returning from the beach at night:

> Once, I remember, the party arrived at midnight; but the unseasonableness of the hour did not repress the impatience of the islanders. The carriers dispatched from the Ti were to be seen hurrying in all directions through the deep groves; each individual preceded by a boy bearing a flaming torch of dried cocoa-nut boughs, which from time to time was replenished from the materials scattered along the path. The wild glare of these enormous flambeaux, lighting up with a startling brilliancy the inner-

most recesses of the vale, and seen moving rapidly along beneath the canopy of leaves, the savage shout of the excited messengers sounding the news of their approach, which was answered on all sides, and the strange appearance of their naked bodies, seen against the gloomy background, produced altogether an effect upon my mind that I shall long remember.

Naturally this is not yet Melville in his great evocative vein, and Stevenson was later to outdo him, just here, in finish and precision of brush stroke, but the passage will serve as a fair example of Melville's painterliness in *Typee* and *Omoo*. Like some other passages in those books, it hints to us—with its romantic chiaroscuro, its violent contrast of deep shadow and high flaring lights, the uncanniness of its moving figures, and its dependence on words like "wild," "startling," "strange," and "gloomy"—hints to us that Melville, in looking at the scenes that passed before him and in reinvoking them, had learned something from such Gothic writers as Mrs. Radcliffe and "Monk" Lewis, and that through them, perhaps also independently, his landscape sense had been formed by the Baroque painters they were always echoing, by Claude Lorrain and Salvator Rosa. Salvator in the Marquesas might have done the nocturne of the fishing party. Baroque, at any rate, most of Melville's landscapes and seascapes certainly are, as well as many of the other scenes he composes like pictures. The hours he spent as a boy poring over the portfolios of prints Allan Melville had brought home had worked a permanent influence on his imagination.

His first two books abound in pictorial effects that can only be described as in some sense romantic; wild and fearful like the gorges, ravines, and chasms of Nuku-Hiva through which he and Toby make their painful way in *Typee*; solemn, deeply shaded, and awe-inspiring, like the tabu groves in Taipi-Vai; uncannily beautiful like another fishing party by torchlight, in *Omoo*, in the sullen surf off Moorea; or in a wholly different vein—the vein of Claude rather than of

Salvator—pastoral, Arcadian, richly reposeful, like the first breathless glimpse of the Paradisal valley of Taipi. Already in these early, experimental books, with varying degrees of success, Melville knows how to cover a gamut of painterly and emotional effects that ranges all the way from the broad and serene to the wild, the grim, and even the grotesque. And indeed it is evident that these contrasts of tone and feeling, especially marked in *Typee*, are conscious and artful, not merely inadvertent, and that they express a native feeling for structure and style that already suggests how much farther Melville may go as an imaginative writer than any of the narrators he is emulating. *Two Years Before the Mast* is a greater book than either *Typee* or *Omoo*, in its strong, sustained austerity of style as well as in its grandeur of feeling; but Melville's books are the unmistakable products of a far more complex and ductile mind than Dana's, and potentially, of course, of a richer creative power. Dana's great book suggests no artistic mode beyond itself; *Typee* and *Omoo* hint constantly at the freer and more plastic form of fiction.

When they first appeared, indeed, they were taxed, or credited, by many readers with being *pure* fiction, and some of these readers, at least, were more imaginative than those who took them for sober fact. It is not only that we now know how long a bow Melville was drawing in both books, especially *Typee;* how freely he was improvising on the mere actualities of his experience; that is an external and mechanical sort of check. The books themselves need only to be read responsively in order to uncover their real quality—their real and equivocal quality of narrative that is constantly vibrating between the poles of "truthfulness" and fantasy. The proportion of sober truthfulness in *Omoo* is doubtless greater than in *Typee*, and the free, fanciful strains in it take the form of playfulness, gay exaggeration, and grotesqueness rather than, as they mostly do in *Typee*, of a heightened "anxiety," on the one hand, and a deliberate idyllism, on the other. But in both books Melville is far too much the born artist not to keep bathing the plain truth in a medium of imaginative intensity.

A few weeks after *Typee* was published, as we have seen, Toby Greene unexpectedly turned up in Buffalo to testify to the veracity of those chapters for which he could vouch, but we must not take his evidence too literally. Melville's story of what happened after he and Toby plunged into the interior of Nuku-Hiva, of the hardships and sufferings they underwent before they arrived in Taipi—this story bears on the face of it the hallmarks of poetic sublimation. Plenty of travelers have undergone greater ordeals than Melville's was at its worst, and one has only, again, to read Mungo Park's account of some of his solitary vicissitudes in order to observe how calmly and even barely the thing can be done. There is nothing calm or bare and certainly nothing austere in Melville's narrative. It is frankly and volubly a tale of tribulation: it abounds in the imagery of physical and mental misery. At the outset Melville and Toby are drenched by a downpour of tropical rain; they find themselves trapped in a thicket of dense, resistant reeds; they are baked by the heat of midday; they scramble up a steep cliff and crawl along a ridge on their bellies to evade detection; they are confronted by a series of "dark and fearful chasms, separated by sharp-crested and perpendicular ridges," up and down which they painfully clamber; they spend the nights in gloomy ravines, shivering with the chill and dampness; and at last they make their way down into the valley by falling, rather than descending, from ledge to ledge of a horridly high, steep precipice. Throughout, they suffer from hunger and raging thirst; Melville, from a painful injury to his leg; and both of them, from "frightful anticipations of evil." We move, in all this, not over the solid terrain of even a romantic island but amidst a dream-imagery of deadly apprehensiveness, baffled and dismayed by obstacle after obstacle, and oppressed continually by a dread of what is before us. Such writing is far less reminiscent of *Two Years* than it is of Mrs. Radcliffe or Poe.

The note of nightmarish foreboding, in any case, is struck recurrently in *Typee*, where it reaches a culmination of intensity in the last chapters, with Melville's gruesome discoveries and his horror lest he should be powerless to escape. It alternates, however, like a theme in music, with the strongly contrasted note of contentment and peace; the contentment and peace of daydreaming. The conflict between wishful revery and the anxiety that springs from a feeling of guilt, in short, goes on throughout the book. In *Omoo*, on the other hand, perhaps because it was written in a period of emotional freedom and effervescence, there is no such inner drama and no such stylistic musicality. The contrasts of tone in the book are furnished partly by the simple alternation between personal narrative and impersonal informativeness, but also by the relatively prosaic setting-off of the hardships and exasperations of life aboard the *Julia* (Melville's name for the *Lucy Ann*) or in the Calabooza Beretanee against the heady pleasures of freedom and vagrancy. The play of fantasy in *Omoo* takes the form not of nightmarishness or even of daydreaming but of an easy and emotionally liberating current of humorous narrative, always slightly in excess, as one sees with half an eye, of the sober autobiographical facts. It usually has the satisfactory effect of throwing a ludicrous light on the representatives of order and authority—captains and mates, consuls and missionaries, resident physicians and native constables. There is still, as a result, an emotional release in reading *Omoo*, as in reading any such book; we take our own revenge on respectability by contemplating the discomfiture of the feeble Captain Guy and the bullying consul Wilson, or by listening to the wily sermon of the Chadband whom Melville describes himself as hearing in the church at Papeete.

It is true that, compared with the billows of almost demoniac humor on which *Moby Dick* is so incredibly sustained, the humor of *Typee* and even of *Omoo* seems gentle and rather tame. Yet one feels at once that it is the expression of a genuinely humorous fancy. One feels it in such accounts as that of the popgun war in *Typee* or of Long Ghost's jolly philanderings in *Omoo*. One feels it even verbally in such remarks as that Captain Guy was "no more meant for the sea than a hairdresser," or in the observation on the ugliness of the ship's carpenter on the *Julia:* "There was no absolute deformity about the man; he was symmetrically ugly." One feels this youthful humor chiefly, however, in the individual characters in whom both books abound, and who are treated with a freedom far closer to fiction than to mere reminiscence. The difference is easily evident when one puts one of Dana's characters—say the young Hawaiian, Hope, or the English sailor, George P. Marsh, a decayed gentleman—side by side with characters like Melville's Kory-Kory or Long Ghost. Dana's portraits have the sobriety and the realism of Copley's in another medium; Melville's come closer to suggesting Cruikshank or Phiz. For the rest, in the period when he was writing *Typee* and *Omoo*, it was mostly the amusing, even lovable oddities and humors of human character that engaged him, not its darknesses and depravities. There are shadows of some intensity here and there; in the brutal Captain Vangs and in the dark, moody, vindictive Maori harpooneer, Bembo; but mostly the scene is animated by such gently comic personages as fussy old Marheyo in Taipi, or the grotesque-looking Kory-Kory, or the poor landlubber sailor, Ropey, on the *Julia.*

Most of them are mere sketches, lightly and hastily drawn; and the most fully realized feminine character, the exquisite Fayaway, is not so much drawn as vaguely and dreamily evoked in wishful water colors. Only one personage among them all is painted at full length; this is the demoted ship's surgeon, Long Ghost, who is the real protagonist of *Omoo* (Melville himself is the protagonist of *Typee*), and who embodies the complete footlooseness, the perfect irresponsibility, which Melville, on one side of his nature, would have liked to attain. A ruined gentleman, well-read and well-

mannered, but lazy, mischievous, reckless, amorous, and rascally, Long Ghost appears in the forecastle of the *Julia* as if
he were a personal materialization of all Melville's longings
for a really unbraced and ungirded freedom. So long as the
mood lasts, Long Ghost sticks by his side, a perfect companion, indeed another self, but at length the mood passes, the
fundamental seriousness in Melville reasserts itself, and
about to join the crew of the *Leviathan* he takes leave both of
the waggish doctor and, to all intents and purposes, of the
beachcomber in himself.

The gesture has an almost allegorical quality. Lighthearted and unprofound as on the whole they are, *Typee* and
Omoo have an undertone of serious meaning. Taken together
they tell the story of a quest or pilgrimage—a pilgrimage not,
certainly, "from this world to that which is to come," but
from the world of enlightened rationality, technical progress,
and cultural complexity backward and downward and, so to
say, inward to the primordial world that *was* before metals,
before the alphabet, before cities; the slower, graver, nakeder
world of stone, of carved wood, of the tribe, of the ritual
dance and human sacrifice and the prerational myth. It was a
pilgrimage that led to no all-answering oracle or consumma-
tory revelation; in that sense it was a failure. But it was a
pilgrimage that Melville's deepest needs had driven him to
make, and he did not return from it empty-handed. There are
passages in *Typee* especially that tell us how really intense,
how far from merely fashionable, was his animus against
"civilized barbarity," against "the tainted atmosphere of a
feverish civilization." He returned to civilization in the end,
but he had had a long gaze at a simpler, freer, gayer, and yet
also statelier mode of life, and this was to serve him, in memory, as a stabilizing and fortifying image. His own creative
power, moreover, at its height, was primeval and myth-making
in a sense that, in his day, was of the rarest: it could never
have been set free, just as it was, if he himself had not made
his descent into the canyon of the past. In touching the body

of Fayaway, Melville had regained contact with the almost vanished life of myth.

His instincts had guided him rightly when they sent him wandering into the young Pacific world, and they guided him rightly when they drove him away from it again and back to civilized society, to resume a burden he had temporarily laid down—the burden of consciousness, of the full and anguished consciousness of modern man. He had taken a long plunge into the realm of the preconscious and the instinctual, the realm of heedless impulse and irreflective drift; he had been refreshed, indeed remade, by it; but he had found there no ultimate resolution of his difficulties. Not in avoiding the clash between consciousness and the unconscious, between mind and emotion, between anxious doubt and confident belief, but in confronting these antinomies head-on and, hopefully, transcending them—in that direction, as Melville intuitively saw, lay his right future as an adult person. The alternative was a lifetime of raffish vagrancy with the seedy Long Ghost, and a kind of Conradian dilapidation at the end. In the last chapter of *Omoo*, saying good-bye to his companion, he insists on Long Ghost's taking half the Spanish dollars which the captain of the *Leviathan* has given him as an advance; a generous but also a proper payment for the wisdom he has acquired in Long Ghost's society. A new cruise awaits him, on another vessel; and in fact, when Melville finished the writing of *Omoo*, he had come to the end of one expedition, in the intellectual and literary sense, and was ready to set out again in a quite different direction.

The writing of *Typee* and *Omoo*, it goes without saying, confronted Melville with literary problems, but they were not problems of intense difficulty, and in solving them he was content for the most part to rely on a literary form that was already fully evolved and perfectly well defined when he began to write. He could do this because what he was aiming to express was an experience, or rather an aspect of that experience, that was relatively unprofound, uncomplex, unproblematic. Other writers of such books had stopped dead in their tracks at just that point, but naturally this was impossible for Melville. Only now, as he later remarked to Hawthorne, was he beginning to be aware of an intense inward development, of an almost painfully accelerated process of unfolding within himself; only now, in his middle and later twenties, was he becoming fully conscious of a thousand intellectual and emotional perplexities, difficulties, enigmas. Month by month, one imagines, as he was writing *Typee* and surely *Omoo*, the need was growing on him to descend deeper and deeper into these obscure and questionable regions of the mind, and to move on, as a writer, from the manner of an American Gautier or Kinglake to a larger, bolder, more complex, and more symbolic manner that would be capable of rendering the richness and the fullness of his maturing thought.

There was little in the literary practice of Melville's generation to make this process of discovery anything but a troubled and wastful one. The romantic tale, as Hoffmann and Poe had developed it, was too purely static and introverted, as well as too confined, ever to have been a natural form for Melville to turn to at this stage; and he could not move, as Hawthorne had done, from the romantic tale to the psychological romance, from "Young Goodman Brown" to *The Scarlet Letter*. The great form of the historical novel had already passed its meridian, and even if it had not, it was only too evidently unprofitable to Melville, for whom the past did not have the emotional and poetic value it had for Scott and Hugo. "The Past is the text-book of tyrants," he says in *White-Jacket;* and though the remark naturally does not exhaust the range of Melville's feelings about history, it helps one to understand his development as an artist. Still less than in the historical romance, moreover, could he find his account in the practice of his great contemporaries, Balzac and Stendhal, Dickens and Thackeray: his imagination shared no common ground with these observers of the social, the contemporary scene, of business, the church, the great world, the modern city. His solution did not lie in the main direction of the nineteenth-century novel.

What he did, as a result, when he came to write *Mardi*, was to grope his way forward toward a new manner by writing alternately in several manners, no one of them quite the right one. The book begins in very much the vein of *Typee* and *Omoo*, though the air of the fictional is now still more pronounced, and when Melville and his elderly companion Jarl desert the *Arcturion* and set off in a whaleboat, one soon finds oneself in the nautical novelistic world of Cooper and Marryat, of *Wing-and-Wing* and *Mr. Midshipman Easy*. Then abruptly, and quite without transition, appears the great double canoe of Aleema and his sons, with the fair Yillah as a prisoner in it, and one steps suddenly into the re-Yillah as a prisoner in it, and one steps suddenly into the region of romantic or transcendental allegory, of *Heinrich von Öfterdingen* and the Blue Flower, or of Huldbrand von Ringstetten and the water-sprite, Undine. More or less at the same time one enters a far less worthy, far weedier literary region than that, but a related one: the region of sentimental symbolism and gift-book prettiness, of "the language of flowers," of the *Atlantic Souvenir* and *Godey's Lady's Book*. Something in Melville responded to the mincing *marivaudage* of conversation at Miss Anne Lynch's, where he sometimes turned up at this period; and just as Poe could make common cause with Mrs. Seba Smith, or Whitman with Fanny Fern, so Melville, with the amaranths and oleanders which Hautia's messengers keep brandishing before Taji, joins hands with Mrs. Fanny Osgood and *The Poetry of Flowers*.

Aleema, Yillah, and Hautia, however, and the romantic-sentimental allegory they embody, make their presence felt only at intervals in the later chapters of *Mardi*. When Yillah mysteriously vanishes, one turns with Melville—or Taji, as he is now called—to the company of the cheerful South Sea king and demigod, Media, and sets out with him and other companions on a voyage round the archipelago of Mardi—in quest, to be sure, of the unforgotten Yillah but also for the sake of visiting one quite independently allegorical island after another. Much of what follows is in the ancient line of philosophical and ethical satire; in the line, not of Novalis and de la Motte Fouqué, and certainly not of Mrs. Osgood, but of Lucian, Rabelais, and Swift. On the whole, this was a somewhat less infelicitous vein for Melville, somewhat less of a pitfall for him, than the other.

Taji's voyage, in any case, reminds one at once of Lucian's fantastic trip beyond the Gates of Hercules in the *True History*, or of Pantagruel's quest for the Oracle of the Holy Bottle, or of Gulliver's voyages to Lilliput and Brobdingnag. When Taji, Media, and the others sail past what Melville calls Nora-Bamma, the Isle of Nods, one thinks of Lucian and his visit to the slumbrous Isle of Dreams. The whole voyage from island to island is full of reminiscences of Rabelais, especially of his last two books. The praise of eating and drinking is highly Rabelaisian in intention, and so in general is all the satire on bigotry, dogmatism, and pedantry. Taji and his friends wandering about on the island of Maramma, which stands for ecclesiastical tyranny and dogmatism, are bound to recall Pantagruel and his companions wandering among the superstitious inhabitants of Papimany; and the pedantic, pseudo-philosophical jargon of Melville's Doxodox is surely, for a reader of Rabelais, an echo of the style of Master Janotus de Bragmardo holding forth polysyllabically to Gargantua in Book I. As for *Gulliver's Travels*, there is something very Swiftian in Melville's Hooloomooloo, the Isle of Cripples, the inhabitants of which are all twisted and deformed, and whose shapeless king is horrified at the straight, strong figures of his visitors from over sea. Hooloomooloo is but one of several reminders of Swift, and in general, though all this was nowhere near the center of Melville's imagination, it was in a vein that was far more natural to him than that of romantic

allegory: some of these Rabelaisian or Swiftian passages—
that on the same Isle of Cripples, as an instance—are done
with a certain vivacity and point.

There are suggestions of other familiar literary modes in
Mardi, but from this point of view the most remarkable
thing about the book is Melville's attempt to endue it with
the enchantment of the exotic and also with the grandeur of
the legendary and mythical by using, throughout, the imagery
of Polynesian life. It was an effort that deserved to succeed
better than it did: Melville, after all, was the first Western
writer of genius who had lived in the South Seas himself, and
he was the first of the actual travelers to go beyond mere narrative and to aim at converting his remembered impressions
into serious, ambitious, and poetic fiction. So the seascape and
landscape of Mardi is that of the Pacific world, of Hawaii or
the Marquesas or Tahiti: a chain of high-peaked islands, set
in their rings of coral reefs and lagoons, abounding in seaside
groves and inland valleys, shaded by the foliage of breadfruit
and casuarina trees, of coco-palms and hibiscus, and dotted
here and there with the thatched and open dwellings of the
natives. These dwellings are furnished with mats and tapa
hangings, with gourds and calabashes; the feasts that are con-
sumed in them consist of breadfruit dishes, baked yams, and
tropical fruits; and the feasters are clothed in tapa tunics and
mantles, in garlands and wreaths; the more aristocratic of
them, in feathered ornaments that are purely Hawaiian. The
sacred edifices, moreover, are not temples but *morais*, like the
great Morai of Maramma, which allegorically suggests St.
Peter's at Rome but pictorially resembles some great Polynesian *morai* like that of Purea on Tahiti.

Nor is the Polynesianism of *Mardi* a matter only of scene:
it is a matter also of custom and conduct, of legend and myth.
It is true that Melville was drawing, in all this, not only on his
own memory but also on the reading he had done both earlier and later, and that many a passage in *Mardi* derives, in
the literal sense, rather from William Ellis's *Polynesian Re-*

searches than from Melville's days in Taipi or Maatea. But in the deeper sense it was those days, those recollected impressions, that made *Mardi* possible: Ellis and the others were only tools for the forming imagination—tools, to be sure, that were not always handled with perfect skill. In any case, the South Sea localism of manners and behavior is inescapable in *Mardi*. The girdle of Teei, which is the symbol of kingship on the Isle of Juam, might have been the *maro-ura* or girdle of red feathers that, according to Henry Adams, was the symbol of chiefship in old Tahiti; and when the common people in Mardi strip to the waist in honor of their chiefs, they are only observing a form of obeisance that in fact prevailed in the South Seas. There chiefs were actually, as they are in Mardi, regarded as gods or demigods, and when the narrator of the novel represents himself as being taken for the returned god Taji, Melville is of course remembering how Captain Cook was taken by the Hawaiians for the returned god Lono. When Mohi, Melville's chronicler, relates the early history of Juam and the struggles betwen Teei and his brother Marjora, one might be listening to some narrative of the violent career of an actual Pomare or Kamehameha. Indeed the precipice of Mondo in *Mardi*, over the brink of which, says Melville, fifty rebel warriors were driven to their deaths, can hardly fail to suggest the real cliff called the Nuuanu Pali, on the Hawaiian island of Oahu, over the brink of which the first Kamehameha did actually drive his worsted enemies.

Beyond all this, however, Melville was feeling his way forward, rather timidly and fumblingly, to a genuinely mythopoeic form by investing his narrative with something of the quality of Polynesian legend and myth. The attempt was on the whole an abortive one, but the important thing is that he made it. The whole tale of the priest Aleema and his lovely captive Yillah suggests an awkward mingling of something that might be a Tahitian or Hawaiian legend with something that might be a German romantic allegory. Yillah herself suggests, on the one hand, some particularly vaporous Mathilda or Undine and, on the other, some legendary Hawaiian maiden, a Kaanaelike or Kamamalau, of whom Melville might conceivably have heard. As the voyagers sail past the islanded crag of Pella, Mohi the chronicler tells a story to account for its being there, and this story recalls a local legend about a mountain near Papetoai on Moorea, which Melville himself had of course seen. On one island or another Taji hears of the names and deeds of various gods, Keevi the god of thieves, for example, or the nimble god Roo. Somehow these unvenerable deities strongly suggest certain real Polynesian gods—or better, perhaps, such a tricky culture-hero as the great Maui, the Polynesian Prometheus, who fished up the various islands of the Pacific with his magic fish-hook. Mardi, at all events, abounds in gods as Polynesia did, and the name of the great transcendent god of Mardi, Oro, was in fact the name of a real deity in Tahiti. Yet it must be confessed that, in all this, *Mardi* remains a sketch, a promise, an intimation, and not a consummated achievement.

It does so partly because, in spite of Taipi and Fayaway, the specific myths and legends of Polynesia remained somewhere near the surface of Melville's mind and imagination; their special quality of feeling and image-making somehow kept them from serving as the vehicles of his deepest experiences; it was only as legend and myth in general that they attracted and liberated him. His own myth-making, when its time came, was to be the expression of his own culture and his own age and not, predictably, that of the neolithic world of the Pacific islands. Moreover, the thoughts and feelings he was attempting to express in *Mardi* were too disparate among themselves and often too incongruous with his South Sea imagery to be capable of fusion into a satisfying artistic whole. In the rush and press of creative excitement that swept upon him in these months, Melville was trying to compose three or four books simultaneously: he failed, in the strict sense, to compose even one.

Mardi has several centers, and the result is not a balanced design. There is an emotional center, an intellectual center, a social and political center; and though they are by no means utterly unrelated to one another, they do not occupy the same point in space. The emotional center of the book is the relation between Taji and Yillah, between the "I" and the mysterious blonde maiden he rescues from the priest Aleema, at the cost of slaying him; the maiden with whom he dwells for a short time in perfect felicity on a little islet off the coast of Odo, but who then vanishes as mysteriously as she has appeared. Taji sets out in quest of her throughout Mardi; he fails to find her on one island after another; he fails, in the end, to find her at all, but he discovers that she has fallen a victim to the witchcraft of the enchantress Hautia, and in ultimate despair, convinced that life without Yillah would be "a life of dying," he turns his prow at last toward the open sea of self-destruction.

In the poetic sense the whole allegory of Yillah is too tenuous and too pretty to be anything but an artistic miscarriage. In the personal and biographical sense, and in connection with the rest of Melville's work, it is extremely revealing. The blonde and bloodless Yillah, who in the language of flowers is associated with the lily, is an embodiment of the pure, innocent, essentially sexless happiness which, given his relations with his mother, Melville longed to find in his relations with some other woman, and which he had some reason to feel he had at one time fleetingly enjoyed. Even then—we do not know why—he had enjoyed it only at the expense of some act of emotional violence, of injury to another; and such happiness as he had had was soon destroyed by the intrusion of the sensual, the carnal, the engrossingly sexual, of which Hautia, symbolized by the dahlia, is the embodiment. With all of this the most intense and anguished emotions of remorse are associated: they drove Melville, in *Mardi*, to an act of symbolic suicide. It is possible that he was expressing thus the emotional history of his marriage to Elizabeth Shaw, which took place during the summer of 1847, perhaps after he had written the first, seagoing chapters of *Mardi*, but certainly before he had written the greater part of the book. It may be that the abrupt break at the end of the thirty-eighth chapter occurred at the time of the wedding and honeymoon, and in any case the allegory of Yillah and Hautia is strongly suggestive of the passage from an idealized courtship to the fleshly realities of marriage. What is not open to doubt is that physical sexuality was charged through and through for Melville with guilt and anxiety.

Meanwhile the middle portion of *Mardi* is mainly occupied by a series of forays in social and political satire, and by quasi-metaphysical speculations, that are at the best only loosely and uncertainly related to the quest for Yillah: the attempt to weave them together into a unified fabric was almost as quixotic as the attempt would be to find a common frame for *Endymion* and *A Connecticut Yankee*. If the fabric of *Mardi* holds together at all, it is only because there is a certain congruity among the various more or less frustrated quests it dramatizes—the quest for an emotional security once possessed, the quest for a just and happy sociality once too easily assumed possible, and the quest for an absolute and transcendent Truth once imagined to exist and still longed for.

The social and political strictures which are so explicitly expressed in *Mardi* are sometimes astonishingly sweeping and severe: they force us to remember that, though the deep centers of his work lie elsewhere, Melville was all along, among other things, a writer of the critical and protestant order to which Carlyle, Thoreau, and Tolstoy belonged. Partly under the sway of writers like this, no doubt, but much more under the bombardment of his own harshly instructive experience— "bowed to the brunt of things," as he says, "before my prime" —Melville had conceived an attitude toward the civilization of his age that mingled in quite special and personal fusion the ingredients of skepticism, humorous contempt, and the anger of an outraged sense of right. It is not great passion, for example, but it is a real enough disdain that inspires his treatment of the fashionable world in *Mardi*—in the allegory of the silly Tapparians and their insipid, formalized life on the island of Pimminee. There is a much deeper note in the satire on militarism as one sees it in the sanguinary war games constantly being played on the Isle of Diranda. There is a deeper note still in the glimpse one has, behind the charming fore-scene on Odo, of the broken serfs and helots who labor in the *taro* trenches and dwell in noisome caves; of the horrors of industrialism on the island of Dominora, which is the England of Dickens and Engels; and of the collared people, toiling under the eyes of armed overseers, in the extreme south even of republican Vivenza.

Vivenza is of course Melville's own country, and *Mardi* expresses, with no attempt at a forced consistency, both the pride he always felt in being an American—"in that land seems more of good than elsewhere"—and the skeptical reservations with which he contemplated America's present and future. It is not that these reservations leave one in any uncertainty where Melville's feelings as a democratic writer lay: the indictment of arbitrary political power and an inhumane or rigidified inequality is unambiguous enough. What he rejects is not the profounder moralities of democracy—they were in his blood—but a cluster of delusions and inessentials that, as he felt, had got themselves entangled with the idea of democracy in American minds; the delusion that political and social freedom is an ultimate good, however empty of content; that equality should be a literal fact as well as a spiritual ideal; that physical and moral evil are rapidly receding before the footsteps of Progress. All this Melville rejects, and he counters it with a group of insights that are by no means always sharp and strong; they are sometimes feeble and sometimes capricious; but in their wiser expressions they take the form of a political and social pessimism that was for him wholly reconcilable with a democratic humanism, though certainly not with an optimistic one. "For evil is the chronic malady of the universe."

So reads, in part, a scroll which the travelers find fixed against a palm tree in Vivenza: it is Melville's somber retort not only to the overweening political hopefulness of his time and place but to its optimistic ethics and metaphysics as well; to the unmodulated affirmations to which Emerson had given the most exaggerated expression: "Through the years and the centuries . . . a great and beneficent tendency irresistibly streams." Melville saw no such tendency in nature or in history; on the contrary, he had failed to find in nature any warrant for the aspirations of humanity ("nature is not for us") and he had failed to find in history—or in his own experience—any warrant for a belief in human perfectibility. Man he had very generally found to be a "pugnacious animal," "but one member of a fighting world," and his discovery had not filled him with confidence in the human outlook. On the whole, experience and reflection had confirmed the dark view of the natural man which his Calvinist nurture had implanted in him. They had not, however, confirmed the metaphysical absolutes of Calvinism, or indeed absolutes of any sort; and the philosophical plot of *Mardi* is furnished by the interaction—which, to tell the truth, is too largely a vacillation—between the longing for certainty, a longing at least as intense as that for Yillah, and the painfully recurring suspicion that, on all the great questions, "final, last thoughts you mortals have none; nor can have."

"Faith is to the thoughtless, doubts to the thinker," says one of Melville's spokesmen in *Mardi*, and in the end Taji himself cannot find spiritual assurance even in the pristine, purified, undogmatic Christianity of Serenia. Meanwhile, however, it is clear that Melville is struggling to avoid "a brutality of indiscriminate skepticism," as he calls it, and no doubt—divided and confused as he was, when he wrote the book, among a host of contradictory emotions and ideas—he came nearest to expressing his basic thought in a speech of

Babbalanja's as he "discourses in the dark": "Be it enough for us to know that Oro"—God—"indubitably is. My lord! my lord! sick with the spectacle of the madness of men, and broken with spontaneous doubts, I sometimes see but two things in all Mardi to believe:—that I myself exist, and that I can most happily, or least miserably exist, by the practice of righteousness."

It is not a very trumpet-tongued conclusion, nor even philosophically a very remarkable one, and indispensable though *Mardi* is to a study of Melville's developing powers—fine, even, as a few passages in it are—the book suffers irremediably, as a work of art, from the intellectual precipitateness and prematurity out of the midst of which it was palpably written. If Melville could have brought himself, at that period, to confide his crowding thoughts to the pages of a personal journal, the result might well have been a gradual burning up of his own smoke and, in the end, the pure lucidity of tragic insight that is consistent with dramatic and poetic wholeness. As it is, what one mostly finds in *Mardi* is not the clarifying solemnity of tragic acceptance; it is the drifting and eddying fog of intellectual worry, vacillation, and indecision, and in consequence there is no imaginative purification in reading it. Doubt and repudiation are great themes, and great books have been written on them; mere indecisiveness is strictly speaking not a theme for a work of art at all, and despite the violent termination of *Mardi*, its general movement is that of indecision rather than of strong denial.

This is what essentially keeps the personages, the narrative, and the symbols themselves from really enlisting our imaginative interest and taking a sure hold on our imaginative attention; most readers will end by agreeing with T. E. Lawrence that *Mardi*, as a whole, is a dull book. A remark of Eliot's may also occur to some of them: "We cannot afford to forget that the first—and not one of the least difficult—requirements of either prose or verse is that it should be interesting." Melville was quite capable of remembering just this, and doubtless it is with a momentary flash of self-criticism that he remarks in *Mardi* itself: "Genius is full of trash." If *Mardi* is a mixture of trash and genuineness, however, it is the sort of mixture of which only genius is capable. The unalloyed metal still remained to be run into the molds.

In both the intellectual and the literary senses *Mardi* had turned out, despite its undeniable qualities, to be a great detour for Melville; in the end it brought him back to his own route but in an oblique and rather wasteful way. His mind was still developing too rapidly and too intensely for him to be long content with the kind of skepticism, impatient and even intemperate, which *Mardi* ended by expressing. There is a lesser skepticism and a larger one, and the skepticism of this book is not yet the latter. In its form and texture, too, *Mardi* was evidently not what Melville was struggling to arrive at; he made no second use of its characteristic manner, and years later he was to voice his true feeling about the book when he remarked that the worst thing he could say about Richter's *Titan* was that "it is a little better than *Mardi*." His central problem as a writer was to find a fictional style in which there would be a particular kind of dynamic balance between fact and form, between concept and symbol, between the general and the particular—"the whole problem is there," as Gide once observed—and Melville had by no means found his solution in transcendental allegory of the Early Romantic type or even in the ancient mode of satirical burlesque he had inherited from Rabelais and Swift. Just how flimsy Yillah and Hautia are as vehicles for Melville's meaning is evident when one reflects for a moment on the essential unnaturalness and unspontaneity, for him, of the flower images that accompany them, the un-Melvillean verbenas and vervain; and as for the Rabelaisian tour of the archipelago of Mardi, it grows more and more perfunctory and essayistic as the book wears on.

Manqué though it was, however, *Mardi* had been written, we may be sure, at the cost of a heavy drain on Melville's psychological resources, and he was not yet ready to move on to another effort of comparable scope and difficulty: time would have to elapse before his highest energies could accumulate their full weight and force. Meanwhile it was a question of lowering his sights a degree or two, and what he did when he went on to write *Redburn* and *White-Jacket* had superficially the air of a return upon himself, a lapse back to the vein he had already worked in *Typee* and *Omoo*, the vein not of metaphysical allegory but of unpretentious reminiscent narrative, vibrating again between the poles of literal autobiography and free fictional improvisation. *Redburn* and *White-Jacket* take us back once more to the ship and the sea voyage, to "real" ships and "real" seas: in the one case, to the deck of an American merchant vessel making an ordinary trip across the North Atlantic; in the other, to the deck of an American man-of-war on its cruise from the port of Callao in Peru, around the Horn, back to its home port on the eastern seaboard. Both books abound in information, in factuality, in solid objects and practical activities, and in all this they recall *Typee* and *Omoo*. But the movement Melville was describing, it need hardly be said, was not a retrograde but a spiral one, and *Redburn* and *White-Jacket*, though they have lost the youthful charm of the earlier books, are denser in substance, richer in feeling, tauter, more complex, more connotative in texture and imagery. Whatever imperfections they may have, they give us the clear sense that the man who wrote them was again on his own track.

The prose, for one thing, is that of a much more mature person and more expert writer. One easily sees how much ground Melville has gained, partly as a result of writing *Mardi*, when one turns from almost any page of the first two books to almost any page of the later ones. Here is a characteristic passage from *Omoo*:

> Toward morning, finding the heat of the forecastle unpleasant, I ascended to the deck, where everything was noiseless. The Trades were blowing with a mild, steady strain upon the canvas, and the ship heading right out into the immense blank of the Western Pacific. The watch were asleep. With one foot resting on the rudder, even the man at the helm nodded, and the mate himself, with arms folded, was leaning against the capstan.
>
> On such a night, and all alone, revery was inevitable. I leaned over the side, and could not help thinking of the strange objects we might be sailing over.

Certainly the nocturnal picture here is pleasantly rendered; the effect of contrasted motion and stillness (the advancing ship, the nodding helmsman, and the like) is quickly and agreeably achieved; the rhythms are easy; the forward movement of the sentences is steady and effortless; the plain, low-pitched diction surges a little, at one moment, to a kind of grandeur in the phrase, "the immense blank of the Western Pacific." But rhythmically the passage achieves little more than easiness; the language is almost neutral and without idiosyncrasy; and the sense of a missed opportunity in the last sentence is acute. There are finer passages in *Typee* and *Omoo*, but virtually nowhere in those books does Melville write as he repeatedly writes in *Redburn* or *White-Jacket*. Is it possible, in such a passage as the following, from *Redburn*, to mistake the gain in rhythmical variety and intricacy, in sharpness of diction, in syntactical resource, in painterly bravura and the fusing of image and emotion into a unity of strangeness, beauty, and dread? It is part of the chapter in which Melville describes his ascent of the mainmast to loosen a skysail at midnight:

> For a few moments I stood awe-stricken and mute. I could not see far out upon the ocean, owing to the darkness of the night; and from my lofty perch the sea looked like a great, black gulf, hemmed in, all round, by beetling black cliffs. I seemed all alone; treading the mid-

night clouds; and every second, expected to find myself falling—falling—falling, as I have felt when the nightmare has been on me.

I could but just perceive the ship below me, like a long narrow plank in the water; and it did not seem to belong at all to the yard, over which I was hanging. A gull, or some sort of sea-fowl, was flying round the truck over my head, within a few yards of my face; and it almost frightened me to hear it; it seemed so much like a spirit, at such a lofty and solitary height.

It is not only the spectral sea-fowl here, flying round the masthead in the darkness, which tells one that, in the progress from *Typee* to *Moby Dick*, Melville has already passed the middle point.

If this holds for *Redburn* stylistically, it holds no less truly for its substance and spirit. The outward subject of the book is a young boy's first voyage as a sailor before the mast; its inward subject is the initiation of innocence into evil—the opening of the guileless spirit to the discovery of "the wrong," as James would say, "to the knowledge of it, to the crude experience of it." The subject is a permanent one for literature, of course, but it has also a peculiarly American dimension, and in just this sense, not in any other, *Redburn* looks backward to a book like Brockden Brown's *Ormond* as well as forward to *The Marble Faun* and to so much of James himself. Wellingborough Redburn sets out from his mother's house in a state of innocence like that before the Fall, a state like that of Brown's Constantia Dudley or James's Maisie Farange, but he has hardly gone a mile from home before the world's wickedness and hardness begin to strip themselves before him. Man, Redburn quickly finds, is a wolf to man. On the river boat his shabby indigence elicits no compassion from the comfortable passengers, but only coldness and disdain. He reaches the city and is very soon victimized by a rascally pawnbroker, a pawnbroker who might have stepped out of *David Copperfield* or *Cousin Pons*. He takes himself aboard the *Highlander* and begins at once to be sworn at, pushed around, humiliated, and persecuted by mates and sailors alike; and the dapper Captain Riga, who had appeared so friendly in his cabin while the ship lay at anchor, now, when poor unsophisticated Redburn attempts to address him as man to man, flies into a rage and flings his cap at him.

Blows and hard words are mostly Redburn's lot on the *Highlander*, yet he suffers not only from the inhumanity of men but from the spectacle of their depravity generally. His feelings about the sailors vacillate, it is true; as individuals he finds some of them generous and friendly; but taking them in the lump, he is conscious chiefly of their drunkenness, their profanity and obscenity, their indurated cynicism and sneering misanthropy. All this accumulated evil, indeed, is focused so concentratedly in the figure of one man, the sailor Jackson, as to raise him to something like heroic stature, the statue at any rate of one of Schiller's Majestic Monsters. The first of Melville's full-length studies of "depravity according to nature," Jackson is stricken, symbolically, with a fatal disease—the penalty for his "infamous vices," as Redburn learns—but this does not keep him from being a pitiless bully and exercising an unchallenged and almost preternatural sway over the rest of the crew, who thus, in their pusillanimity, pay tribute to the principle of pure evil in him. He for his part feels nothing but malevolence toward them; nothing but malevolence toward Redburn, if only because he is young, handsome, and innocent; and indeed "he seemed to be full of hatred and gall against everything and everybody in the world." His enmity toward the boy sets the rest of the crew against him too, and Redburn begins to feel a compensatory hatred growing up in himself against them all; but meanwhile, day by day, his ears are assailed by the bitter talk of a man who is "spontaneously an atheist and an infidel," and who argues through the long night watches that there is "nothing to be believed;

nothing to be loved, and nothing worth living for; but every-thing to be hated, in the wide world."

There is a touch of Svidrigailov or old Karamazov in this Jackson, and there is a touch of the Dostoyevskian also in Redburn's feeling that there was "even more woe than wick-edness about the man." He is so impressive a figure, one sees, partly because so much of Melville's own bitterness and dis-belief entered into his composition. Jackson is easily first among the personal embodiments of evil in this book, but in addition to him and to all the personages, and more overpow-ering than any of them, there is the infernal city of Liverpool, a near neighbor of the City of Destruction itself. That older allegory is bound to occur to one's mind in thinking of *Red-burn* and Liverpool, but even so it was not until the nine-teenth century that the great city, any great city, the great city *an sich*, could become just the kind of symbol it did be-come of human iniquity. In imagining Liverpool as he did, Melville was wholly at one with the deepest sensibility of his age, and in his wonderful series of Hogarthian evocations—in the dark, begrimed, polluted streets, the great prisonlike warehouses, the squalid dwellings, the loathsome haunts of vice and crime, and the beggars, the quacks, the crimps, the peddlers who populate these infested purlieus like moral gro-tesques—in all this there is a power quite comparable to that with which Balzac's Parisian Inferno is rendered, or Baude-laire's *fourmillante cité*, the London of *Bleak House* and *Our Mutual Friend*, or the Dublin of *Ulysses*. Melville's Liv-erpool, too, like his Lima, is a City of the Plain.

In such a setting as this there is no mere enigma even in the one chapter of *Redburn* in which Melville seems to be indulg-ing in deliberate mystification—the chapter in which he represents Redburn as being carried off to London on an un-explained errand by his new friend Harry Bolton and taken by him to "Aladdin's Palace." This is an Orientally luxurious pleasure-house of some ill-defined sort, where they spend a melodramatic night, and where Harry appears to lose most of his remaining funds at the tables. Aladdin's Palace is the opulent counterpart of the "reeking" and "Sodom-like" dens in Liverpool where Redburn's shipmates indulge their squalid vices; the walls of one room are hung with pornographic paintings to which Melville suggests various learned parallels, but most of these he himself invented as he composed the passage; and their real purpose, like that of the whole chapter, is to dramatize the horrified Redburn's feeling that "this must be some house whose foundations take hold on the pit," and that "though gilded and golden, the serpent of vice is a serpent still." He fails to see another stick or stone of London, and one more drop is thus added to his cup of disappointment; but his experience of evil has been extended in still another direction, and by the engaging Harry, too. The conflict between wishfulness and revulsion is evident enough. For the rest, though the chapter is not without a genuine vein of dreamlike intensity, it is vitiated as a whole by the kind of unnaturalness into which Melville so easily fell with such themes.

Meanwhile, *Redburn* abounds in the imagery not only of moral evil but of disease, disaster, and death. The voyage itself, here as elsewhere, is a metaphor of death and rebirth, of the passage from childhood and innocence to experience and adulthood; the crossing, to and fro, of a sea in the waters of which one dies to the old self and puts on a new. As if to enforce this intention irresistibly, the *Highlander's* voyage outward and the voyage home are both initiated by a scene of violent death. During the first long night watch that Redburn stands with his mates on the voyage out, he is terrified when all at once a sailor, suffering from delirium tremens, dashes up the scuttle of the forecastle and flings himself to his death over the bows of the vessel. The boy Redburn is then poetically identified with this sailor when he is made to occupy the dead man's bunk. Still more ghastly than this is the discovery, in the first dogwatch of the voyage homeward, that a Portuguese sailor who had been thrown, apparently dead drunk, into a bunk as they left port, is literally dead, and that his corpse is now flickering with a hideous phosphorescence. Neither incident, it appears, occurred on the actual voyage that the young Melville made; both are inventions, and all the more eloquent for being so.

Inventions, too, no doubt, are at least some of the other disastrous episodes of the voyage and of the stay in Liverpool: the collision between the *Highlander* and another vessel, in the darkness, which just fails to be fatal; the sighting of a dismantled, waterlogged schooner in the Irish Sea, with dead men lashed to the taffrail, the victims of storm and starvation (an echo, possibly, of *Arthur Gordon Pym*, but not an improvement on it); the murder of a prostitute at a bar in Liverpool by a drunken Spanish sailor; and the epidemic that, on the homeward voyage, destroys many of the inmates of the overcrowded, unwholesome steerage, and throws the refined cabin passengers into a cowardly panic of terror and selfishness. In these last scenes, as nowhere else in his work, Melville resorts to the symbolism of plague and pestilence that had proved, or was to prove, so expressive for a long series of modern writers, from Defoe and Poe to Thomas Mann; and though for him, as for most of them, the literal pestilence has a moral or spiritual reference, it is characteristic that for him, almost alone among such writers, it has a democratic and humanitarian reference also.

All these elements in *Redburn*, at any rate, are "symbolic" in the sense that, at their best, they are imagined and projected with an intensity that constantly pushes them beyond mere representation, and that makes them reverberate with a more than prosaic force in the reader's own imagination. Nothing like this had been true of *Typee* or *Omoo:* if there are symbols in those books, they are there only in the loose sense in which one would find them in any piece of writing that lifted itself even a little above the level of a mere record. The sense of symbol in *Redburn* is unmistakably more acute than in anything of Melville's that preceded *Mardi,* and moreover there are two or three points in the book at which one sees Melville moving toward an even franker and more direct form of symbolism, one which he himself would doubtless have called "allegorical," but which is far from being allegorical in the sense in which Yillah and Hautia had been. It is a question now, not of bodying forth emotional and intellectual experience in deliberately poetic characters and fables, of elaborating dramatic symbols that have obvious analogies in the realm of thought and feeling. It is a question of endowing ordinary objects, ordinary incidents, with a penumbra of feeling and suggestion that imparts to them a symbolic character. One might describe these as antiromantic or shrunken symbols; they have something of the quality of what is called witty imagery, and they were to become more and more idiosyncratic for Melville.

One of them, here, is the old-fashioned glass ship which Redburn's father had brought home from France and which the boy's imagination had hovered over until the object converted his vague longings into a definite purpose of going to sea. On the very day on which he actually left home for his voyage, the little glass figurehead of a warrior had fallen from the bows of the ship into the waves below it, and there he still lies: "but I will not have him put on his legs again, till I get on my own." In very much the same vein of feeling is the old guidebook to Liverpool which, as we have seen already, had proved so helpful to Redburn's father in his perambulations about the city, but which now proves as misleading and even pervertive as every guidebook is that has had its day. Most striking of all, however, and happiest in its imaginative quality is the old gray shooting-jacket that Redburn's elder brother gives him as he sets out from home; the moleskin shooting-jacket with big horn buttons, long skirts, and many pockets, that brings down upon Redburn so much derision from fellow-passengers, shipmates, and Englishmen; which shrinks day by day, particularly after a rain, until he finds it more and more uncomfortable to wear; and which comes to be for him an obsessive emblem of his lost gentility and social humiliation. Redburn's shooting-jacket puts one in mind of that other shabby garment, the old clerk's overcoat in Gogol's famous tale, and indeed, in his characteristic preoccupation with clothing, especially shabby and uncomfortable clothing, Melville suggests the Russians more than any other English or American writer quite does. For the "insulted and injured" there is of course a natural metaphor in old, cheap, and ill-fitting clothes.

Bitter as the feeling in this is, however, and despite the underlying gravity of the symbolism generally, *Redburn* is anything but a lugubrious book as a whole, and it has probably never made any such impression on its readers: the current of animation and vivacity on which it is sustained is purely inspiriting; if this is "pessimism," it is pessimism of the most tonic sort. The book abounds in self-pity, certainly, but distinctions have to be made even here, and there is a kind of self-pity that is more bracing than what passes for restraint and austerity: on the whole, the self-pity in *Redburn* is clearly of that order. Melville's feeling, moreover, for light and shade did not fail him in the writing of *Redburn* as it had done in the writing of *Mardi*. There is the familiar ballast of prosaic information, for one thing—the chapter, for example, on the furniture of the quarter-deck—and there is a good deal of Melville's characteristically smiling and low-toned humor. The account of Max the Dutchman, who has a sober and respectable wife in New York and an equally sober and respectable one in Liverpool, and whose wardrobe is kept in order by the launderings of both spouses—Max the Dutchman is in Melville's happiest vein. He had always had a taste for the burgherlike humor of the little Dutch masters—Teniers, Brouwer, Jan Steen—and in passages like this he approximates it, though in a softened form. In its richness of emotion and variety of tone, *Redburn* generally is the most likable of Melville's secondary books; and it is only because he was so rebelliously conscious how much higher he was capable of going that Melville could have spoken of it contemptuously as "beggarly *Redburn*."

Taken as a whole, *White-Jacket*, which he now went on to write, is something of a drop in quality after *Redburn*; it bears somewhat the same relation to that book as *Omoo* bears to *Typee*. Neither *Redburn* nor *White-Jacket*, and especially not the latter, was written with the concentrated conviction of Melville's whole nature: increasingly he was resentful of the necessities that forced him to write in what seemed to him an inferior strain. Both these books, he said in a letter, he had done simply as jobs, for the sake of making money, as other men are forced to saw wood, and at a time when what he earnestly desired was to write "those sort of books which are said to 'fail'." This, naturally, is a biographical fact, not a critical one, and we cannot be affected by Melville's own feeling in judging either *Redburn* or *White-Jacket*; but the biographical fact has an explanatory interest nevertheless. The earnest desire Melville expressed in his letter was soon to be fulfilled; meanwhile, he seems to have been writing at a murderous rate of speed, and *White-Jacket* itself appears to have been dashed off in the incredible space of two and a half months. It is little wonder that, in writing it, Melville should have lifted from other books not only information (as he had always done) but whole scenes and episodes, without always justifying the theft by improving on what he took. In at least one case he did so, but the symptoms of hurry and fatigue are all too evident elsewhere.

Hitherto he had intuitively succeeded in finding pretty much the true balance between narrative and factuality, between the imaginative and the informative, and in *White-Jacket* he continues to alternate the two—but now in what seems a relatively perfunctory and even wearied manner. The current of personal narrative is simply not full enough or strong enough to buoy up and float along the solid and sometimes rather lumpish blocks of straight exposition and description—straight information about the American navy generally and the individual battleship in particular. Not quite for the first time, but for the first time oppressively, one is conscious of the slight streak of pedantry that was always latent in Melville's passion for facts, and that when his imagination was not deeply engaged betrayed him into dullness and jejuneness. In proportion to the whole, one hears too much, in *White-Jacket*, about the gundeck and the berthdeck, the starboard watch and the larboard watch, the quarter-deck officers and the warrant-officers, and so on. In matters of organization and routine such as these Melville was not genuinely interested, or was interested only with the least creative facet of his imagination, and the result is that he largely fails to endow these things with imaginative life.

The book suffers too, more than the earlier books had done, from the humanitarian note that dominates it as it dominates no other work of Melville's. It is hardly worth saying that, on ethical grounds, one cannot fail to share Melville's indignation. Whatever the personal basis for it, he could not have taken firmer ground than he did when he cried out against "the social state in a man-of-war," the atrocious evil of flogging, and the like. All of it does the utmost credit to Melville's humanity. What was amiss was not this, certainly, but for the time being Melville's sense of form, his literary instinct. In speaking of *White-Jacket* one is tempted to paraphrase Flaubert's remark about *Uncle Tom's Cabin* and Negro slavery, and to ask: "Is it necessary to make comments on the iniquities of the Navy? Show them to me; that is enough." *White-Jacket* is not a novel, to be sure, but it is not a mere pamphlet either; it is an imaginative work of a very special and precarious sort, and it would have gained incalculably if Melville had made his protests far less insistent and less explicit, and if he had dramatized them much more. At least one of the flogging scenes, for example, seems terribly true, but none of them is comparable in repellent power to the one scene with which Dana, in *Two Years*, contents himself; and Melville dilutes the force of his protest partly by his repetitions of the shocking image and partly by his detailed comments on the evil. His moral passion, as so often happens, had asserted itself overaggressively at the expense of his inventive and dramatic gift.

It did not keep him, however, from continuing in *White-Jacket* the search for a right symbolic method that he had carried on in the two books that came before it. This search now led him, confusedly enough, in two directions, one of them a sterile, one a fruitful direction. It was an unhappy inspiration, as it was very probably an afterthought, that induced him to transform the man-of-war itself into the particular kind of symbol that the subtitle, "The World in a Man-of-War," indicates. From time to time as the book advances there are hints that the battleship *Neversink* is a kind of Microcosm of the universe; in one of the later chapters it is specifically remarked that "a man-of-war is but this old-fashioned world of ours afloat"; and finally Melville appends a short epilogue in which the analogy between a battleship and the Macrocosm is explicitly enforced. Just as the *Neversink* sails through the sea, so the earth sails through the air, "a fast-sailing, never-sinking world-frigate, of which God was the shipwright." But the port from which the Macrocosm sails is forever astern; unlike most battleships, that frigate sails under sealed orders, "yet our final haven was predestinated ere we slipped from the stocks at Creation." There are parallels, too, between the social arrangements on a man-of-war and the state of society itself, and though "we the people," like the common seamen in the Navy, suffer many abuses, the worst of our evils we blindly inflict on ourselves.

There are fine touches in this epilogue, like the strangely Kafkaesque suggestion that an abused sailor would appeal in vain, during this life, "to the indefinite Navy Commissioners, so far out of sight aloft." Yet on the whole the macrocosmic symbolism of the man-of-war world is as infelicitous in its way as the allegory of *Mardi* is in its. It is not only hackneyed

in itself—the thought of Longfellow's Ship of State is dangerously near at hand—but treated just as Melville treats it, it is
far too simply pictorial and its ethical bearing is made far too
ponderously explicit. What is it indeed but a curiously belated, anachronistic example of what the sixteenth and seventeenth centuries would have called an Emblem—a highly pictorial allegory with a significance that is frankly and unequiv-
ocally enforced? Ships under full sail on calm or stormy seas
appear from time to time in the sometimes charming cuts
that illustrate the old emblem books, and there is an allegorical ship, allegorical of the soul and its destiny, in the third
book of Quarles's *Emblems*. Melville felt a natural affinity, as
some other writers of his time did, for the literature of the
Baroque era, and sometimes it proved to have a genuinely
quickening influence on him. But the emblem in a nineteenth-
century literary setting was as inappropriate as a sixteenth-
century woodcut would have been as an illustration; it was
not in those terms that Melville's problem would find its
proper solution.

He was much closer to his own true vein in inventing the
symbol that gives the book its title, the white jacket that, in
lieu of a genuine pea jacket or grego, he represents his young
hero, or rather "himself," as concocting out of an old duck
shirt before the *Neversink* sets sail from Callao. He does so in
order to protect himself from the boisterous weather they are
sure to encounter as they round Cape Horn. "An outlandish
garment of my own devising," the jacket is ample in the
skirts, clumsily full about the wristbands, and of course white
—"yea, white as a shroud." He darns and quilts the inside of
it in the hope of making it truly waterproof; but, in spite of
this, in rainy weather it proves to be as absorbent as a sponge,
and thus "when it was fair weather with others, alas! it was
foul weather with me." It is such an ungainly, eccentric garment that it brings down constant ridicule on the wearer's
head, and worse than that, evokes a kind of superstitious hatred on the part of the other sailors. On one occasion they take

White-Jacket himself to be the ghost of the cooper, lost overboard the day before, when they see him lying on the main-royalyard in the darkness; as time goes on, some of them are convinced that other deaths in the crew can be laid to the jacket, and White-Jacket himself begins to feel that the accursed garment has "much to answer for."

He has tried to persuade the first lieutenant to let him have some black paint to cover it with, but in vain. And this is a great part of his misery, for most monkey jackets are of a dark hue and keep their wearers from being too easily visible, especially at night. When, on the other hand, an officer wants a man for some particularly hard job, "how easy, in that mob of incognitoes, to individualize *'that white jacket,'* and dispatch him on the errand!" White-Jacket tries to free himself of the wretched thing by swapping it with a messmate and even by putting it up at auction, but no one will have it, and he begins to imagine that he will never be free of it until he rolls a forty-two-pound shot in it and commits it to the deep. This thought, however, is too much like the thought of his own death, and he refrains. But when the cruise is almost over, the jacket very nearly proves to be his death after all. White-Jacket is sent up the mainmast one night to reeve the halyards of a stun-sail, and while he is trying to do this he loses his balance and, entangled about the head by his jacket, falls rushingly from the yard-arm into the sea. Down he plunges, down into the deathlike waters of the deep. After some seconds, however, he shoots up again to the surface, and attempts to strike out toward the ship, but the fatal jacket, looped about him as it is, almost destroys him. He saves himself only by cutting himself out of it with a knife and ripping it up and down "as if I were ripping open myself." It sinks slowly before his eyes, and White-Jacket returns to life. He does so because he has in fact ripped open an aspect of himself, thrown it off, and allowed it to sink in the sea; the aspect of himself that is mere uniqueness and differentness, mere protective-unprotective self-assertion, easy to identify and indi-

vidualize in any mob, and white, fatally white, as white as a
shroud.

It is a magnificent symbol of the lesser Self, the empirical
Self, the Ego; a far finer symbol for its purpose than that of
the man-of-war for its, and it is so partly because it is homely
and unhackneyed, partly because it is inexplicit, and partly
because, though it has an interpretable meaning, that meaning remains elusive and slightly equivocal. The jacket was
probably sheer invention on Melville's part, though he alleged in a letter to Dana that it was a real jacket. It does not
matter in the least. In its setting the thing has the air of the
only kind of reality that counts. Sheer invention, however, so
far as Melville's external experience went, is certainly the
great scene just alluded to, in which the jacket plays so nearly
fatal a role. In literal fact no such mishap befell Melville on
the *United States*. The ship's log is silent on the affair, and besides it has long been known that the whole scene is a rewriting of a passage in a little volume called *A Mariner's Sketches*
by an old Yankee sailor named Nathaniel Ames, which had
been published in Providence twenty years earlier.

It was a passage that was bound to catch Melville's attention as he read the book: the nightmarish image of falling to
one's destruction from a high place had appeared before in
his own writing, and what psychiatrists call hypsophobia was
as characteristic for him as it was for Poe. He had reached the
head of Taipi-Vai, according to his own story, by a series of
horrifying falls from ledge to ledge of a dreamlike precipice;
and in *Redburn*, in the passage already quoted, he represents
his horror of "falling—falling—falling" when he is sent up to
loosen the skysail. Harry Bolton on the voyage home suffers so
terribly from this phobia that he refuses ever to climb the
mast a second time, though he is permanently disgraced for
it. And even earlier in *White-Jacket*, Melville or his fictional
persona has nearly fallen to his death from the main-royalyard when the superstitious sailors below him suddenly lower
the halyards. It takes no great penetration to detect in this re-

curring image the unconscious impulse to suicide, and the great scene in *White-Jacket* owes its inescapable power, as the scene of White-Jacket's near-flogging does, to the fact that, though it never occurred in the physical world, it did certainly occur in the inner one. The self-destructiveness in Melville expressed itself thus as well as in other ways.

Meanwhile, for all its limitations, *White-Jacket* has stretches of admirable writing in it, of which this scene of the fall from the yard-arm is one. It is already a famous case, but it remains an especially illuminating one, of Melville's genius for transmuting an uninspired model into something greatly expressive. Nathaniel Ames's own account of his fall from the futtock shrouds—oddly enough, it was on the same frigate, the *United States*—though it has several touches of strong realistic truth, is essentially as pedestrian as one would expect it to be if one heard it from the lips of the old seaman himself. Melville transformed it as Shakespeare sometimes transformed Holinshed or North's Plutarch: keeping the facts and the narrative order and even some of the details of feeling, but imparting rhythmicality, and a wonderfully connotative one, to what had had no rhythm at all; working small miracles of linguistic expressiveness ("the strong shunning of death shocked me through"); and intensifying the whole emotional value of the incident through an accompaniment of powerful images—"the speechless profound of the sea," "the maelstrom air," and "some inert, coiled fish of the sea." When he finds in Ames a matter-of-fact sentence like this:

> I kept going down, down, till it appeared to me that the seven fathoms and a half, (the depth of water at our anchorage,) had more than doubled since we let go our anchor;

Melville remakes it thus:

> The blow from the sea must have turned me, so that I sank almost feet foremost through a soft, seething, foamy lull. Some current seemed hurrying me away; in a trance

I yielded, and sank deeper down with a glide. Purple and pathless was the deep calm now around me, flecked by summer lightnings in an azure afar.

Much of the effect of this extraordinarily hypnotic passage is due to the delicate skill with which Melville avails himself of phonetic color—the color, here, of labials and sibilants especially and the closed sound of long e—but much also to the subtly responsive rhythms (conveying the delicious sense of movement downward through a liquid medium, in such gently protracted phrases as "through a soft, seething, foamy lull"), as well as to the synaesthetic use of a word like "lull" for an experience of the sense of touch, and the sudden shift from the sense of motion to the perception of color in the fine words, "purple" and "azure."

Admittedly this whole scene of the descent into the sea and the re-emergence from it is a rare peak in Melville's early prose; it is the finest writing in the ornate style that he did before *Moby Dick*, and one can account for it only by remembering that it sprang from a profound inward experience of life and death in conflict. But it is not the only passage of brilliant narrative writing in *White-Jacket*, despite the dead calm of many chapters. In an entirely different key, the key of relaxed and indulgent humor, the scene called "A Man-of-War College," in which the schoolmaster of the *Neversink* lectures to his flock of restless midshipmen on the refinements of naval strategy, is written with admirable ease and charm. In still another and a darker style, that of indignant, satirical caricature, Melville never went beyond the great scene of "The Operation"; the scene in which the pompous and unfeeling surgeon of the *Neversink*, Dr. Cadwallader Cuticle, performs an unnecessary amputation upon an injured foretopman, under which the wretched man dies. There is an inevitable suggestion of Smollett both in the name and in the character of the surgeon, as there is in the whole chapter; yet after all Melville did not write with the particular kind of harsh, brilliant, indefatigable speed and vigor one associates with the author of *Roderick Random*. Indeed, the passage has an essentially different quality from any of the scenes aboard the *Thunder* in that novel, a quality not so much of choleric energy as of mingled pity and detestation, revulsion and ruthlessness, humor and hatred. It would be easy, too, to say that Melville was writing in much the same style in which, for example, Rowlandson drew when he made his monstrous print of "The Amputation"; but the real feeling in Melville is in fact no more that of Rowlandson—broad, gross, and grotesque —than it is that of Smollett. It is a feeling in which anger at the spectacle of cruelty is underlain by a still stronger sorrow at the spectacle of evil generally.

On these more intangible grounds *White-Jacket* represents no retreat from or palliation of the insights expressed in *Redburn*. One must confess, in fact, that the later book is the more richly counterpointed, in a moral sense, of the two. The World in a Man-of-War is, at the one extreme, quite as black a world as that in a merchant vessel or a great seaport; it is a world, on the whole, "charged to the combings of her hatchways with the spirit of Belial and all unrighteousness." A world of which the ferocious Articles of War form the domineering code could hardly be other than a basically brutal and un-Christian one, and brutal and un-Christian, with its ultimate dedication to purposes of bloodshed and destruction, the microcosm of the *Neversink* is. What follows morally is what could be predicted: overbearing arrogance on the part of most of the officers, genteel rascality on the part of others, petty insolence even in the boyish midshipmen, and cringing subservience or sullen vindictiveness on the part of many of the sailors—for Melville, committed as he is to the rank and file as over against their superiors, cannot and will not represent the human reality as different from what he has found it in experience. He does not spare himself the task, painful though he obviously finds it, of hinting at "other evils, so direful that they will hardly bear even so much as an allusion"; evils that involve some of the common seamen in "the sins for which the cities of the plain were overthrown."

The portrait of Bland, the knavish master-at-arms, though it is less completely dramatized than that of Jackson, is at least as subtle analytically; and his well-bred, unvulgar, "organic" scoundrelism is both more inexplicable and more profound than Jackson's understandable blackguardliness. Yet morally speaking, despite all this, *White-Jacket* has a higher *relievo* and a more complex truth than *Redburn*. There is the moral relief of goodness in *Redburn* but it is too largely associated with passiveness and even effeminacy; Redburn himself remains too much the mere victim, embittered but not very resistant, and Harry Bolton is a more extreme case than he. The stage in *White-Jacket* is occupied by a much more richly representative cast of characters. Not all the officers are bullies or martinets. Mad Jack, a junior lieutenant, is a paragon of generous, manly seamanship, and Colbrook, the handsome and gentlemanly corporal of marines, has the extraordinary courage to intercede for White-Jacket when he comes so close to a flogging. Some of the midshipmen are "noble little fellows," and as for the common seamen, there is the self-respecting old Ushant, there is Nord the silent and meditative, and above and beyond all there is of course the "incomparable" and "ever-glorious" Jack Chase, the heroic captain of the maintop, a far more masculine image of virtue than the pathetic Harry. It is quite in keeping with his love for Jack Chase, moreover, that we should feel the vein of iron in White-Jacket as we never quite feel it in Redburn. Melville, as he wrote the book, had at least for the time recovered from the despairing mood of *Mardi* and from the largely resentful mood of *Redburn*. White-Jacket, it is true, would have gone to his death rather than submit to a flogging, but he would have done so in an act of protest; and in a later scene, when death by water would have come so easily, he has the still greater courage to cut himself out of his fatal garment and return to life.

New York and Pittsfield

IN THE FALL OF 1844 Melville was at home again in
Lansingburgh: the long return from Taipi-Vai was now
complete, and one whole phase of Melville's life, the
phase of turning outward, was over. Young as he still was—he
was only in his mid-twenties—a long period lay before him
during which his life would be quite peculiarly an inward
one. External action, movement in space, physical danger and
hardship, these were behind him once for all; what lay before
him was action of the mind, movement in the realm of
thought and feeling, and the dangers of the spirit. Into the
short space of four or five years Melville had crammed more
"experience," more sheer activity, more roughing of it, than
has been the lot of any but a small handful of modern writers;
in all the five decades that were left to him, his outward life
was to be more uneventful even than Hawthorne's or Whitman's. Meanwhile, he was to pack into the space of six or
eight years, those that followed his return, more emotional
and intellectual experience than even most writers of great
gifts have packed into similar periods; and the result, the result of this violent and excessive alternation of the outward
and the inward, of physical and spiritual exertion, was a prematurity of agedness. From a certain point of view it might
be possible to regret that this was true, for it meant great bit-

terness to Melville as a person; but it was too much in the nature of things, too much in his *own* nature, not to be, as he himself would say, somehow predestinated—"Ourselves are Fate"—and meanwhile the predestination that decreed the accomplishment of *Moby Dick* was hardly a lamentable one. How many are the literary careers that, taken as a whole, present so full and so intense a picture of development as the seven years in Melville's life that intervene between the writing of *Typee* and that of *Pierre?*

One reminds oneself, with a certain effort, that seven books were written during those seven years; that there was no self-repetition in any of them, and that one of them was a work of the highest order. Shelley, at less than thirty, felt that he had lived for ninety or a hundred years of the ordinary span; and it is not surprising if Melville, in his mid-thirties, makes on us already an impression of the superannuated, the all-but-spent. There was a baffling complex of reasons for this, but in the mean time, though Melville's life abounded in strains and pressures, it abounded too in great rewards. In addition to the intense pleasure in writing itself, there was surely a great fulfillment, for the nameless and rather dubious son of Maria Melville, in stepping at once, with his first book, to the very forestage of recognition and literary celebrity. For how many doubts and humiliations must that not have reimbursed him! Recognition not only in his own country but in England too, and recognition that was not withdrawn, essentially, as his second book followed the first, and the fifth book followed the fourth. Most readers, to judge partly by the review in the *Living Age*, seem to have found *Omoo*, "unlike most sequels," equal to its predecessor; and though there was more than a shade of coolness and bewilderment in the reception of *Mardi*, the reviewer in *Graham's*, who may have been the young Bayard Taylor, found it "full of those magical touches which indicate original genius." Hawthorne told Melville's friend Evert Duyckinck, who must have passed the word along, that he thought *Mardi* a rich book, "with depths here and there that compel a man to swim for his life." And resentful as Melville himself was of the necessity that forced him to write *Redburn* and *White-Jacket*, he could not in reason have been disappointed in their reception. *White-Jacket* especially evoked little but enthusiastic commendation.

His prompt and pleasant success as an author, moreover, brought him very soon into a kind of literary society; not one, certainly, with a single great exception, that was to respond to any of his deeper needs or to enrich his mind in any serious sense, but one nevertheless that, for a certain interval, surrounded him with a mild and friendly medium that must have warmed his fingers as he wrote. Melville had hungered for literate companionship during all his wanderyears; he had pounced like a seagull on men such as Long Ghost and Jack Chase who promised to satisfy this hunger, however imperfectly; and now, naturally, he was not unduly exacting in his choice of intellectual friends. He made the most, very cheerfully, of what the New York of the 'forties had to give him. It was not what Transcendental Concord might have given him, or even Whiggish Boston or Cambridge, but he did not, as he said, "oscillate in Emerson's rainbow," and never could have done so; and still less could he have found himself at home in the discreet orbit of Ticknor and Prescott.

He was of course not in the important sense "at home" in New York either, but during these few years of his youthful authorship, Melville seems to have found something congenial in the particular tone of prim Bohemianism and more-than-half-feminine sociality of the age of the Literati. Negotiations with his publishers over the manuscript of *Typee* had brought him into relation with one of their editors, the well-connected young *littérateur*, Evert Duyckinck, who was to be his Leigh Hunt. A sedate Leigh Hunt, to be sure, but in his mild and minor way a man of letters, and one who was to prove a genuine friend to Melville. Recently editor of the *Arcturus*, Duyckinck was soon to help launch one of the very first literary weeklies in the country, the *Literary World*.

Even now Poe was praising him for his "almost quixotic fidelity to his friends," and Lowell, in the *Fable for Critics*, later described him as a ripe scholar and a "neat" critic, "who through Grub Street the soul of a gentleman carries." In fact Duyckinck was too complete a gentleman to see very deeply into Melville's mind; but this did not keep him from having the most spontaneous appreciation of Melville's more evident qualities as a writer, or from befriending him in the columns of the *Literary World* in the most systematic and sympathetic way.

He had an excellent library both of contemporary writers and of old books, and could not have been more generous than he was in giving Melville the run of it. On Saturday evenings, moreover, at his house on Clinton Place, Duyckinck was in the habit of giving small and quietly convivial supper parties for his circle of literary friends, agreeable fellows and momentary lights like Charles Fenno Hoffman, George P. Morris, and Cornelius Mathews; and here Melville could listen, as he enjoyed doing, to the literary gossip and knowing conversation of the town. He even, for a brief spell, ventured into quarters where it is still harder for us to see the companion of Toby Green and Long Ghost, and allowed himself to be lured on a few occasions into the society of those lady literati, those Knickerbocker *précieuses*, for whose company Poe had such a taste. Poe and Melville, disappointingly enough, seem never to have come together; but Melville did sometimes appear at the refined evenings at Miss Anne Lynch's, in her house on Waverley Place, where he would have encountered a score or more of celebrated poetesses, and even a handful of poets: Mrs. Osgood, Mrs. Ellet, Mrs. Seba Smith, as well as N. P. Willis and Bayard Taylor and possibly some elder eminence like Bryant. On such evenings the younger guests might dance a quadrille while the artist Darley passed round a portfolio of his illustrations for *Margaret*, and Grace Greenwood might later recite her lyric, "Ariadne," or Miss Sedgwick read aloud some new poem of Elizabeth Barrett's.

There was a famous Valentine's party at Miss Lynch's—the one at which Sarah Helen Whitman read her fateful tribute to "The Raven"—when Melville was certainly present, and when, amid a flurry of mutual tributes in verse, a valentine to Melville, the production of Bayard Taylor, was read: it expressed the unwittingly ironic hope that the smiles of the tropic seas might be his through life,

> And may some guardian genius still
> *Taboo* thy path from every ill.

Prehistoric as it all sounds, it was not very different at some points from New York literary society today. In any case it is evident enough how superficial its meaning for Melville must have been. Superficial, yet not quite nonexistent, as we have seen. Somewhere on the circumference of his mind there was a freak of taste that enabled Melville to chat, no doubt seriously, with pretty little sentimental Fanny Osgood or the touchingly ambitious saloniste Anne Lynch herself, just as there was a freak of taste that enabled Flaubert to exchange serious literary talk with the shallow Louise Colet. This was real enough to come to the surface of Melville's work on occasion, as it certainly did with Poe again and again. The allegorical lilies and languors of *Mardi* are evidence of this; so, too, are a few limp passages here and there in *Redburn*, and even after *Moby Dick* some of the insipidities of *Pierre* suggest that Melville had not utterly purged himself of the *Godey's Lady's Book* rubbish.

In the mean time, after apparently living for the better part of three years at home in Lansingburgh, Melville, in the summer of 1847, had married and removed to New York. His marriage was a step not wholly easy to account for or understand, and with the passage of time it was to prove the source of much anguish to both Melville and his wife. Yet it lasted for more than forty years, until his death, in a spirit of genuine devotion and loyalty on both sides, and was perhaps a tenderer relation at the very end than it had been at any earlier time. The girl Melville married, Elizabeth Shaw, was a daughter of the most eminent jurist of his century, Lemuel Shaw, the Chief Justice of Massachusetts, the man who, among a hundred contributions to legal thought, had rendered the first really decisive opinion favorable to trade unionism. The thing, indeed, least difficult to understand in the whole connection is Melville's choice of Judge Shaw as a father-in-law. The Chief Justice had been, for one thing, an intimate friend of Melville's father, and as a young man had fallen in love with Allan Melville's sister Nancy, whom he would have married except for her early death. This had been an intense grief to him, and for many years he had not married at all; but the affectionate friendship with Nancy Melville's family continued uninterruptedly, even after Allan Melville's death, and it was a natural token of this that Melville should have dedicated his first book to his father's oldest friend. Lemuel Shaw had more than once held out a generous hand to the bereaved family, and in fact he was a man not only of great force and massive substance but of an almost childlike tenderness of heart and gentleness of feeling. Melville's interest in Elizabeth Shaw may well have been deepened by his need of Judge Shaw's paternal presence.

Herman and Lizzie had doubtless been friends from childhood, and there was something almost cousinly in the marriage, something extremely expressive of Melville's emotional dependence on his near relations, his deep-seated diffidence toward outsiders, especially of the other sex. Only in this setting of family closeness and long continuity, indeed, is his marriage at all understandable. There is nothing anywhere to suggest that Lizzie Melville was, like Sophia Hawthorne, a woman of remarkable intelligence in her own right, or that there was anything in her temperament that could be described as fascinating or romantic. Her letters, in both the earlier and the later years of her marriage, are quiet, colorless, matter-of-fact, and even ordinary: they are those of a well-bred, moderately well-educated, nice Boston girl or woman, whose mind is mainly preoccupied with questions of family health, family visits, the interchange of gifts, and the mats on the floor of Herman's room. In her husband's work there is no doubt that she took genuine pride, but it cannot have been a very understanding one, and her husband himself, deeply though she loved him, Lizzie Melville must have found again and again a terrible enigma. She was to accompany him, nevertheless, with unfaltering fidelity, through very deep waters indeed.

As for Melville himself, there was doubtless, in his feeling for Lizzie, a very large strain of the brotherly, even of the filial; it is true that he called her at the beginning by the romantic name of Oriana, but plain Lizzie soon took the place of this, and in his old age, for poetic purposes, he was calling her by the equally homely name of Winnie. Meanwhile, in the earliest days of their marriage, it is hard not to form the impression that Melville was half-consciously or unconsciously protesting against the relation in which he found himself. Most of *Mardi* was written after the summer of 1847, yet the book is peppered with protests against the marriage state and praises of bachelorhood. The native Samoa, for example, whom they pick up at sea, had at one time, says Melville, "meditated suicide—I would have said wedlock." On the island of Mondaldo the voyagers assist at a characteristic native wedding; the nuptial rites include the binding of the bride's hands with a strong cord, disguised in flowers, and the tying round the groom's waist of an equally strong cord, also flower-bedecked, to the end of which is attached a great stone, "very much carved and stained." At a much later stage of the voyage, as they are supping with the optimistic king Abrazza, Media, Mohi, and Babbalanja unite in celebrating the satisfactions of bachelorhood, and indeed Babbalanja has already repeated to the rest of them the will of the great sage Bardianna, who had remained single throughout life, and before his death had bequeathed to his "sensible" friend Solo, who had signified similar intentions, "the mat for one person, whereon I nightly repose." It is not easy to believe that Melville entered upon marriage without the most disturbing, even if unconscious, conflicts.

Five years later, when he was writing *Pierre*, he was insensible enough to his wife's feeling to speak of "the disenchanting glasses of the matrimonial days and nights." If he expected Lizzie to read his books, he must have been curiously indifferent to their effect on her, unless indeed he "wished" that effect. And the truth is that the masculine and the feminine elements in Melville's own nature were far too precariously balanced, far too unreconciled with one another, for marriage to be anything but excruciatingly problematic both for him and for his wife. All the more so since he could not have had more than the dimmest, most flickering awareness of the reasons for his difficulty. He was conscious enough, no doubt, of the ardor and intensity of his feelings for members of his own sex, but the possibility that such emotions might have had a sexual undercurrent can only with the utmost rarity, and then fleetingly, have presented itself to his consciousness. On the one occasion when he alludes to what would now be called overt homosexuality, in the passage in *White-Jacket* about the morals of the sailors, Melville speaks in a tone of extreme, indeed exaggerated, horror; and then, with an extraordinary flash of what can only be called unperceiving perception, he proceeds at once to associate these abhorrent facts with those of incest, especially incest between mother and son. He associates the two only as manifestations of a similar viciousness, but it is as if he saw, and refused to see, that his own malady had its roots, or some of them, in his unhappily intense relations with his own mother.

Years later, in a poem called "After the Pleasure Party," Melville dealt in a curiously bold manner, for his time, with the theme of repressed sexuality and the vengeance it takes on life and spirit:

> Nothing may help or heal
> While Amor incensed remembers wrong.

What is very striking is that the poem is written from the point of view of a woman, a middle-aged woman who, after a life devoted to science, to astronomy, is tormented and humiliated by her sudden erotic obsession with a young man: " 'Tis Vesta struck with Sappho's smart." For years this woman's mind has literally been on "higher things," on the stars, and now she learns to her bitter cost

> That soon or late, if faded e'en
> One's sex asserts itself.

In writing this poem Melville could hardly have been conscious how much of himself he was revealing. Nor could he have been at all conscious, in the books he wrote before and during the early years of his marriage, how freely he was confessing the ambiguity of his feelings for his own and the opposite sex. In *White-Jacket* he had simply eliminated the feminine altogether, as he came so close to doing in *Moby Dick;* the scene is entirely occupied by the officers and crew of the *Neversink*, and the womanly is virtually never allowed to intrude itself even in thought or imagination. Nothing so thoroughgoing occurred in the earlier books. In *Typee* and *Omoo* a number of lovely Polynesian maidens move across one's field of vision, and no reader is likely to forget the enchanting Fayaway, the ancestress of so many South Sea beauties in literature and in the films since her time. Yet, with the exception perhaps of Fayaway, these maidens seem less real than the handsome young Marquesan, Marnoo, who might have posed for the statue of "the Polynesian Apollo," or the comely young Tahitian, Kooloo, who makes himself Melville's *taio* and then jilts him so shamelessly. Kooloo appears briefly in *Omoo*, and one must also remember in that book the beautiful young Englishwoman, Mrs. Bell, whom Melville sees with such romantic emotions at Papetoai. Yet Mrs.

Bell too is seen only for a moment, and then on horseback, a not very feminine situation.

The only woman in *Mardi*, except for the allegorical characters, is the dreadful shrew, Annatoo, and Melville disposes of her very quickly and rather vengefully by drowning. The feminine principle asserts itself strongly in *Mardi* nevertheless; in its ideal aspect, as Yillah, and in its sensual one, as Hautia; and of course it is vital to Melville. Yet it comes into conflict, obscurely and uncertainly, with Taji's strongly emotional relation to the old Hebridean sailor, Jarl, his chum, as Melville calls him. Jarl is in effect a foster-father to Taji, and it is understandable that he should take so strong an aversion to the lovely Yillah when Taji turns to her, and that he should prove a living sacrifice to Taji's pursuit of the phantom maiden. The avengers of Aleema's death succeed in overtaking Jarl and slaying him. "Slain for me! my soul sobbed out"—and Taji, rent apart by his conflicting needs, does indeed lose both his comrade and his mistress. At the end he sees nothing before him but suicide.

Some obscure sense of the conflict between comradeship and romantic love, and even of their mutual destructiveness, lay behind this cloudy allegory. The pattern is not repeated in *Redburn*. Here it is a struggle, rather, between comradeship and the mere impersonal brutality of circumstance or fate. The forlorn Redburn does find a companion in the graceless but lovable Harry Bolton, only to lose him in the end to the unpitying seas. Meanwhile, Redburn has not put all thought of the opposite sex from his mind. As he wanders about the countryside near Liverpool, he comes upon an English cottage where he is hospitably entertained at tea by an old countryman and his wife, and loses his heart to three rosy maidens, their daughters, "three charmers, three Peris, three Houris!" He pretends, indeed, that he still remains a bachelor on their account, and clearly they are wishful phantoms, if nothing more; but compared with Harry Bolton, who seems to owe everything to reality, the three charmers have an oddly literary, second-hand, gift-book quality: they seem to have stepped out of *Lalla Rookh* or some engraving in the *Token*.

There is always a certain factitiousness or unreality in Melville's feminine characters, except when, like Mrs. Danby, the boardinghouse keeper in *Redburn*, or Mrs. Hussey of the Try-Pots in *Moby Dick*, they are middle-aged or elderly. And he is always at his easiest and most unconstrained when he can leave the land and the world of women quite behind him and launch himself upon the high seas in the midst of men and boys exclusively. Yet if this is true for him as a writer, it is not the whole truth for him as a person: the masculine element in his nature was too strong for that, and he could not, as Whitman could, hold the feminine at a safe and simple distance while he organized his emotional life around his male companionships. He could not, for one thing, given all his connections, abandon himself genially to the declassed and rather raffish Bohemianism that Whitman found so congenial. Marriage was doubtless inescapable for him, and in the long run it was to prove a healing and preservative force: it was to his marriage perhaps that he owed his long and productive survival. In the mean time, however, the clash between one group of needs and another was terribly intense, and emotionally speaking (not on other grounds) this is the central fact behind his work.

Shortly after his marriage Melville had settled with his young wife in a house on Fourth Avenue in New York between Eleventh and Twelfth Streets, and here they were to live, with Melville's sisters and sometimes his mother as part of the household, for the next three years. In 1849 their first child, a boy named Malcolm, was born, and the pressures on Melville, as financially responsible head of a large and growing family, became steadily more severe. It was chiefly for this reason that, in the fall of that year, Melville thrust the manuscript of *White-Jacket* into his carpetbag and set out for England: in London he could hope to make some more advantageous arrangement with an English publisher than he could do at a distance. The trip had no very profound effect on Melville's development: it was too late in the day for that. But it was not a bad thing for his self-regard to land in England again, after ten years, not now as a shabby unknown, but (as he said with a certain grimace) as the "author of 'Peedee' 'Hullabaloo' & 'Pog-Dog'." It is true that, for the author of three or four successful books, it must have been humiliating to have to hawk the manuscript of his fifth book about among seven or eight publishers before finally coming to terms with Bentley. But meanwhile he was treated with consideration and even hospitality everywhere; he met no very great celebrities, but he dipped a little into London society, literary and otherwise; he met the forbidding old Lockhart at dinner at Murray's, but refused to kowtow, he says, to a man he knew to be "a thorough-going Tory & fish-blooded Churchman & conservative"; he encountered Kinglake at breakfast at Samuel Rogers's; and—what he enjoyed more than either—he dined, with many thoughts of Lamb and the Old Benchers, with a group of carefree bachelors in the rooms of a cousin of Murray's in the Temple.

The love of personal freedom, in fact, kept struggling throughout the trip with Melville's homesick thoughts of his wife and baby. On the whole, he was in a high-spirited, vacationing mood. On the packet boat going over, while the other passengers lay seasick, he strode about the deck or clambered up the mast with the agility of a young sailor; played card games and shuffleboard; and best of all, sat up until all hours drinking whiskey punches and talking metaphysics—"fix'd fate, free will, foreknowledge absolute"—with a young German-American scholar named Adler, whom he liked heartily, and whom he saw again and again in London and Paris. The passion for travel and sight-seeing was still strong in him; he belonged to the innocent age of unapologetic guidebooks and catalogues, and both in England and on the Continent he was indefatigable in making the rounds of churches and museums, castles and fortresses, theaters and zoos. The sight of London from one of the bridges, overhung with coal smoke, make him think, like an earlier Eliot, of Dante and the dolorous City of Dis. The Lord Mayor's show struck him as "a most bloated pomp," and on the following day he was outraged by the spectacle at the Guildhall when the poor were allowed to enter and make off with the leavings of the banquet. In Paris he was deeply affected by a visit to the Hôtel de Cluny and especially by the Thermes or ruinous Roman baths below it. Brussels struck him as a dull place, but Cologne fascinated him, and at Coblenz he was stirred by the magnificent pile of the fortress of Ehrenbreitstein across the Rhine. The ruins on the Drachenfels seemed to him glorious—"but," he added to himself defiantly, "the river Rhine is not the Hudson." Sights such as these were full of meaning to the poet in Melville, and some of them were later to re-emerge in his work.

Back in England, he was strongly tempted to prolong his stay by several weeks when he had an invitation from the Duke of Rutland to make him a visit at Belvoir Castle. He would very much have liked to see for himself "what the highest English aristocracy really & practically is," and he realized that it might mean "material" for his books. What Melville would have done, however, with material that suggests Disraeli or Thackeray much more than it does him will never be known. The longing to rejoin Lizzie and Mackie was stronger now than the desire to see a ducal household from within, and once he had struck his bargain with Bentley he lost no time in taking passage on another packet boat and returning with as much speed as might be to New York. Early in February he was back at home again on Fourth Avenue, and within the month, probably, he had set to work on still another book.

He was not to finish it, however, in the city. Some need had grown up in him to return to the country surroundings in which so much of his boyhood had been spent, and in the summer of 1850 he and Lizzie, with the baby, decamped from New York and went to stay at Pittsfield in his Uncle Thomas's old house, Broadhall, which his uncle's widow was now conducting as a summer hotel. So strong did the pull of these earlier scenes prove to be that Melville made up his mind to move from the city entirely, and in the autumn, with money that Judge Shaw advanced him—for his own finances were extremely shaky—he bought a big, old-fashioned, eighteenth-century farmhouse, not far from his aunt's, and moved into it with his family of dependents. The old house, which he named Arrowhead from some relics he dug up on his new property, was to be his home for the next thirteen years. It stood, with its plain square lines and its great chimney, in the midst of pastures and hayfields, elms and maples, with an apple orchard and a wooded hill to the south, and northward, across the meadows that sloped down to the Housatonic, a magnificent prospect of Mount Greylock, twelve miles away. On this north side of the house, in fact, he built a large piazza giving on the near meadows and the distant hills; and here, in winter, as he strode back and forth with frosted beard while the north wind drove the floury snow about him, he could almost imagine that he was not on land after all but at sea again, pacing the sleety deck, weathering Cape Horn. Even in summer, indeed, it gave him a sea-feeling to sit on this piazza and gaze out across the rolling meadows, over which the still August noon brooded like a calm upon the Line.

At Arrowhead, for the first year or two, Melville's life was a mingling of the bucolic, the literary, and the social. He made no claim to being a serious farmer, but winter and summer there were chores to do about the place, a horse and a cow in the barn to be fed and watered, wood to be cut in the woodlots nearby and split for firewood, apples to be picked for cider and hay mown in the meadows. As soon as possible, that first fall or early winter, Melville settled down earnestly to his book again, shutting himself in his room after breakfast, and emerging only at half-past two when Lizzie or his sister Augusta knocked at the door, by request, until he was forced to leave off. Meanwhile, he had by no means abjured society. The Berkshire towns, Pittsfield, Lenox, Stockbridge, in the midst of which he was living, were by no means isolated villages but pleasant country towns with a cultivated social life of their own, and there were always a certain number of literary people, not all of them perhaps of the highest distinction, within reach. Unconventional as he was rapidly becoming in social intercourse—there were people who disliked his "irreverent language," for example—Melville in these months was much of the time in a mood of high spirits and even conviviality; Duyckinck and others came up for visits from the city; one hears a good deal about champagne, gin, and cigars, about overnight excursions to the summit of Greylock, carriage drives to the Shaker village of Lebanon, costume parties at the Morewoods', and picnics on the shores of Lake Pontoosuc.

It was during the first summer back in Pittsfield, while Melville was still staying at his aunt's house, that the most fateful of all these outings occurred, the outing that brought Melville and Hawthorne together. Hawthorne had been living for some months in a little house on the shores of Stockbridge Bowl in Lenox, and it was at Stockbridge one day, as guests of David Dudley Field, that the two men met. It was a day—the fifth of August, 1850—that some of those present remembered for years as a specially happy one. It began in the morning with an expedition to Monument Mountain nearby. Just before they reached the top of the mountain a shower came up which drove them all for shelter beneath a ledge of overhanging rock, damp and mossy, and here Cornelius Mathews read aloud Bryant's poem on "Monument Mountain." A little later, the sun came out again and they climbed on to the summit, where Melville, boyishly elated, perched on a narrow rock that jutted out like a bowsprit and began pulling and hauling at imaginary rigging. Back at Field's in the village, they sat down to a bounteous feast, well moistened with wines, during the course of which Dr. Holmes, who was present, took it into his head to argue the superiority, physical at least, of Englishmen to Americans, only to find himself vigorously assailed, some say by Hawthorne, some by Melville; perhaps by both. The meeting had brought a shock of happy recognition to the two men, and when, in the afternoon, the party set out again to scramble through the Gothic shades of the Icy Glen, Hawthorne was in such exceptional high spirits that for once he shed all reticence, and in the dank gloom of the little ravine one heard his rich voice shouting out warnings of inevitable destruction to the whole party.

The two of them had struck up a friendship at a particularly fortunate hour, and it ripened quickly. A few days later Hawthorne was writing to his friend Bridge that he liked Melville so much he had invited him over to Lenox for a few days' visit—by no means a routine procedure on Hawthorne's part. As for Melville, this meeting with the older writer—Hawthorne, fifteen years his senior, was in his mid-forties—found him in a state of quite special responsiveness; it was a cardinal moment, intellectually and emotionally, in his life. Association with pleasant fellows and small *littérateurs* like Duyckinck, Willis, and Mathews, was well enough, but almost certainly it was beginning to pall on Melville, conscious as he was of being engaged at last on a task commensurate with his powers; and moreover he had only just begun seriously to read Hawthorne's work (not yet *The Scarlet Letter* but the *Mosses*) and to hear in it the voice of the first American writer who had moved him profoundly, at a depth to which Cooper and Dana had never penetrated. Probably just before the Stockbridge party, though possibly just after it, he had sat down at Pittsfield and written for the *Literary World* a long, excited essay about Hawthorne's work, in which he expressed the sentiment that, up to that point, the American who had evinced in literature the largest brain with the largest heart was Nathaniel Hawthorne. Now he had encountered Hawthorne in person; the current of sympathy and mutual interest had passed between them like a magnetic force; and on Melville's part the sense of personal fulfillment was solemn and even mystical. "I feel," he wrote later, "that the Godhead is broken up like the bread at the Supper, and that we are the pieces."

It was more than a year after their first meeting that Melville wrote this; it was after several meetings, indeed, and in response to a deeply understanding letter that Hawthorne appears to have written him about *Moby Dick*. He would not have spoken so earnestly as this in the earlier months of their friendship; not so quickly as that were the barriers of shyness and reserve between two such men to be broken down. But even at the beginning, on Melville's side, there was undoubtedly a sense that he had come upon another man to whom he could address himself with a fullness and a straightness that had no precedent in his experience. What told him this was not only Hawthorne's personal presence but his work. What mattered most was that, at least as Melville believed, there was a mind, a creative mind, in America, to which he could feel at once inherently akin; he had not hitherto had that good luck. Essentially he felt himself, and no doubt increasingly, a spiritual alien in the midst not only of the Duyckincks and the Willises but of the Emersons and the Thoreaus, their superiors, the best minds. Where among them all was there any recognition of the fact of tragedy, any awareness of that dark half of the globe that more and more seemed to Melville an immitigable reality, not to be conjured away by transcendental spells? Something of this he might indeed have found in Poe, but he seems never to have done so, and doubtless he was always repelled by the glitter and the artifice that bulk so large in Poe's equivocal genius.

Now he had found, in the unlikely form of the sketches and tales of *Mosses from an Old Manse*, the resonance of the somber strain his ears had been listening for. How different from *Knickerbocker's History* or *The Pioneers*, from *Nature* for that matter, were "Young Goodman Brown," "The Bosom Serpent," "Earth's Holocaust"! How appalling, yet how profound, the moral of this last!—that after all the out-worn, empty forms and follies have been burned to ashes, and nothing is left but the all-engendering heart of man, yet so long as *this* remains unconsumed, the great conflagration has gone for naught. "Now," Melville had said in his essay, "it is that blackness in Hawthorne . . . that so fixes and fas-cinates me." It fixed and fascinated him because it mirrored a blackness that lay within himself, and moreover it fortified him in his resolve to let that dark hue have full expression in his work. "Already I feel that this Hawthorne has dropped germinous seeds into my soul. He expands and deepens down, the more I contemplate him; and further and further, shoots his strong New England roots in the hot soil of my Southern soul."

It is an astonishingly sexual image, but probably only such an image could adequately have expressed Melville's feeling, for the moment, of receptiveness and even passivity in the ac-ceptance of impregnation by another mind. How deep and decisive the effect of all this was on the composition of *Moby Dick* one can only guess: it seems likely to have been very great. Melville wrote his essay on Hawthorne's *Mosses* late in July or early in August of 1850, a few days before or after he actually encountered Hawthorne in the flesh. Months ear-lier, in May, he had written to Dana that he was halfway through his "whaling voyage," and Duyckinck, writing to his brother on the seventh of August, spoke of Melville's new book as "mostly done." Yet *Moby Dick* was not actually fin-ished until late in July 1851, and though sixteen or seventeen months seems a prodigiously short period for the composition of such a book, it would have been a rather unaccountably long period at the pace at which Melville had been writing.

One of the possibilities is that he rewrote much of it, and stroked in all the lines far more boldly, after reading Hawthorne's book and meeting him. Certainly he talked with his new friend about what he was doing. Even before *Moby Dick* was finished, Hawthorne conjured up, in *A Wonder Book*, the image of Herman Melville, "on the hither side of Pittsfield," sitting at his study-window and "shaping out the gigantic conception of his 'White Whale'." The sense of Hawthorne's sympathetic and understanding nearness, at all events, cannot have been less than vital, and it implied far more than the usual friendliness and good will when Melville dedicated the book to him at last.

Meanwhile, though both men were too much preoccupied for constant meetings—Hawthorne during much of this time was busy with the *Seven Gables*—their intimacy had blossomed quickly, and with only five or six miles between them, a series of visits between Arrowhead and the red cottage had taken place. Julian Hawthorne could remember years later a winter's day when "Mr. Omoo," with a shaggy coat and bushy brown beard, had plowed his way over from Pittsfield through the snow to call upon them, accompanied by a black Newfoundland dog on whose back the Hawthorne children were allowed to ride. There were two or three days in the middle of March when Hawthorne, with the *Seven Gables* behind him, took Una over to Arrowhead for a visit, and the two friends, deterred from long walks by the inclement weather, spent their time lounging about in Melville's barn, smoking and talking metaphysics by the hour. They even discussed the possibility of an expedition to New York together, which never came to realization. Late one August afternoon, however, the following summer, as Hawthorne, a temporary bachelor, was returning on foot with Julian from the post office in Lenox, a man on horseback came along the road, saluted him in Spanish, and then, not being recognized at once, renewed his salutation, and Hawthorne recognized his friend. Together they made their way back to the red cottage, and after a bite of supper, and when Julian had been put to bed, the two men, violating all Sophia's tabus, sat smoking cigars in the living-room and having a talk about time and eternity, "and all possible and impossible matters," that lasted far into the night.

Sophia Hawthorne would have been outraged by the cigar smoke, but she had the most understanding appreciation of Melville both as a person and as a writer. In a letter to her mother she described him about this time as a man with a warm heart, a soul, and an intellect, very tender and modest; and she added that she was not sure that he was not a very great man. Puzzlingly to her, his eyes were not large or deep or particularly keen; indeed, not remarkable eyes in any way; and yet at times, when his intermittent animation lapsed, they would take on a singularly quiet expression, an indrawn, dim look that gave one the feeling that at that instant he was taking the deepest note of what was passing before him. For the rest, his nose was straight and rather handsome, his mouth expressive of sensibility and emotion, and he himself tall and erect, with an air of freedom and manliness. In conversation, especially in story-telling, he was sometimes incomparably vivid and animated, full of gesture and force, and quickly lost himself in his subject. There was one evening when Mr. Omoo related to Sophia and her husband the story of a fight he had once witnessed between two Polynesian braves, in which one of them had performed prodigies of valor with a heavy club. When their guest had gone, Hawthorne and Sophia looked high and low for the club with which Melville had been "laying about him so," and gradually became aware that it had existed only in his imagination and theirs.

Curious that the story the Hawthornes best remembered should have been one involving a combat and a club. The dealing of blows—if not with clubs, then with harpoons and lances—was an essential aspect of Melville's imaginative life at the time, and the retaliation for injury an essential aspect of his emotional life. Nevertheless, and despite the deepening strain of his inward and outward problems, it was in such an atmosphere of warmth and appreciation as this, at least in the direction of Lenox, that Melville composed his greatest book.

The Whale

HOW LONG, when Melville settled down to write his "whaling voyage," the conception of *Moby Dick* had been present to his mind, it is impossible to say. He did not keep notebooks, as Hawthorne did, and one cannot, as one can with *The Scarlet Letter*, detect what appears to be almost the first germ of the romance in its pristine form and then trace its slow, embryonic maturation over a period of ten years or even more. The whole process, with *Moby Dick*, was certainly far more condensed and rapid than that. Yet the opening chapters of *Mardi*, three years earlier, had made it plain that the image of the Sperm Whale was beginning to lift itself more and more compulsively in Melville's imagination: one can now see that sooner or later that image would have had to be appeased. Not only so, but it is evident that, if he did not encounter some unlikely break, stoppage, and reversal in his whole development as a writer, Melville was bound eventually to transmute into fiction the experience of those many months during which he had been a foremasthand on the *Acushnet*, the *Lucy Ann*, and the *Charles and Henry*. Clearly they had been the months of most intense meaning for him in all his wanderyears, more intense even than the months in the islands, and now, after *Redburn* and *White-Jacket*, they remained the one great chapter in his active life that had not been fully embodied in his work. Their having been thus postponed is what partly tells us that they *were* the richest in meaning: he had shied away from them, after a few chapters of *Mardi,* with an abruptness that speaks volumes about his sense of unreadiness. The turn *Mardi* had taken, moreover, had been a turn away from realistic narrative toward a more poetic, more mythical form; but on the whole the experiment had proved a fiasco. In the next two books Melville had proceeded at a more cautious pace, but he had by no means relapsed to the prosaic straightforwardness of *Typee* and *Omoo:* he had drawn close to a symbolic manner far more deeply expressive of his own genius than the allegory of *Mardi* and far truer to the stuff of his own experience. Now, with *Redburn* and *White-Jacket* behind him, he was ready not only to return finally to the enriched remembrance of his whaling past, but ready too to incorporate it in a high form, a form in which prose and symbol might be completely fused in a powerful, polyphonic whole.

This dependence on his own experience, in the obvious and outward as well as in the inner sense, this reliance on reminiscence, is one of the traits of Melville's particular gift; a second is his extraordinary dependence on the writings of other men. These traits, even when taken separately but especially when taken together, characterize him as a unique, or all but unique, figure in his period. It points to something very potently archaic in his genius to say that in a certain sense he was hardly an "inventive" writer at all; that he should rather be described, like some minstrel of the heroic era or some tragic writer for the ancient stage, as an essentially convertive or transmutative poet. All invention, of course, is a complex form of transmutation, but there is a genuine difference of quality here nevertheless; and it means something to speak of the great novelists of the nineteenth century—Scott, Balzac, Dickens, Dostoevsky, Hardy—as wonderfully originative writers; originative in the sense of creating their thickly populated worlds out of materials that for the most part are at least once removed from their own personal histories, and that depend only very secondarily on the writings of other men. They draw heavily enough, in another sense, on those writings; but what they draw is not their matter, dramatic and presentational, but their literary means, their resources of form, their structure. It is the large structure of *Moby Dick*, on the contrary, that is, for the nineteenth century, completely originative. For his matter, Melville turned first to his private memories and then to books.

It is eloquent of the curious mingling in his nature of passivity and active creativeness that he should have done so. The White Whale himself is no invention, in the nineteenth-century sense; he is—to remain, for the moment, near the surface—the complex product not only of a thousand impressions Melville must have had of the actual Sperm Whale, but also of his recollections of Reynolds's magazine article, "Mocha Dick: or The White Whale of the Pacific." Touches in that article had lingered somewhere in his memory, as touches in Coleridge's endless readings in travel literature had lingered in his, and (as in Coleridge's case) had doubtless ceased even to be consciously recollected. Melville could not wholly have "forgotten," however, that, according to Reynolds, Mocha Dick had so deeply affected the superstitious imaginings of the sailors that they had come to think of him "rather as some ferocious fiend of the deep, than a regular-built, legitimate whale." Melville had changed the name itself slightly, it is true, either because he had actually heard another form of the name in the forecastle talk of his fellow sailors, or because he wished to avoid the incongruous associations of the word "Mocha," or because he wished somehow to evoke the White Whale's magnificent mobility. The seeds so carelessly dropped by Reynolds, in any case, had fallen on unpredictably creative soil.

Nor was it the Whale alone that had been given to Melville by this special collaboration of experience and reading. The great image of the ultimate catastrophe itself, the destruction of the *Pequod* by Moby Dick, had come to him in a somewhat comparable way. He himself had never, so far as one knows, undergone literal shipwreck, but soon after the *Acushnet* sailed from Fairhaven he had begun to hear his shipmates in the forecastle tell tales about the famous and fearful case of the whale-ship *Essex* of Nantucket, which in 1820, on the equatorial cruising-grounds in the Pacific, had been stove and sunk by a huge Sperm Whale. The captain and the crew of the *Essex*, it is true, unlike Ahab and his men, had escaped from the wreck in their boats, but in the weeks that followed they had undergone the most gruesome hardships and sufferings, and in the end only the Captain, George Pollard, with the first mate, Owen Chase, and three hands had made their way back to Nantucket. When, twenty years later, according to some notes of Melville's, the *Acushnet* had been ten or eleven months at sea, they had had a "gam" with another Nantucket craft, and Melville had then made the acquaintance of "a fine lad of sixteen or thereabouts," who proved to be a son of Owen Chase, and who, says Melville, lent him a copy of the little book his father had written, the *Narrative of the Most Extraordinary and Distressing Shipwreck of the Whale-Ship Essex*. The reading of this strange and terrible story on "the landless sea," and not far from the scene of the disaster itself, "had a surprising effect on me," he says; and this effect was deeply re-enforced when, not long after, the *Acushnet* spoke still another Nantucket ship, the *Charles Carroll*, and found that Owen Chase himself was its captain.

He had come aboard the *Acushnet* at that time, and though Melville, as a mere foremasthand, was in no position to converse with him, he had been strongly affected by this glimpse of a man who, already in his own lifetime, had taken on in the eyes of whalers a legendary and almost preternatural stature. Chase proved to be in fact a man of curiously prepossessing appearance, rather tall, well-made, and with a handsome face, "expressive of great uprightness & calm un-

ostentatious courage." Doubtless he was the noblest example
Melville was to encounter of that almost Viking grandeur of
type which, as he says in *Moby Dick*, Nantucket sometimes
produced; doubtless he seemed "a mighty pageant creature,
formed for noble tragedies." Certainly his figure hovered before Melville's imagination as he wrote *Moby Dick*, and certainly also did the image of the *Essex* on its fatal day—on
that day when the great Sperm Whale, enraged as it seemed
by the sufferings of his companions, already attacked, had
come bearing down upon the ship not once only but twice,
horrible in aspect, and as if animated by a calculating malice,
had stove in the bows, grazed the keel, and then swum off to
leeward as the doomed vessel began to go down. Mocha Dick,
Owen Chase, and the foundering *Essex*—such was the powerful constellation of images that, gathering together in Melville's imagination from actuality and from books, had massed
itself into one whole and become the intense nucleus of his
novel.

What remained to do even then, however, was very far
from being a matter simply of spontaneous invention or free
fictive improvisation upon his great theme. Melville had always striven, as we have seen, to impart to his books the utmost density and substantiality; the quality that Ortega describes as "imperviousness.' He had instinctively felt that, as
Ortega says, "to enjoy a novel we must feel surrounded by it
on all sides," that "the great novels are essentially lavish of
particulars." And now, in his largest effort, he set to work in a
manner that suggests the collaboration of the minstrel and
the systematic savant. *Moby Dick* was to be "a mighty book,"
and not even "a mighty theme" was to be enough for it; a
mighty labor of at least informal scholarship was also required. What Melville knew from firsthand experience about
whales and whaling was not to suffice him; much as it may
have been, it was to be re-enforced, rounded out, and made
precise by reliance on other writers. There was something of
Zola's pertinacity, though very little of Zola's program, in the

manner in which he went about his *enquête*. By buying them
or borrowing them from libraries, he seems to have laid his
hands on most of the books then available on such subjects;
he ended by making particularly heavy draughts on three or
four: the Rev. Henry T. Cheever's *The Whale and His
Captors*, Thomas Beale's *Natural History of the Sperm
Whale*, the younger William Scoresby's *Journal of a Voyage
to the Northern Whale Fishery*, and a rather spirited book he
reviewed for Duyckinck's paper, *Etchings of a Whaling
Cruise*, by J. Ross Browne, a young Kentuckian who had
shipped on a whaler from New Bedford a year or so later
than Melville. "I have swam through libraries," he says
proudly, and not without reason, in *Moby Dick*.

For the most part it was solid information that he drew
from these books, information about the anatomy and the
ecology of the whale, and about the history and the methods
of the whale "fishery." He had made use of similar authorities
in writing *Typee* and *Omoo*; but on the whole, in those
books, he had done hardly more than reproduce or paraphrase his originals. Now, in *Moby Dick*, working at the
height of his shaping power, Melville was almost incapable
of leaving any piece of information in its raw state of un-
resonant factuality, and with rare exceptions Beale's and
Cheever's facts are Melville's metaphors. If Cheever baldly
remarks that the fin on the back of a finback whale resembles
the gnomon on a sundial, Melville, appropriating the image,
endows it at once with metaphorical richness by associating it
with a reminiscence from Isaiah: "On that Ahaz-dial the
shadow often goes back." If Beale prosaically describes ambergris as "nothing but the hardened faeces of the spermaceti
whale," Melville proceeds to convert the fact into the complex ironies and solemnities of the chapter on "Ambergris";
"Now that the incorruption of this most fragrant ambergris
should be found in the heart of such decay; is this nothing?"
But he does not limit himself to the transformation of arid facts
into metaphors and symbols: one can never predict when

some piece of pedestrian exposition will furnish him with the germ of a great dramatic scene. In Scoresby, for example, he came upon the account of a method by which, when a ship's compass has been reversed in its polarity by lightning, a new compass can be improvised by percussion. Upon this hint Melville wrote the majestic scene in which Ahab, after the ship has passed through a typhoon, demonstrates that he is "lord of the level loadstone."

Perhaps no writer has ever worked at a more intense pitch of imaginative anabolism than Melville did during these wonderful months. Literary fare could hardly be jejune enough to deter him from consuming it and then transmuting it into the tissue of heroic poetry. Even from so small and journalistic, though lively, a book as Ross Browne's he was capable' of taking cues; and we perhaps owe "The Town-Ho's Story," in this literary sense, not so much to the lays of Demodocus in the *Odyssey* as to the tales-within-a-tale with which Browne's sailors regale one another, especially one called "Bob Grimsley's Ghost." If so, the distance between Browne and Melville in poetic quality is something like the distance between Geraldi Cinthio and Shakespeare. And one soon exhausts both the interest and the critical importance of Melville's or any such writer's "sources": they are worth an allusion only because, compared with most of his contemporaries, he drew upon them so heavily and sublimated them with such power. More intangibly, moreover, he had found creative nourishment in a long list, not of prosaic authorities, but of great books and writers of the sort toward whom he had always been drawn. In this connection two books are worth a word or two, the *Lusiads* of Camoëns and the plays of Shakespeare.

He had come to Camoëns and his great poem, according to *White-Jacket*, through the enthusiasm for it of Jack Chase; certainly he knew the *Lusiads,* and knew it well, in the surprisingly energetic version that Mickle had made in heroic couplets. It was, as he had found, the greatest of all modern poems about the sea, the greatest of all such poems perhaps, except the *Odyssey*, and in its extraordinary fullness and density of detail, its bitingly and blowingly saline quality, a more purely seagoing poem even than Homer's. Camoëns, as Melville knew, had been not only a soldier but a sailor also, and for the Portuguese poet too the high seas, the wastes of ocean, had ended by becoming powerfully, primordially symbolic. The sense of spatial vastness, of remote oceanic horizons, is intense in the *Lusiads;* and so too is the sense of the fearfulness and peril of the untamed forces of nature, the forces that Camoëns embodies in the mythical figure of Adamastor, the Spirit of the Cape, the monster who attempts to wreak destruction on Gama and his men, and whom Melville alludes to in *Billy Budd.* The *Lusiads* abounds in the imagery of nautical terror—of waterspouts and corposants, of cold and darkness, of raging tempests, thunderbolts, and turbulent seas. No great poem is more solidly and unbookishly realistic, yet this realism, faithful though it is, harmonizes in the richest way with the expressions of a strong myth-making phantasy. It is hard indeed not to feel that *Moby Dick* would have been somewhat different from what it is if Melville had not known the *Lusiads.* In his old age, certainly, he wrote two small poems about Camoëns in which he clearly identified himself, in his obscurity and solitude, with his great Portuguese predecessor.

As for Shakespeare, it is already a familiar fact that the reading and rereading of his plays, in the months before and during the writing of *Moby Dick*, affected Melville profoundly. What this reading signified to him can hardly be suggested in a few sentences. One can, it is true, make the negative remark that, like many men of his time, Melville was little interested in or affected by Shakespeare the writer for the theater; for what he calls, in the essay on Hawthorne, "the tricky stage"—true as it was that this alone had made Shakespeare's "mere mob renown." Nor was it mainly the poet who had populated a whole phantasmal world with superreal personages, Shakespeare the creator of character, who acted on Melville's own creativeness. What he most vitally found in the plays was not dramatic effectiveness or individual psychology but "those deep far-away things in him; those occasional flashings-forth of the intuitive Truth in him; those short, quick probings at the very axis of reality." What he found was Shakespeare "the profoundest of thinkers," the man most fearlessly capable of hinting at "the things which we feel to be so terrifically true" that no merely good man would ever speak them. Shakespeare, in short, the Shakespeare of *Lear* and *Hamlet* and *Timon*, confirmed and strengthened Melville in his own sense of the dark destructive forces—the ferocity, the hard selfishness, the cunning cruelty —that are so often operative in actual men and women; confirmed him too in the intuition that there is something wild, arbitrary, and irrational in the very structure of things, and that innocent men suffer at its hands as flies suffer at the hands of wanton boys. Yet all this did not, on the other hand, blind him to the Shakespeare for whom man was in action like an angel and in apprehension like a god.

To speak of the structure and the texture of *Moby Dick* is to embark upon a series of paradoxes that are soberly truthful and precise. Few books of its dimensions have owed so much to books that have preceded them, and few have owed so little; not many imaginative works have so strong and strict a unity, and not many are composed of such various and even discordant materials; few great novels have been comparably concrete, factual, and prosaic, and few of course have been so large and comprehensive in their generality, so poetic both in their surface fabric and in their central nature. In form alone *Moby Dick* is unique in its period, and that too in a sense more special than the sense in which every fully achieved work of literature is unique. Such a book could only have been written by an American, and an American of Melville's generation, working as he did in a kind of isolation from the central current of European writing in his time—an isolation quite consistent with his keeping abreast of it intellectually—and, while losing something in consequence, gaining something indispensable he could not otherwise have had.

Given his kind of creative power, Melville was wholly fortunate in his literary derivations and development. As we have seen, his springboard had never been the English or European novel, not at any rate in its great characteristic mode, the mode of the social novel, the novel of manners, the novel of "real life." He belonged to a society that was in some of its aspects too archaic to find a natural place for forms so advanced as these, and his own origins, as if he belonged to the Bronze Age or at least to the Age of Migrations, were partly in oral story-telling, the story-telling of sailors and travelers, and partly in forms that were either subliterary or at the best on a modestly and hesitantly literary level. He had begun as a writer of reportorial travel books, books that were simply further examples of the "journal" or "narrative," and in a certain sense he continued to be such a writer in *Moby Dick*. It is wholly natural that Owen Chase's *Narrative* should have been so vital to him, and that one pole of *Moby Dick* should be constituted by the informative chapters on whales and whaling. Melville's need as an artist was to take the small, prosy, and terribly circumscribed form he had inherited, and somehow make it a vehicle capable of bearing a great imaginative weight, of expressing a great visionary theme. His problem was to find the bridge between J. Ross Browne and Camoëns. He had quite failed to find it in *Mardi*; he had run away from his true matter in pursuit of an allegorical will-o'-the-wisp, and the result had been fiasco. A better wisdom had come to him in consequence; a better sense of his own right path. His own right path was, as Emerson would say, to "ask the fact for the form": to remain faithful to his own crass, coarse, unideal, and yet grandiose material—the life of American whalers—and to make of its unpromising images his symbols, of its hardly malleable substance his myth.

It is what he does in *Moby Dick*. There is no question here of chimerical priests and maidens, of symbolic blooms and allegorical isles and Spenserian bowers; no question of symbols wilfully imposed upon the meaning from without; no question of what Melville himself now calls "a hideous and intolerable allegory." In their stead one finds a fable almost bare in its simplicity and, on the surface, journalistic in its realism; the fable of a whaling vessel that sets out from Nantucket and, like some actual whaling vessels, comes to a disastrous end on the cruising-grounds near the Line. This tale is launched in pages so homely in their substance, despite their intensity of expression, that its earliest readers might almost have doubted whether they had to do with a "novel" or only with another and rather more dashing "narrative." It comes to a close in pages in which we are still encountering men like the bereaved Captain Gardiner and the vessels like the *Rachel* of Nantucket. The skipper and the mates of the *Pequod* hail from Nantucket or the Cape or the Vineyard; all the characters, including the pagan harpooneers, and even perhaps the Parsees, are such men as might have been found, though some of them rarely, on an actual whaler of the 'forties. In their company we sail over well-known whaling routes, past familiar capes and headlands, giving chase not to fabulous monsters but to Sperm Whales and Right Whales of the sort that men had taken by the thousands, and having glimpses as we do so of other creatures—sharks, squid, swordfish, seahawks—such as Owen and Cuvier had classified. In short, with one or two great exceptions, the substance of *Moby Dick* is as faithful to sober fact as that of Owen Chase's or Ross Browne's book; if the impress on the imagination is that of a high poetic form it is not because the poetry is "allegorically" imposed on the stuff, but because the stuff is allowed to render up its own poetic essences.

It does so partly because the organizing structure of the fable—the Voyage, with its clear beginning and its predestined catastrophe—is at once so firm and simple and so large and free in its elasticity: like the structure of the *Odyssey* or the *Lusiads*, it is both strict and pliable. It is a fable, moreover, which, though it took shape in the most natural way out of a set of dense facts and tough, unromantic conditions, could nevertheless be made concrete and dramatic through a group of basic, primary symbols (the sea, the quest, the great "fish," the ship, the watery tomb) and of incidental or secondary symbols (the sword-mat, the monkey-rope, the sharks, and others) that are both immediate and primordial, both local and archetypal, both journalistic and mythopoeic. They are, moreover, at the same time wonderfully various and powerfully interrelated, so that the balance, as Coleridge would say, between "sameness" and "difference" is all but perfect. In any composition less completely integrated there might seem to be a hopeless incongruity between Ahab's pipe and the mystic Spirit-Spout, as between the jolly, unimaginative Stubb and the satanic Fedallah: in the setting of *Moby Dick* they are no more incongruous than, in the *Odyssey*, the swine of Eumaeus and the magic veil that Ino bestows on Odysseus.

Such analogies are inescapable because, after every necessary thing has been said about Melville's homely and prosaic derivations, in the bookish sense, one has to go on to say that the design and the texture of *Moby Dick*, both of them so unlike those of the classical novel of the age, abound in reminiscences of forms that are somewhat, or even very, remote from the nineteenth century. There is no doubt that this is in part the result of a conscious and artful process. There is no doubt that Melville deliberately undertook to intensify, to elevate the narration of his tale—to express the strangeness and the grandeur that were latent in it—by resorting, at one point or another, to traditional styles that had no association in anyone's mind with the Novel. The most evident examples of this, familiar to every reader of the book, are the stylistic devices that came to him from his reading of Shakespeare and other Elizabethan playwrights. Everyone is struck at once, of course, by the stage directions that accompany some of the chapters (*"Enter Ahab: Then, all"*); by the soliloquies that Ahab or Stubb or Starbuck, like Macbeth or Timon, delivers; by the chapters indeed ("Midnight, Forecastle" or "The Deck"), which are literally in theatrical form or in a form but one degree removed from it.

Some of these passages, just in themselves, are far from being very successful in execution; Melville, one feels, would have written badly for the stage, whenever he had lived. His imagination was profoundly nondramatic. Yet even so, and however oddly, the book as a whole gains something vital from these chapters, including the weaker ones, as other books have been strengthened by their imperfections. It gains as a musical composition does by shifts of rhythm and modulations of key: the total structure is by so much the more various, complex, and irregular as a result, and the threatening monotony of movement, in this as in other ways, is forestalled. Moreover, the peculiar immediacy that the dramatic style always produces is achieved, especially in such tense chapters as "Ahab and the Carpenter" and "The Deck towards the End of the First Night Watch."

This is so true, and the verbal echoes of Shakespeare are sometimes so striking, that certain writers have argued that the book has a structural rise and fall like that of Elizabethan tragedy, and a movement from scene to scene that ends by producing the five familiar "acts"; a movement that is marked thus by the great scene on the quarter-deck, by the meeting with the *Jeroboam*, the meeting with the *Samuel Enderby*, the "fourth-act" climax of "The Candles," and lastly the catastrophe itself. Scenes such as these are certainly among the moments of highest tension in *Moby Dick*, but they are dramatic only in a loose and metaphorical sense, as the scene of Dido's suicide in the *Aeneid* might be said to be dramatic; and the fact is that the structure of the book has only a superficial analogy with that of tragedy or of drama in general. The vital character of dramatic structure, as one need hardly say, is concentration; the vital character of this book's structure is expansiveness. A tragedy, in form, is ideally close, swift, and undivertible; *Moby Dick*, on the contrary, though in its own sense firm and unwasteful, is structurally open, loose, slow-paced, and ample. There are certainly tragedies that look in this direction—*Lear* and *Antony* do, and they made a great impression on Melville— but such tragedies, like some other Elizabethan plays, strain beyond the limits of that form.

If one must look for analogies that will do a little to express the effect *Moby Dick* has on us in form—and they can do no more than that at the very most—it is not to tragedy that one should turn but to heroic poetry, to the epic. And this for reasons that are not narrowly literary. The kind of life Melville was raising to the fictive level in this book was not the kind that has ever furnished, or could furnish, the stuff of plays or novels; it was a life in some of its aspects reminiscent of that led by the Achaean peoples in the days of their folk-wanderings or by the Germanic peoples in the days of theirs; the whole of American life at the time, with all its differences, was something like that. European migrants, from the sixteenth to the nineteenth century, had reverted in the Western world to a state of things that had much in common with an archaic, a "heroic" age. Here there had reappeared, as in the Bronze Age and the Age of the Vikings, a population of brawlers, boasters, and bullies, as well as of proud, touchy, self-reliant, heroic individuals; and among them there had reappeared a habit of story-telling, of recitation and legendary reminiscence, shot through with a love of the grandiose and never wholly free from an undercurrent of superstitious fear—fear of the hostile and mysterious powers in savage nature, in forests and seas, in wild animals. The life of trappers, hunters, and frontiersmen was of that sort, and the life of whalers equally so. This is part of the complex truth to which Fedallah points when he riddlingly says that the wood of Ahab's hearse "must be grown in America."

If any aspect of this world, and specifically that of whale-hunting, was to be embodied in a mighty book that would really render its essential character, such a book would inevitably take on some of the qualities of epic poetry. And so *Moby Dick* does, both in structure and in more intangible ways. In sober fact, of course, the book is not a heroic poem but a work of its own age; yet it genuinely helps to define the formal quality of *Moby Dick* if one says that what he feels in its spacious narrative movement is not unlike what he feels in the narrative movement of the *Iliad*, of the *Odyssey*, and even of the more "literary" poems that derive from them, the *Aeneid*, the *Lusiads*. It is quite true that there is no curving back upon itself of the narrative line as there is in all but the first of these; the line in *Moby Dick* is straight ahead and undeviating, like that in the *Iliad* or in *Beowulf*. Yet the movement forward, as in all such poems, is not from climax to climax in the sharp dramatic sense, but from one wave-crest to another, from one chase or encounter to another, from cruising-ground to cruising-ground, from departure to arrival, from storm to calm. It is in short an undulant, not a peaked and valleyed line, and as a result the book has an epiclike pattern that, at least in quality, cannot be mistaken; it suggests the threefold design of the *Iliad*, or the sixfold design of the *Odyssey*, or the fivefold design of the *Lusiads*.

Exactly what the pattern is no two readers would probably agree, and in a certain sense it does not matter: what matters is the stylistic principle itself. Some readers, however, would doubtless concur in feeling that the narrative of *Moby Dick* is conducted through a series of four basic "movements," one of which is disproportionate to the others in mere bulk. All the introductory chapters, up to the sailing of the *Pequod* on that bleak Christmas day, form a clear and defined movement, like that of the first four books of the *Odyssey*. A second unmistakable wave is the one that comes to its crest in the scene on the quarter-deck, when Ahab nails the doubloon to the mainmast. The whole central portion of the book, from the sunset scene in Ahab's cabin to the encounter with the bitterly misnamed craft, the *Delight*, forms a third movement; in this there are surely no breaks so marked as the first two. The fourth movement naturally begins with "The Symphony" and comes to a close with the catastrophe itself—the Epilogue forming a kind of musical coda, not wholly unlike the burning of Hector's body on the funeral pyre in the last few lines of the *Iliad*. It is certainly true that within the long third section one is conscious of other crests and troughs; the section occupies more than two-thirds of the whole book, and of course it is not written along an unvarying line. The crests are simply less high and the troughs less deep than the others; but they are there, and they are not very disproportionate among themselves. To one reader's feeling there are six of these lesser crests: the "first lowering" for a whale, the encounter with the *Jeroboam*, the passage of the *Pequod* through the Straits of Sunda and its emergence upon the Java Sea ("The Grand Armada"), the typhoon and the corposants, and finally the meeting with the *Delight*.

Meanwhile the principle of variety is observed and its effect achieved not in pitch only but in pace and key also. For surely what the descriptive and expository chapters on whales and whaling do is partly to slow down the tempo and partly to provide for a change of key. They suggest the passages of deliberate quietness and even dullness in all very large poems, and they are placed and spaced with beautiful compositional tact—the first of them ("The Advocate") appearing at the very opening of the second main movement, and the last of them ("Does the Whale Diminish?"), very near the opening of the fifth section of the third movement. The "intense *Pequod*" is now sailing northward through the China Sea; it is about to head eastward and sail through the Bashee Channel into the open Pacific; it is drawing nearer and nearer to its doom, and from this point on there can be no retardation of the narrative speed and no distraction from the spectacle of the fated cruise.

In the strictest sense Melville had no great model for the

introduction of these magnificent non-narrative chapters; they sprang from his own creative feeling for composition and chiaroscuro; their only model was his own practice in his earlier books, especially *White-Jacket*. In its formal whole-ness, indeed, as one has to repeat, *Moby Dick* is unprece-dented and unique. No great poet has ever, before or since, brought zoology and poetry together in an even comparable way. Other great poets, however, have brought poetry to-gether with the tangible facts of armament or equipment in a manner that *Moby Dick* does suggest, and again not for merely literary reasons. It is not Bronze Age warfare or hunt-ing that is Melville's subject, as it was Homer's and the others', but it is an industry that had some of the aspects of warfare and certainly of the archaic hunt; and in the loving manner in which Melville lingers over his imagery of lances, harpoons, and cutting-spades, of whaleboats, whale-lines, and blubber-hooks, of cutting-in and trying-out and stowing-down, there is a shade of feeling that carries one far out of the nineteenth century and recalls again the epic minstrel and the way he lingered over his imagery of javelin and sword, shield and breastplate, chariot and ship, and such practical activities as sailing, hunting, plowing, and the per-formance of obligatory rites.

Of all this Melville cannot have been wholly unaware, and in the chapters in which the *Pequod* buffets its way around the Cape of Good Hope, it is hard not to feel that there is a conscious recollection of Gama and his men, in the *Lusiads*, heading eastward around the same howling Cape. From time to time, moreover, Melville launches upon the kind of sus-tained and formal similes that everyone recognizes as Ho-meric or Virgilian, and that have in *Moby Dick*, as in the *Iliad* or the *Aeneid*, an effect either of aggrandizement or of peaceful relief. The homeliest and most unexpected of these is the simile in which the whaleman's trained capacity to predict the route of the whale he is chasing is compared to the ordinary citizen's capacity to predict the arrival of a train on "the mighty iron Leviathan of the modern railway." More pastoral and more traditional than this is the familiar passage that brings together the picture of a school of Right Whales, sluggishly moving through a field of brit, and that of "morning mowers" slowly advancing their scythes through the wet grass of a marshy meadow. And the noblest, surely, of Melville's "epic" similes is that in which, in the chapter on "The Grand Armada," the great school of Sperm Whales hurrying through the Straits of Sunda is likened to an army accelerating its march through an unfriendly defile in the mountains, "all eagerness to place that perilous passage in their rear."

The imagery of armies and of warfare in fact is recurrent in *Moby Dick*, and for evident reasons. It keeps us from forgetting that butchery and carnage are close to the center of the theme, yet it lifts even them to a level on which the imagination can accept them. In general, however, the metaphors —and the allusions that have a quasi-metaphorical role— point in two opposite directions and, as a result, enhance the duality of tone that is so profound an aspect of the book's character. There are the metaphors that, like some of the similes, ennoble and aggrandize the texture of the narrative; and there are those that, like others, diminish or subdue it or even make it humorous. On the one hand, we are repeatedly put in mind of royalty or imperial dignity, of Czars and Sultans, or of the great figures of legend or history (Perseus, Alexander, the Crusaders, Tamerlane) or of Biblical story. Some of the most profound intuitions, moreover, are embodied in metaphors of architectural or monumental grandeur (the ruins of Lima, "the great dome of St. Peter's," the halls of Thermes below the Hôtel de Cluny) or in metaphors of naturalistic power and beauty ("the unabated Hudson," "one insular Tahiti," "the flame Baltic of Hell," or, perhaps most memorably of all, the meadows under the slopes of the Andes). All this is true, but it is also true that there is a constant contrapuntal play of shrunken or diminishing metaphors, and that these have a decidedly Shakesperean or at any rate Elizabethan rather than an epic quality, as when Ahab hoots at the gods as mere pugilists and cricket-players, or "Death himself" is likened to a postboy, or a Sperm Whale and his spout are compared to a portly burgher smoking his pipe of a warm afternoon. Close to these in feeling are the images that come from nineteenth-century industry or technology, the images of drilling and blasting, of mining, of cogged wheels and mechanical looms and magnetic wires, and even the "Leyden jar" of Ahab's "own magnetic life."

These latter metaphors are not without a suggestion of some of the metaphysical poets or of twentieth-century poetry; at other points in *Moby Dick* one is reminded, by the constant recurrence of imagery from animal life, of *Lear* and *Timon* on the one hand and on the other of Melville's contemporaries, the naturalistic novelists, Balzac and Zola. The Sperm Whale of course is one of the great primary symbols, and actual creatures of the sea, squid and sharks and swordfish, appear not as metaphors but as secondary symbols. In addition to these, however, which are given by the very subject, almost the whole range of animal life, wild and domestic, seems to have been scoured for images. Ahab himself is likened to a tiger, to a grizzly bear, to a wolf, a moose, a sealion, a walrus; and Pip even calls him "that anaconda of an old man." There is a steady, stately parade of elephants throughout the book; these greatest of land beasts are deliberately evoked as attendants, so to say, upon the greatest animal of the sea. The pagan harpooneers and the Parsees are sometimes, like Ahab, compared to tigers, and in the famous chapter on "The Whiteness of the Whale" everyone will remember the polar bear, the unspottedly white albatross, the sacred White Dog of the Iroquois, and the spectral White Steed of the Prairies. And indeed, as these allusions suggest, there is both a likeness and a difference between Melville's animal metaphors and either Shakespeare's or Balzac's. It is true that, like those writers (in their wholly dissimilar ways), he sometimes intends to suggest an analogy between the ferocity or the bestiality of men and that of beasts; but Melville's intention is more ambiguous than theirs, and it is quite as much for the sake of imparting to his theme a certain majesty, a certain grandeur, a certain strangeness of beauty, that he introduces his often splendid animals and birds.

Certainly nothing could be more eloquent of the incandescence out of which *Moby Dick* was written than the variety and the idiosyncrasy of the metaphors with which it is animated; nothing, perhaps, except the equally extraordinary resourcefulness and inventiveness of Melville's language. For this there is nothing in his earlier books to prepare us fully, though there are hints of it in the best passages of *Redburn* and *White-Jacket*. In general, however, the diction in those books is the current diction of good prose in Melville's time; it has a hardly definable personal quality. Now, in *Moby Dick*, it takes on abruptly an idiosyncrasy of the most unmistakable sort; it is a question now of Melvillean language in the same intense and special sense in which one speaks of Virgilian language, of Shakesperean, or Miltonic. It is a creation, verbally speaking; a great artifice; a particular characterizing idiom; without it the book would not exist. One of its hallmarks, as in all the other cases, is the "signature" furnished by favorite words; the favorite nouns, adjectives, and adverbs that end by coloring the fabric of the book as strongly as the use of a favorite range of hues affects the manner of a painter. Like Virgil, with his *pius, ingens,* and *immanis,* or Shakespeare, with his *rich, brave, sweet,* and *gentle,* Melville has his own verbal palette: it is chiefly made up of the words *wild, wildly,* and *wildness, moody* and *moodiness* ("moody Ahab," especially), *mystic* and *mystical, subtle, subtly,* and *subtlety, wondrous* ("most wondrous philosophies"), *nameless, intense,* and *malicious* ("malicious agencies"). One has only to cite these words to suggest how intimately expressive they are of *Moby Dick's* dark, violent, and enigmatic theme.

It is a matter, however, not only of characteristic words, familiar in themselves to readers of Melville's time and ours, but of characteristic *kinds* of words and of words that are again and again his own coinages or at least of a great rarity. One feels, as in all such cases, that the limits of even the English vocabulary have suddenly begun to seem too strict, too penurious, and that the difficult things Melville has to say can be adequately said only by reaching beyond those limits. He does so, perhaps most strikingly, in the constant use he makes of verbal nouns, mostly in the plural, and usually his own inventions; such nouns, for example, as *regardings, allurings, intercedings, wanings, coincidings,* and the nouns one gets in the strangely connotative phrases, "nameless invisible *domineerings*" and "such lovely *leewardings*." Almost unanalyzable is the effect these have of uniting the dynamism of the verb and the stasis of the substantive. And so of the other abstract nouns Melville loves to use in the plural—*defilements, tranquillities, unfulfilments,* "sorrow's *technicals*," and "unshored, harborless *immensities*." In their very unliteral pluralized form these characteristic abstractions become an elusive kind of inverted metaphor. Very different and less metaphorical, but almost as special in their effect, are the nouns Melville habitually constructs with the suffix *-ness* (*localness, landlessness, aborigalness, inter-indebtedness*) or *-ism* (*footmanism, sultanism, Titanism,* and the Carlylean *vultureism*).

Quite as abundant as the unfamiliar nouns are the unfamiliar adjectives and adverbs that do so much to give the style of *Moby Dick* its particular unconformable character. And again, just as verbal nouns are Melville's most characteristic substantives, so adjectives and adverbs based on present or past participles are his most characteristic modifiers; participial adjectives such as *officered, cymballed, omnitooled, un-*

ensanguined, uncatastrophied, "last, *cindered* apple" and
"*stumped* and *paupered* arm"; and participial adverbs such
as *invokingly, intermixingly, gallopingly, suckingly, post-
ponedly,* and *uninterpenetratingly.* These however are only
the most characteristic of his modifiers; a complete list would
have to include such rarities as *unsmoothable, familyless,
spermy, flavorish, leviathanic,* and *unexempt* (which might
have echoed in his mind from *Comus*) or (for adverbs) *di-
agonically, Spanishly, Venetianly,* and *sultanically.* And even
beyond these one would have to glance at the sometimes odd,
sometimes magnificent compounds, almost always adjectival,
that give so vibrating a life to the pages of the book: "a *valor-
ruined* man," "the *message-carrying* air," "the *circus-running*
sun," "*teeth-tiered* sharks," and "*god-bullied* hull." There
is an energy of verbal inventiveness here that it is hardly too
much to call Aeschylean or Shakesperean.

It does not, curiously, express itself in the formation of unfamiliar verbs so typically as in these other ways; this is a
kind of anomaly in a style of which the capacity to evoke
movement, action, and all kinds of kinaesthetic sensations is
so great. Melville, indeed, uses familiar or not unfamiliar
verbs, again and again, with beautiful force; yet the impul-
sion of some of his finest passages of vehement action depends
only partly on these; it depends at least as much on other
parts of speech, as a characteristic paragraph such as this will
suggest:

A short rushing sound leaped out of the boat; it was
the darted iron of Queequeg. Then all in one welded
commotion came an invisible push from astern, while
forward the boat seemed striking on a ledge; the sail collapsed and exploded; a gush of scalding vapor shot up
near by; something rolled and tumbled like an earthquake
beneath us. The whole crew were half suffocated as they
were tossed helter-skelter into the white curdling cream
of the squall. . . .

Nothing could be finer than a sound leaping out of a boat, or than the "something" that "rolled and tumbled beneath us," but the effect of the passage obviously depends on the vigor with which quite ordinary verbs are used, and at least as much on the vitality of the nouns and adjectives ("welded commotion," "invisible push"). Only rarely, but then sometimes with irresistible effect, does Melville create his own verbs, or virtually create them: "who didst *thunder* him higher than a throne," "he *tasks* me, he *heaps* me," "my fingers . . . began . . . to *serpentine* and *spiralize*," and "skies the most effulgent but *basket* the deadliest thunders." In all these cases, of course, he has boldly made verbs out of nouns or adjectives; and indeed, from this point of view, the manner in which the parts of speech are "intermixingly" assorted in Melville's style—so that the distinction between verbs and nouns, substantives and modifiers, becomes a half unreal one—this is the prime characteristic of his language. No feature of it could express more tellingly the awareness that lies below and behind *Moby Dick*—the awareness that action and condition, movement and stasis, object and idea, are but surface aspects of one underlying reality.

There is a passage in *Moby Dick* in which Melville deprecates the possibility that some ignorant landsmen will scout at the White Whale as "a monstrous fable, or still worse and more detestable, a hideous and intolerable allegory." It is quite plain that the remark has two edges and is meant to be ironical; it is plain, too, however, that Melville was in fact earnestly avoiding what we should now call allegory, in the sense in which we would use it of *Mardi*. The word "symbolism," in its literary bearing, had not come into use at the time *Moby Dick* was written; it was nearly twenty years before it did so, although Emerson had already dwelt with extraordinary eloquence and subtlety, in the essay on "The Poet," on the role of symbols both in experience and in art. If

Melville had had the word, no doubt he would have used it in his own thinking about the book; as it was, he was limited to the older and less suitable one. As almost always happens in literary history, the *thing* had come before the term for it; and so, when Melville answered an appreciative letter of Sophia Hawthorne's, a month or two after *Moby Dick* had appeared, he expressed himself in this manner: "I had some vague idea while writing it, that the whole book was susceptible of an allegorical construction, and also that *parts* of it were—but the speciality of many of the particular subordinate allegories, were first revealed to me, after reading Mr. Hawthorne's letter which, without citing any particular examples, yet intimated the part-and-parcel allegoricalness of the whole."

There is a little touch here of the serious artist's particular sort of frivolity and disingenuousness, as one is pleased to find; it was the right tone for Melville to take, now that his book was well behind him. But of course he had had much more than a "vague idea" while writing *Moby Dick* that his fable, his images, his personages were the bearers of complex and unstatable meanings that no prosaic apprehension of them, even one that would be appropriate to other literary forms, could account for. Emerson's remarks had been highly symptomatic, as some of Carlyle's had also been, and the poetic mind in America was already symbolist in everything but the program, as Poe's and Hawthorne's work had shown and as Whitman's was soon to show. Unlike these others as he was in the special grain of his mind, Melville was at one with them in the conviction they all shared, the conviction that "objects gross" are only provisionally real, and that the eventual reality is the "unseen soul" they embody. In that familiar sense they were all "transcendentalists": their assumptions were those of romantic idealism, and their literary practice was in entire keeping with these. Ahab of course is only putting it all in his own manner when he speaks to Starbuck in a familiar passage thus: "All visible objects, man, are but as pasteboard masks. But in each event—in the living act, the undoubted deed—there, some unknown but still reasoning thing puts forth the mouldings of its features from behind the unreasoning mask." Or later, apostrophically: "O Nature, and O soul of man! how far beyond all utterance are your linked analogies! not the smallest atom stirs or lives on matter, but has its cunning duplicate in mind."

Such is Melville's personal version of the doctrine of Correspondences that lay below so much romantic and symbolist writing, as a similar doctrine of analogies lay below medieval allegory. That he entertained some such view has long been a familiar fact, and there is nothing remarkable now in saying that *Moby Dick*, in a sense that does not quite hold for any other American book, is a symbolist prose romance. Its leading images are symbols in the strict sense, not allegorical devices or emblems; symbols in the sense that their primal origins are in the unconscious, however consciously they have been organized and controlled; that on this account they transcend the personal and local and become archetypal in their range and depth; that they are inexplicit, polysemantic, and never quite exhaustible in their meanings. "The profounder emanations of the human mind," said Melville himself a little later in *Pierre*, "never unravel their own intricacies"; and he cannot have been unaware that his own book would present difficulties to the unraveler. Many of these have long since been disentangled, yet something always remains to be added, however slight, to any cluster of interpretations, however rich. It may be useful here to speak of *Moby Dick* and its meanings by adopting our own version of Dante's "fourfold interpretation" (which is of course inapplicable) and suggesting that the intricacies of the book may be reduced to four planes of significance; that these may be called the literal, the oneiric or psychological, the moral, and the mythic.

Of the first of these, the literal, not much (by definition) demands saying. What is chiefly important is not to allow ourselves to forget that it is there, just as it is in Dante's poem, and that the literary critic, like the Biblical exegete, must remember Pascal's salutary warning against two errors: "1. To take everything literally. 2. To take everything spiritually." Taking everything in *Moby Dick* "spiritually" means not taking it spiritually enough; the intangible meanings of the romance would not be so wide-reaching and deep-plunging as they are if they were not embodied in a fable of which virtually every detail has a hard, concrete, prosaic, and even naturalistic substantiality. There are some exceptions to this, as the principle of contrast demands; the Spirit-Spout is one of them, and the actual make-up of the crew is another. Miscellaneous as the real crews of the whalers were, we are not intended to suppose literal-mindedly that any one of them ever included as harpooneers a Gayhead Indian, a Negro, and a Polynesian, as well as a boat's crew of Parsees, and along with them a Maltese sailor, a Tahitian sailor, an Icelandic, a Chinese, a Danish sailor, and so on. Yet all these freedoms with realism are dilatations of fact, not pure fantasies; even the Spirit-Spout doubtless had its origin in the surely quite breath-taking sight, at sea, of a Sperm Whale's jetting spout beheld at some distance on a moonlight night. The mere *scaffolding* of *Moby Dick*, as hundreds of readers have felt, would remain firm and stable if there were no question of symbols whatever.

The literalness of the book has another facet, however, to which justice has not been done. It is the facet provided largely by the factual chapters about whales and whaling. The true purpose of these chapters is to provide the book with an even intenser literalness than it otherwise has, and this on a serious intellectual level. This literalness, not of course stylistically but in substance, is that of systematic and exact knowledge; it is the literalness of the natural and especially the biological sciences. It is all, or much of it, translated into imaginative or humorous terms, and Melville insists on having his joke by arguing that the whale is not a mammal but *"a spouting fish with a horizontal tail."* Yet the motive behind these chapters remains a serious one. Transcendentalist though he was at the center of his mentality, Melville had too tough and too capacious a mind to fall willingly into mere vaporous and subjective idealism. He was a romantic idealist with a passion for actuality, for precise knowledge, for facts; he was an intuitionalist who wished, in his essential reliance on the nonrational and the superrational, not to fall a victim to mindlessness; not to forswear the sanctions of the intellect. "Undeniably," says Bardianna in *Mardi*, "reason was the first revelation; and so far as it tests all others, it has precedence over them . . . so far as it goes, for us, it is reliable."

A passage like this, one hurriedly notes, must be seen in the context of Melville's whole work; taken by itself it is misleading: the fact is of course that Melville was no simpleminded idolater of what Wordsworth had called "our meddling intellect." There was a painful division in his mind, as in the minds of many of his contemporaries, between his distrust of the discursive reason and his respect for it; he suffered deeply from the inner dissociations of his age. Yet his aspiration, like Thoreau's for example, was to triumph over them; to do justice both to "visible objects," masks as they are, and to the immaterial reality that, as he believed, lies behind them. It was an impossible task, so profoundly split, so dualized was the mind of his time, and his own as representative of it. But it was a task of which Melville intuitively felt the momentousness, and as a result *Moby Dick*, symbolist romance that it is, draws close at one pole to the bias of naturalism. The White Whale is a symbol, certainly, and even some of the details of his anatomy contribute to what he symbolizes; but their literal value is there all the while, and we must know how to give the proper, prosaic attention even to a half-humorous classification (the Folio Whale, the Octavo Whale, and so on), to the measurement of the whale's skeleton, to the facts about his blubber, his sense-organs, his spermaceti, and his flukes. We are in the company, and should recognize it, not only of Coleridge and Carlyle and Emerson but of Linnaeus and Cuvier.

We leave their company abruptly, however, when we move beyond the reading of *Moby Dick* as literal narrative and exposition, and begin to read it as what, on one plane, it is, an oneiric or dreamlike projection of Melville's unconscious wishes and obscure inward contests. *On one plane* the book is this, and on that plane only; for of course *Moby Dick* is not a dream but a work of imaginative art, and this means that it is the product of a complex creative process of which a great part has been conscious, deliberate, reflective: the formless spontaneity of an actual dream, along with much else, has been transcended. It shares with a dream, however, its sources in the unconscious, its dependence on irrational symbols, and its power to give expression to deep, instinctive, irrational fears and desires. How much of the sway it exercises over us depends on this!

When we read *Moby Dick* in this manner we are conscious of being presented at the very outset with one dominating oneiric image, the image of self-destruction; and then, as the action unrolls itself, and Ahab advances slowly to the forescene, we are given its counterpart and equivalent, the image of murderous destructiveness directed outward against the Other. From one point of view, what is dreamlike in the book may be said to move back and forth between these two poles, the suicidal wish, the longing for self-extinction, and its necessary antithesis, so deeply dependent upon it emotionally, the desire to inflict death upon what is, or what one imagines to be, the source of one's suffering. To undergo a kind of suicide is the motive that, along with the idea of the Whale (so closely bound up with it), impels Ishmael in the first place to go off to sea. Whenever, he says, he finds himself involuntarily pausing before coffin warehouses, and bringing up the rear of every funeral he meets, then he accounts it high time to get to sea as soon as he can: "With a philosophical flourish Cato throws himself upon his sword; I quietly take to the ship." There follows a series of hypnotic meditations on the allurements of the sea, of water generally, in which that element figures, though in a complex and iridescent way, as a symbol of death; of a return to the primal liquidity, oblivion, nonbeing. The sailing of the *Pequod* is to be for Ishmael a temporary passage out of existence.

Meanwhile, however, the death-wish has met with a check and a corrective; Thanatos has entered into a contest with Eros, and Ishmael, in his deathful loneliness encountering the savage Queequeg, has formed a solemn friendship with him, formed what he calls a marriage; the longing to love and to be loved has evoked its own oneiric symbol, and from this point forward Ishmael gradually ceases to be the man committed wholly to death. A dreamlike "displacement" occurs, and the accent shifts to Ahab, another embodiment of the self, and to Ahab's will to death, which expresses itself not directly as the conscious purpose of suicide, but indirectly as the purpose to wreak destruction on Moby Dick. It is true that Ishmael succumbs with part of his being to Ahab's ferocious hate: "A wild, mystical, sympathetical feeling was in me," he says; "Ahab's quenchless feud seemed mine." But the verb is "seemed" not "was," and already there is the possibility of Ishmael's recovering the will to live.

From this point on we are only intermittently and in flashes aware of him. It is Ahab in whom the most intense emotions of the dream are now concentrated. He is what our wildest, most egoistic, most purely destructive malevolence could wish to be, this old Quaker skipper from Nantucket; obsessed to the point of monomania with the will to destroy the hated thing, yet free from all mere smallnesses, "a grand, ungodly, godlike man." He is our hatred ennobled, as we would wish to have it, up to heroism. Moreover, he has in fact been terribly and vitally injured by Moby Dick. The Whale, in what looks like conscious malice, has reaped Ahab's leg away with his frightful, sickle-shaped jaw, and Ahab must now rely on a dead, artificial leg made of a Sperm Whale's jawbone. A kind of castration, in short, has been not only imagined and dreaded but inflicted, and the phallic source of vital potency has been replaced by an image of impotence and lifelessness, constructed from the skeleton of the injurer himself. Not only so, but in a kind of redoubled, repetitive, dreamlike manner, we hear that this apparently impotent limb has itself turned upon Ahab, and that before the sailing of the *Pequod* he had been found one night fallen in the streets of Nantucket with his artificial leg so twisted about that it had smitten his groin like a stake and almost pierced it.

A profound sexual injury is transparently symbolized here, and Ahab's "ivory" leg is an equivocal symbol both of his own impotence and of the independent male principle directed cripplingly against him. It had been fashioned from the polished bone of a Sperm Whale's jaw, though not of course from Moby Dick's own: what, then, does Moby Dick himself, on this deep instinctive plane, shadow forth? It would be easiest to say simply the father, the father who imposes constraint upon the most powerful instincts, both egoistic and sexual; the father also who threatens even to destroy the latter by castration and may indeed, in all but the literal sense, carry out the threat. On the deepest level, this is the oneiric truth about Moby Dick, but it is Melville with whom we have to reckon throughout, and for whom we have to remember how soon, and how overbearingly, the paternal role was played by Maria Melville. On every ground we are forced to confront a profound ambiguity in Moby Dick and to end by confessing that he embodies neither the father merely nor the mother but, by a process of condensation, the *parental* principle inclusively. Of his basic maleness there can be no question, not only because we are everywhere reminded of his preternatural power and masculine strength but because, in detail, we are required to contemplate the "battering-ram" of his head, the highly prized spermaceti with which it is so richly stored, his phallus ("The Cassock"), and his tail (with its "Titanism of power"); there is even a suggested association with the phallic serpent-god of the Ophites. Yet along with all this we cannot ignore a certain bisexuality in the image, if not literally of Moby Dick, then of the Sperm Whale generally; a bisexuality that is conveyed to us partly by the glimpses we have into his "beautiful" mouth and "the great Kentucky Mammoth Cave of his stomach"—that stomach in which, as Father Mapple's sermon reminds us, Jonah was swallowed up as in a womb—but also, and chiefly, by the obstetric imagery of the chapter (LXXVIII) in which Tashtego falls into the liquid depths of a Sperm Whale's severed head and is rescued or "delivered," like a baby, by Queequeg.

Moby Dick is thus the archetypal Parent; the father, yes, but the mother also, so far as she becomes a substitute for the father. And the emotions Moby Dick evokes in us are the violently contradictory emotions that prevail between parent and child. Too little, curiously, has been made of this; what dominates most accounts of the White Whale is the simple vindictive emotion that Ahab is alleged to feel toward him, and of course there can be no question of his Oedipal bitterness toward Moby Dick: his conviction that the Whale is the embodiment of "all the subtle demonisms of life and thought"; in short, "all evil." Yet hatred of this obsessive and even paranoid sort is but the deformation of a still more deep-seated love, and Ahab is as tightly bound to Moby Dick as an unhappy child to a parent too passionately loved. The emotion, however, that the Sperm Whale inspires is not restricted to Ahab's monomaniac vengefulness: from the very outset we are conscious also of Ishmael's feelings, and though at one pole these are identified with Ahab's, at the other they are by no means the same. They are, at any rate, more openly and obviously contradictory: the "grand hooded phantom," as it swims before Ishmael's fancy, may inspire a kind of fear but it inspires also an intensity of mystical longing that is something like love. It is a sort of love that lies behind that passionate preoccupation with every detail, however trifling, that characterizes the regarded object, and it is a sort of love, though an imperfectly fulfilled one, that brings Moby Dick before our imaginations as a creature of "majestic bulk," "pervading dignity," and "appalling beauty."

In his role of archetypal parent, in fact, Moby Dick is the object of an excessive and an eventually crippling love, as Maria Melville was for her son; and the consequence is the vital injury symbolized by the loss of Ahab's leg, an injury to the capacity for heterosexual love. Both Ahab and Ishmael suffer in this way, but Ahab far the more terribly of the two. Ishmael, by somehow preserving a complexity of feeling toward the White Whale, has preserved also his capacity for selfless love even though this is directed toward his own sex and even toward a member of his own sex, Queequeg, who embodies both the grandeur and the limitations of the primitive, the prerational, the instinctive. Nevertheless it is love that Ishmael deeply feels toward Queequeg, and it is the imagination of an even more comprehensive love that comes to him as he sits before a tub of cooling spermaceti, squeezing its congregated globules back into fragrant fluid, and washing his hands and his heart, as he does so, of "our horrible oath." The capacity to imagine an all-embracing love, which proves to be Ishmael's salvation, Ahab has fatally lost. He has lost it so far that he has succeeded in hardening his heart even toward his young wife and their child, whom he has frankly deserted; what wretched vestiges of pure human feeling are left in him go out only to the small black boy Pip, and to him reluctantly. Ahab is dedicated now to mere destruction, and he ends by attaining his suicidal wish and meeting his death by water. Ishmael, thanks to his rejection of mere hatred, survives the wreck; is picked up before he drowns by "the devious-cruising *Rachel*," the vessel that is itself a symbol of bereaved motherhood. In the end, the dream embodies a will to live triumphing over the will to die.

Meanwhile the unconscious and instinctive sources of the

fable have expressed themselves in still other oneiric symbols. The very setting of the whole narrative, on board a ship from which of necessity everything female has been excluded, is itself dreamlike and wishful. Of all the countersailing vessels the *Pequod* meets, only one is an image of prosperity and jolliness, and this vessel is revealingly named the *Bachelor* —that "glad ship of good luck" which is heading back to Nantucket laden to its very bulwarks and mastheads with abounding spermaceti. The weapons with which the Sperm Whale is attacked and slaughtered are appropriately phallic symbols —harpoons, lances, cutting-spades, and the like—and if there were any uncertainty about the nature of Ahab's injury, on this instinctive plane, it would not survive a careful scrutiny of the doubloon he nails to the mainmast as a promised reward for the man who first sights Moby Dick. This golden coin from Ecuador bears on its exposed side three unmistakable symbols in the form of three Andean mountain-peaks, one of them flaming like a volcano, one bearing a tower on its top, and the third a crowing cock. Queequeg, gazing at it, as Stubb watches him from a little distance, glances from the coin to his thighbone, "comparing notes," and seems, as Stubb fancies, to find something in that vicinity: "I guess it's Sagittarius, or the Archer." The coin that is to reward the sailor who first glimpses the White Whale, and who proves to be Ahab himself, is one that symbolizes, among other things, the virility that Moby Dick has destroyed.

The moral meanings of *Moby Dick*, though of course they transcend its oneiric meanings and exist in a sense on another plane, are by no means independent of them: on the contrary, the unity of the book is so masterly that only by artifice can we disentangle its various strands of significance. From the oneiric point of view Ahab is the suffering and neurotic self, lamed by early experience so vitally that it can devote itself only to destructive ends and find rest only in self-annihilation. No reader of the book, to be sure, could fail to feel how imperfectly this clinical description fits the grandiose captain of the *Pequod*: he embodies a form of sickness, certainly, but in doing so he embodies also, and on a higher imaginative plane, a form of tragedy. The two, however, originate and eventuate together.

Ahab is not only the sick self; he is, for his time and place, the noblest and most complete embodiment of the tragic hero. He is modern man, and particularly American man, in his role as "free" and "independent" Individual, as self-sustaining and self-assertive Ego, of forcible will and unbending purpose all compact, inflexible, unpitying, and fell, but enlarged by both his vices and his strength to dimensions of legendary grandeur. About Ahab's moral largeness there can be no uncertainity: the cleansing effect of *Moby Dick* depends vitally upon that. He is described as not only "grand" but even "godlike," and godlike—in a sense that is at once Greek and Yankee, at once classical and contemporary— everyone feels him to be. He has such Areté, says Melville in effect, as a grim and shaggy old whale-hunter from Nantucket can have, and that is much; his very appearance suggests a demigod: "His whole high, broad form seemed made of solid bronze, and shaped in an unalterable mould, like Cellini's cast Perseus." He calls himself "proud as a Greek god," and indeed his pride is noble enough to endure the comparison. In its highest expression it is the heroic self-trust and self-regard of the modern Western man asserted in the teeth of all that would overbear and diminish him, whether natural or beyond nature. This is what Ahab affirms in the Aeschylean scene in which he defies the flaming corposants: "I own thy speechless, placeless power; but to the last gasp of my earthquake life will dispute its unconditional, unintegral mastery in me. In the midst of the personified impersonal, a personality stands here."

This is the very rapture of ideal individualism: neither Carlyle nor Emerson nor Nietzsche ever uttered it more loftily. Yet even as he pronounces his great tirade Ahab is dimly and bitterly aware that what he says is not true: what stands there is not, in the high sense, a personality, but only a proud and defiant will. Ahab has long since ceased to be a personality, if that word is to be understood as signifying a human being in all his wholeness and roundness. He has ceased to be anything but an Ego; a noble Ego, to be sure; a heroic one; but *that* rather than a Self. He is no longer a free mind: his thought has become the slave of his insane purpose. He is no longer emotionally free: his heart has become the slave of his consuming hate. Nor is he any longer morally free: his conscience too has allowed itself to be deadened and stupefied by the compulsive quest for Moby Dick. Just how empty, in this sense, is his claim to be a "queenly personality," he himself betrays when he exhibits what his monomania has done to his very conception of humanity, of "a complete man after a desirable pattern." In the scene with the old carpenter, who is making a new leg for him, Ahab, half soliloquizing, half addressing the carpenter, imagines such a man as, first, physically gigantic, and then as having "no heart at all, brass forehead, and about a quarter of an acre of fine brains."

Fine "brains," yes, as who should say "fine nerves"; not a fine and free intelligence, disinterestedly committed to the search for impersonal truth; what Ahab wants is hardly more than an anatomical organ that will act efficiently and mechanically in the service of his overbearing will. How much he cares for the intellect, in any serious sense, he demonstrates vividly enough in his destruction of the quadrant and his imprecation against science: "Science! Curse thee, thou vain toy. . . ." The capacity for pure thought had once been in him, and even in his ruin, as he leans over the bulwarks of the predestinated ship, on the day before they encounter the White Whale, Ahab has a moment of something like speculative freedom: he allows himself, in his transitory and final weakness, to wonder what unearthly thing it is that, "against all natural lovings and longings," is impelling him forward to what he knows is disaster. Even now, however, he does not sincerely wish to find the answer: what he wishes is to judge himself ultimately blameless and irresponsible, and in the next breath he gives his evasive reply: "By heaven, man, we are turned round and round in this world, like yonder wind-lass, and Fate is the handspike." No wonder that, a minute later, he sees the satanic Fedallah's eyes leering up at him from their watery reflection.

It is partly his momentary gleams of insight, nevertheless, that preserve Ahab's tragic stature even in his perdition. He has penetrated to one of the fatal truths about himself when he uses the phrase, "against all natural lovings and longings." His ideal man would have "no heart at all," and he himself has striven with terrible success to destroy his own great na-tive capacity for love. To have yielded to it—to have yielded to what is clearly his ardor of affection for his wife and child, to his love for little Pip, to his spontaneous movement of com-passion for the bereaved Captain Gardiner—this would have been to open a breach in the massive wall of his self-suffi-ciency; and so rigid is his egoistic fixity that he cannot afford or admit the slightest concession to a self-forgetful thought. The idea of pure independence has become an insanity with him: the thought of dependence in any form is a torment. It enrages him that he must be a debtor to "this blockhead" of a carpenter for a bone to stand on: "Cursed be that mortal in-terindebtedness which will not do away with ledgers. I would be free as air; and I'm down in the whole world's books." Again, with his wonderful, intermittent self-knowledge, Ahab is right: he is not genuinely independent, but on the contrary peculiarly dependent, and on the whole world. It is a sterile dependence, however, not a creative one, because it is imposed from without by circumstance, not accepted from within by the ethical imagination; and Ahab has his reward. He gets not independence but isolation; and, since he is after all human, it is unendurable. He has lived, as he himself says, "in a desolation of solitude," and it destroys him. He has re-fused to accept the interdependence that is the condition of genuinely human existence, and we can at least imagine that, like Jonah in Father Mapple's sermon, "he feels that his dreadful punishment is just." Objectively it is so.

The wild joy of self-assertion was never more contagiously rendered than in the great scene on the quarter-deck. The misery of self-assertion was never more terribly conveyed than in the stern and solemn chapters with which *Moby Dick* approaches its catastrophe. It is the succession of the one emotion by the other that imparts to the book its primordially tragic quality. In our identification with Ahab we have undergone the double movement of aggression and submission, of self-assertion and self-surrender, that is the secret of the tragic release, and we are freed by it. This is what Melville himself meant by the familiar remark in a letter to Hawthorne: "I have written a wicked book, and feel spotless as the lamb." In the person of Ahab he had accepted the ultimate penalty, which he knew to be a just one, for his egoistic strivings.

The tragic error for which Ahab suffers is an archetypal one; it has both its general and its particular aspects, both its placeless and its local application. The raging egoism Ahab embodies has something in common with the Hubris of Greek tragedy, as it has also something, and still more, in common with the Christian sin of pride; but it is neither quite the one nor quite the other. There is something of Prometheus, of Agamemnon, of Oedipus in Ahab: he is guilty of an inflated arrogance similar to theirs, a similar conviction of his superiority to the mass of ordinary men. The true antithesis of Hubris, however, is moderation, and moderation is no cardinal virtue in Melville's calendar; Starbuck embodies that, and Starbuck hovers between a golden *mediocritas* and plain mediocrity. So with the sin of pride: we are far closer to Ahab's error here, as with Melville's deep spiritual derivation from Calvinist Christianity we are bound to be. Father Mapple's sermon is intended to make us understand that Ahab, like Jonah, has in a certain sense sinned through his proud refusal to obey God's will, or its equivalent; pride and disobedience, in at any rate some dimly Christian senses, are at the root of Ahab's wickedness. The true antithesis of spiritual pride, however, is Christian humility; and this is only somewhat closer to Melville's positive thought than moderation is. A purely Christian submission and endurance, indeed, he describes in the chapter on "The Tail" as merely negative and feminine virtues, though they are, he adds, the peculiar practical virtues of Christ's teachings.

No, neither moderation nor humility is the true alternative to Ahab's error, and this because his error itself is not really Hubris and not really, in the strictest sense, spiritual pride. It is something closer to Ahab's actual world than either. Without an awareness of the gods' displeasure and jealousy in the offing, there is little intensity left in the idea of Hubris, and the conviction of the sinfulness of spiritual pride is at any rate transformed when the dogma of Original Sin is discarded. There was a level of Melville's complex mind on which the jealousy of the pagan gods could seem terribly real to him; there was certainly a level on which he was capable of darkly "believing" in Original Sin. In the fullest conscious sense, however, he believed in neither. What he felt as a menace in himself, and what he saw at work in the scene about him, was very like what Hawthorne felt and saw: a complex moral reality of which one pole was a pure and strong affirmation of the grandeur of the individual, and the other pole a wild egoism, anarchic, irresponsible, and destructive, that masqueraded in the kingly weeds of self-reliance. It is no accident that Ahab, as a whale-hunter, represents one of the great exploitative, wasteful, predatory industries of the nineteenth century; from this point of view the Whale embodies nothing so much as the normally innocent and indifferent forces of wild nature—the forests, the soil, the animal life of land and sea—that nineteenth-century man was bent on raping to his own egoistic ends. On the last day of the chase, in spite of what he has suffered at their hands, Moby Dick seems intent only on swimming as swiftly and as straight as possible away from the *Pequod*. "See!" cries the good Starbuck to Ahab. "Moby Dick seeks thee not! It is thou, thou, that madly seekest him!"

The alternative to Ahab's egoism is not, then, the ideal of "Nothing too much," nor is it a broken and a contrite heart. On one level it is an intuition that carries us beyond morality, in the usual sense, into the realm of cosmic piety; on the usual ethical level, however, it is a strong intuition of human solidarity as a priceless good. Behind Melville's expression of this, one is conscious of the gravity and the tenderness of religious feeling, if not of religious belief; it came to him in part from the Christian tradition in which he had been nurtured. The form it took in him, however, is no longer specifically Christian; as with Hawthorne and Whitman, it was the natural recoil of a sensitive imagination, enriched by the humanities of romantic idealism, against the ruinous individualism of the age. It is Melville's version of Hawthorne's "magnetic chain of humanity," of Whitman's "manly attachment": so far, it is an essentially humanistic and secular principle.

Ishmael, again, whose very name suggests a desperate estrangement, becomes nevertheless the narrative agent of these affirmations. Solitary and embittered as he first appears to us, Ishmael seems scarcely to have hardened the outermost surface of his heart: even before he has departed from New Bedford, his distrusts and his resentments have yielded to the outgoing affectionateness of "this soothing savage," Queequeg; and on the passage over to Nantucket he responds at once to the meaning of one of Queequeg's acts. A silly bumpkin, who has jeered at the outlandish appearance of Ishmael's new friend, is flung overboard by a sweep of the boom, and in spite of the fellow's behavior Queequeg risks his life in order to rescue him. When it is all over he leans back against the bulwarks of the little schooner as if to say: "It's a mutual, joint-stock world, in all meridians. We cannibals must help these Christians."

Ishmael is soon bound to Queequeg, and rejoices to be

bound, in a relation of tenderest fraternity; this involves risks, appalling risks, as he learns, but these risks he is glad to take. As an oarsman under Queequeg, it becomes Ishmael's scary duty, when the body of a whale is lashed to the side of the ship, to bind himself to one end of a monkey-rope at the other end of which Queequeg is bound; secured by this, Queequeg stumbles back and forth on the whale's slippery back attempting to cut a hole in it for the insertion of the blubber-hook. As Ishmael leans over the bulwarks holding on to his end of the rope, it comes over him that he and Queequeg are now wedded indeed, and that if poor Queequeg should sink to rise no more, both honor and usage demand that Ishmael should descend with him into the depths. "My own individuality was now merged in a joint-stock company of two"—a sobering but also a softening thought. "Well, well, my dear comrade and twin-brother, thought I, as I drew in and then slacked off the rope to every swell of the sea— what matters it, after all? Are you not the precious image of each and all of us men in this whaling world?"

It is true that, in feeling this, Ishmael feels also how far he is from having a perfectly free will, how dependent he is on the mistakes and the misfortunes of other men. Yet the two kinds of dependency are here merged into one, and it is the creative dependency of fraternal emotion that prevails.

Deep as are the psychological meanings, and serious as are the moral meanings, of *Moby Dick*, they by no means exhaust between them the richness of its interest or the scope of its significance. In the end, as one reflects on the book, one is aware that one must reckon with the most comprehensive of all its qualities, the quality that can only be called mythic. Few words even in our time have been used more glibly than the word "myth"; it has ended by taking on some of the hollow sanctity of the mystic syllable Ôm in the mouths of the unenlightened. When one uses it, however, in association with *Moby Dick*, it means something precise and indispensable; and it is used here in the sense of an imagined narrative in which the leading roles are played by divine or god-like personages, engaged in symbolic actions amid symbolic objects; which embodies some form of the conflict between human wishes and nonhuman forces, and which has its roots in a philosophically serious desire to comprehend the meaning of nature and the destiny of man. The literary expression toward which myth in this sense typically moves is the epic or some closely comparable form.

If *Moby Dick* has a strongly mythic character, it is partly because the human setting out of which it emerged, as we have repeatedly seen, reproduced many of the conditions of a myth-making phase of culture. There was much in Melville's own experience too—his life among the Taipis and Tahitians, as well as much else—that, along with the bias of his own creative faculty, led straight in the mythic direction. There was a mingling in his nature, as in that of every greatly endowed poet, of the primitive and the highly civilized; of the naive and the literate, even the bookish; of the primitive capacity to "think" in symbols and the cultivated capacity to deal in abstractions. He was unique, moreover, among American writers of his time in the particular quality of his intellectual and moral seriousness; unique in his troubled preoccupation with problems that Emerson and Thoreau simply passed by, and that Hawthorne was intellectually too incurious to consider deeply. Like a truly myth-making poet's, Melville's imagination was obsessed by the spectacle of a natural and human scene in which the instinctive need for order and meaning seems mainly to be confronted by meaninglessness and disorder; in which the human will seems sometimes to be sustained but oftener to be thwarted by the forces of physical nature, and even by agencies that lie behind it; in which goodness and evil, beneficence and destructiveness, light and darkness, seem bafflingly intermixed. In none of the great formulations that were available to him, neither in Calvinist Christianity nor in romantic optimism, could Melville discover a myth that for him was adequate to the lighting up of these obscurities.

Moby Dick is his endeavor to construct his own myth. The personages of the fable, ordinary as they begin by seeming, very soon take on the large outlines and the poetic typicality of figures in legend or edda. They are engaged, moreover, in an action that is profoundly archetypal—that is, in a voyage by sea that is also a hunt or a quest, and that reaches its culmination in an all but complete catastrophe. As they do so they move among primordial forces in which their destinies seem involved almost as if they were Greek or Norse or Polynesian demigods or heroes—forces such as the sea that is both the source of life and the extinction of it, the solid land that is both safety and peril, the spires of flame that must be defied but also worshipped, the wind that is sometimes "glorious and gracious" and sometimes tainted and cowardly, the sun "like a royal czar and king," and the moonlight or starlight that serves to irradiate the mystic Spirit Spout. So intense is the animation, so nearly personal is the vitality, of these elemental forces that hardly a step would be needed to transform them into actual deities. Melville himself indeed remarks that the Greeks gave the sea a deity of its own; he calls the northeast wind by its Greek name, Euroclydon, and Ahab defies the fire of the corposants in language that leaves no doubt of its mythic deification. Nowhere, however, is Melville's myth-making power at work in a more truly primordial sense than in the creation of the White Whale himself.

Here chiefly, in the aggrandizement of a huge and fearsome animal to deiform proportions, does Melville surpass all other poets of his century in the rejuvenation of myth. On this ground he is quite incomparable; no other writer of the century can be set beside him. He himself could not wholly have realized how deep a descent he was making into the quarry of the past by penetrating so far as he did into the region of animal existence. He had some sense of this, but it was a flickering one: unavailable to him in his generation was the knowledge of primitive thought and belief that enables us now to see Moby Dick for the deeply primordial symbol he is. Only a man who had himself been a hunter of wild beasts —only a man who had been in at the kill of a tormented Sperm Whale—could have re-entered so far into the intense and complex feelings with which the primitive hunter regards the animals about him and especially his chief prey; into that lost, archaic mingling of fear and gratitude, of resentment and veneration, in which all the savage's emotions toward the animal are steeped, and which leads him again and again to endow it with an awful divinity. Of all this Melville had little or no "knowledge" but a penetrating intuition. The three pagan harpooneers on the *Pequod*, Queequeg, Tashtego, and Daggoo, have all seen Moby Dick before; when Ahab speaks for the first time of the White Whale to his crew, they and they alone are at once aware what creature it is that he means.

"Your true whale-hunter is as much a savage as an Iroquois," Melville himself says, and he adds: "I myself am a savage." Certainly in his half-fearful, half-worshipful attitude toward the Sperm Whale he was closer to the primitive than to the civilized mind; and he gives us his own clues to this when he identifies the Whale with the dragons of Perseus and St. George, or recalls that the Hindu god Vishnu was incarnate in a whale. Yet he probably did not know, literally, that for many primitive peoples—for peoples as remote from one another as the Annamese, the Tongans, and the Unalit Eskimos—the whale is, or once was, the object of a solemn cult, a sacred animal as truly as the cow or the bear was elsewhere. He probably had not heard that some of these peoples prepared themselves for a whale-hunt by fasting for days beforehand, by bathing themselves repeatedly, and by other rites; that some of them, after a whale's life had been taken, propitiated his ghost by holding a communal festival; and that others, when a dead whale was washed ashore, accorded it solemn burial and preserved its bones in a small pagoda near the sea.

Melville knew that whiteness in animals had often been a mark of special sanctity; he alludes to the sacred White Dog of the Iroquois and the White Elephant of Pegu; did he know, however, that the White Whale itself was so superstitiously regarded by the Eskimos of Bering Strait that a hunter who had helped to kill one was forbidden to do any work for four days thereafter, and that the shore where a dead White Whale had been beached was thenceforth tabu? It is of no real importance whether he knew of these things or not; in the contemplation of the great white monster and its mystic ways, he could rely upon a deeper and more primeval knowledge than any he could have acquired from Tylor or Frazer. His imagination ran before the anthropologists; he forefelt, as other poets have done, what the savants would later confirm.

He could rely, in all this, upon the aboriginal myth-making fancy, still strong in his own nature, for which birds and beasts were not simply "lower animals" but creatures somehow identifiable with the beneficent or the malignant potencies of all nature; the fancy that again and again transformed these creatures into gods—eagle-gods, bear-gods, fish-gods, and the like. Even among nineteenth-century whalers generally there may have survived, obscurely and dumbly, much more of this fearful and worshipful emotion than has ever been supposed, and Melville may be pointing to this when he makes Starbuck say of the heathen crew of the *Pequod* that the White Whale is their "demigorgon"—Demogorgon, as he should have said if he meant the mysterious infernal deity to whom Milton and Shelley allude, but he may well have been confusing Demogorgon with the creative Demiurgos of Platonic or Gnostic thought. In any case, there can be no doubt about Moby Dick's deific attributes. There is something godlike in the mere crude fact of his physical

magnitude, his "majestic bulk." Physically he is the greatest
of all animals that have ever existed, and in proportion to his
vast magnitude is his potency, the potency that exhibits itself
in his terrific speed, in the dreadful strength of his great jaw,
and in the "Titanism of power" with which he wields his
massive tail. He is not only physically huge and appallingly
powerful, but—as one realizes when one reflects on the problem of his spout—there is in his whole being a "great inherent
dignity and sublimity." Moby Dick is godlike in his beauty
too, and when, after so many months of search, we at last
sight him, gliding swiftly and mildly through the sea, he
seems more beautiful even than Zeus himself swimming in
the shape of a white bull, with Europa, toward his nuptial
bower in Crete: "not Jove, not that great majesty Supreme!
did surpass the glorified White Whale as he so divinely
swam."

Beautiful he may be, yet to the whalemen who have encountered him, or even to those who have only heard of such
encounters, there is something so terrible, so mysterious, in
the ferocity and the apparently intelligent malignity with
which Moby Dick has rounded upon his attackers, that they
have ended by refusing to believe that such a creature is fit
prey for mortal man. Some of them have persuaded themselves that he is actually ubiquitous; that he has been sighted
in opposite latitudes at the same instant of time; and not only
so, but that he is immortal, and that no lance forged of earthly
iron can ever destroy him.

Certainly the penalty for attacking him seems always to
have been death and destruction in some frightful form, yet
Moby Dick appears never to have sought these encounters
himself, and to have dealt out ruin only when provoked by
his pursuers. Demoniac as he can be when hunted and har-
pooned, he himself seems rather to evade than to seek these
meetings, and perhaps, as the commonsensical English ship-
surgeon, Dr. Bunger, suggests, what Ahab takes for the White
Whale's malice is only his awkwardness. In any case, if we

regard Moby Dick not as an individual but as representative of a species, as an archetypal Sperm Whale, it is not mainly of his malice that we are reminded but of his unintentional beneficence. On occasion he may have been the apparently conscious cause of much evil and suffering, but certainly he is also the source of great and even priceless goods. For many men, both primitive and civilized, his flesh and his spermaceti have served as food. When ambergris is found in his bowels, ignoble as that derivation is, the Sperm Whale becomes the bestower upon mankind of the precious sweetness of perfume. His chief gift to them, however, has not been sweetness but light: it is of spermaceti that the best candles are made, and with sperm-oil that the best lamps are lighted. Illumination, not darkness and terror, is Moby Dick's great boon to humanity. And when we meditate on this fact, we are less sure than we would otherwise be that the mad Gabriel of the *Jeroboam* is as mad as he seems when he warns Captain Mayhew that Moby Dick is the Shaker God incarnated.

However this may be, he is certainly not the God of orthodox or even of modernist Christianity. That is the meaning of his whiteness, of that "visible absence of color" which is at the same time "the concrete of all colors," and hence is the symbol of "a colorless, all-color of atheism from which we shrink." That beautiful and frightful whiteness appeals to our souls so powerfully because it may symbolize both the most spiritual of things, even the Christian Deity, and also the things most appalling to mankind. It cannot, and in Moby Dick it does not, reassuringly and finally symbolize the Christian God, transcendent and absolute, and, however mysterious in His workings, a God of absolute love and justice and truth. A cosmic scene lorded over by the White Whale is one from which the soul-freezing possibility of an ultimate atheism is never wholly absent, and of course it was terribly present to Melville's spirit when he wrote the book. Moby Dick's whiteness, however, may and does symbolize not only negation and denial but "all colors"; all positive goods, fulfillments, benefits. It is a symbol of profound and irreducible ambiguity, but that ambiguity has a pole of lightness as well as a pole of darkness.

The White Whale is a grandiose mythic presentation of what is godlike in the cosmos as this could be intuited by a painfully meditative and passionately honest poetic mind in the heart of the American nineteenth century. Moby Dick is an Animal God such as only the imagination of that century in the Western world could have conceived and projected; a god in Nature, not beyond it; an immanent god in some sense, not a transcendent one; an emergent deity, not an Absolute; a deity that embodies the physical vastness of the cosmos in space and time as astronomy and geology have exhibited it; a deity that represents not transcendent purpose and conscious design but *mana*; energy; power—the half-conscious, half-unconscious power of blind, restless, perhaps purposeless, but always overbearing and unconquerable force. There is terror in such a conception, as indeed there is, on one side, in the Calvinist conception of a transcendently powerful and justly wrathful God; and Moby Dick owes something to the deity of Calvin and Edwards. He is not that deity, however, if only because nothing assures us that he is capable of loving man as Calvin's God loved him despite his sinfulness; we cannot imagine Moby Dick as conferring upon mankind the ultimate gift of free and unmerited grace. Yet terrible though Moby Dick is in his apparent and perhaps real indifference to men, he is also sublime, sublime as the cosmos itself is, in its unimaginable magnitude, its appalling beauty, and the demiurgic creativity of power that seems everywhere to be at work and alive within it.

This is a nature myth such as only a nineteenth-century imagination, obsessed with the spectacle of impersonal force and ceaseless physical change, could have created, though Melville had unconsciously drawn, in creating it, on a whole complex of thoughts that had come to him from reading, or reading about, Job, the Stoics, the Gnostics and Manicheans,

Spinoza, and the men of science. It is a myth such as other minds of the nineteenth century were groping toward, and one can see dim analogies to Moby Dick in Schopenhauer's blind irrational Will, in Herbert Spencer's Unknowable, and still more truly in Hardy's Immanent Will or Urging Immanence. In the traditional Christian God, the omniscient and loving Father, Melville had now lost all confident belief; *that* God survived in his mind, when he wrote *Moby Dick*, only as a symbol of human fraternity and the quasi-religious sense of equality: "The great God absolute! The centre and circumference of all democracy! His omnipresence, our divine equality!" The language here seems traditional enough, but it is unsupported by anything else in the action or the imagery of the book, and the truth is that the God of Melville's fathers has yielded place, at every other point, to the godlike and portentous White Whale.

The mating of romantic idealism with the masculine sense of reality in Melville's mind has begotten here a myth that approaches, if it does not quite overtake, a naturalistic theism. The question remains: If Moby Dick embodies the deific principle in nature, what spiritual meaning can he have for mankind as an object of worship? The answer would have to be that, in the fullest sense of worship, he could have a very uncertain one, if he could have one at all. It is evident that, like Spinoza's God, Moby Dick cannot be imagined as, strictly speaking, either loving man or hating him; and, conversely, he is hardly conceived as sustainedly and satisfyingly inspiring that "intellectual love" which, according to Spinoza, the free man himself can feel toward God. A positive attitude he does nevertheless inspire, though certainly it is in the end a more austere and far less solacing attitude than that of happy and confident worship. The great clue to this, again, is the symbolism of the doubloon that Ahab nails to the mainmast. This coin was minted in the republic of Ecuador, "a country planted in the middle of the world, and beneath the great equator, and named after it; and it had been cast midway up the Andes, in the unwaning clime that knows no autumn." Arching over the mountain peaks stamped on it, one sees a segment of the zodiac and "the keystone sun entering the equinoctial point at Libra."

Obsessed with his proud and impious interpretation of the symbols on the coin, Ahab quite fails to understand its still deeper significance, quite fails to see that the coin he himself has nailed up is an emblem, not, to be sure, of ethical moderation in the Greek sense, but of the Double Vision; the vision, so to say, of the equatorial line from which one may look out on both North and South with equal comprehensiveness; the balanced vision of the sun itself as it enters the constellation of Libra or the Scales. This is the vision, surely, with which a wise man would contemplate Moby Dick, stoically accepting the fact that the White Whale, the cosmic force, has again and again unconsciously wrought havoc and destruction, and will doubtless continue to do so; but recognizing too that Moby Dick is, or may be made to be, the source of much genuine good—of nourishment, of fragrance, of light—and that, though "I know him not, and never will," one can glory in the spectacle of his sublimity.

That is what Ishmael has revealed a capacity to do, and it is the deepest reason for his rebirth from the sea. Ahab, on the other hand, has shown no such capacity; on the contrary, he has persisted in identifying Moby Dick with "all evil," and piling upon the whale's white hump "all the general rage and hate felt by his whole race from Adam down." But this is both madness and wickedness. Evil exists, it is true; essential Evil; it is no illusion, as Emerson would have it, but a dense and unexorcisable reality. So far as the reality of Evil is that of suffering, Moby Dick is indeed the source of much of it; but that is only one aspect of his dual nature, and moreover, so far as the reality of Evil is moral, so far as Evil connotes an evil will, then Moby Dick does not embody this at all: the one who does embody it is Ahab's own harpooner, the diabolic Fedallah, to whom Ahab has surrendered his moral freedom, and whom Stubb quite properly identifies as the devil in disguise. "One cannot sustain an indifferent air concerning Fedallah." One cannot, indeed, for he is a principle of pure negation, of hatred instead of love, vindictiveness instead of charity, destruction instead of creativeness. Ahab has sold his soul to the fire-worshipping Parsee, the Parsee who, in this case, worships fire not as a symbol of light and truth but as a symbol of raging and destructive Evil. Moby Dick, however, is indestructible, and the upshot of their impious onslaught upon him is not his but their destruction.

There would be a religious solace in this thought if one could believe that Moby Dick, with his immunity and immortality, were in conscious, benevolent collaboration with the forces of love in their struggle against the forces of hate. As it is, one must be content with the consolations of philosophy in *Moby Dick*, or rather with those of a philosophical mythology; one cannot avert one's eyes from the fact that good and innocent men—Starbuck, Queequeg, and others—are involved in Ahab's doom. One can tell oneself that mad and wicked men inevitably wreak their own destruction in attempting to thwart the workings of "nature"; one cannot tell oneself that wise and virtuous men are preserved from suffering and fatality. They only *may* be, as Ishmael is.

Something else, however, is suggested in the book, though only obscurely, and this is something that takes us closer, if not to religion in the fullest sense, at any rate to a certain form of natural piety. Some years after he had written *Moby Dick*, Melville was sufficiently struck by a sentence of Spinoza's, quoted by Matthew Arnold, to mark the passage in his copy of Arnold's essays. The sentence is this: "Our desire is not that nature may obey us, but, on the contrary, that we may obey nature." Already in *Moby Dick* there had been an intimation of this cosmic submissiveness. The desire to understand, to fathom, the whole truth about the White Whale—the desire that is manifest at every turn in the explanatory and meditative passages—this is at least the true beginning of wisdom. The willingness to submit, to accept, to "obey," in that sense, would naturally follow. Father Mapple, indeed, in his sermon—employing, of course, the familiar language of faith—makes provision for this when he says that "all the things that God would have us do are hard for us to do. . . . And if we obey God, we must disobey ourselves; and it is in this disobeying ourselves, wherein the hardness of obeying God consists." The "will" of nature, even if there is something godlike in it, is hardly synonymous with God's will in the Christian sense. Yet *Moby Dick* seems to say that one might arrive at a kind of peace by obeying it.

The Lee Shore

BUOYED UP by the coffin life-buoy of the foundered *Pequod*, Ishmael had floated for a day and night "on a soft and dirge-like main," and had then been picked up by the devious-cruising *Rachel*, searching for her missing children. Ishmael had undergone a certain death, and he had survived it. The question now was whether he could long survive the life that lay before him. To put it more literally, the question now was whether Herman Melville would survive not only the shattering ordeal of writing such a book but the even more stringent "ordeal by existence" that remained to him. For a period of at least five years, as both he and his family were in some sort aware, the wordless inner debate over that question went on. In the end, it was resolved on the side of life, not of death, but the two forces had been terribly evenly matched, and Melville survived by the scantiest margin. For the rest of his days he must have had the look of a man who, as was said of Dante, had been in the Underworld.

It had taken him a little more than a year to write *Moby Dick*, yet in every sense but the literal one it was as if half a lifetime had passed. In the months before he had begun the book, and even at times while he was at work on it, Melville must have struck those who encountered him as still essentially a young man. This is what his London journal suggests to us, and there is much the same impression of youth and high spirits in some of the glimpses we have of him at Pittsfield and Lenox. After *Moby Dick* we virtually never have that impression again; already it is a middle-aged man who looks out at us from the letters or memories of people who saw him in these years; of Mrs. Morewood, his neighbor, for example, who found him, that first winter, "more quiet than usual," or of Maunsell Field, the New York lawyer, who thought of him as "the most silent man of my acquaintance." Like so many creative people, he had remained young longer than most men, and then, when a kind of agedness came, it came swiftly, so swiftly that he himself could feel it coming. His sense of life had been so effervescent, early in the winter when he had been writing *Moby Dick*, that he could ask Duyckinck, in a letter, for "fifty fast-writing youths" to assist him in the writing of that many books, all of which he had in his head. Yet even the next summer, before the book was quite finished, he could remark in another letter, to Hawthorne, alluding to his rapidity of development: "I feel that I am now come to the inmost leaf of the bulb, and that shortly the flower must fall to the mould."

He had solved a great artistic problem in writing *Moby Dick*, and in doing so he had *imagined* a great solution for his intellectual and even his emotional problems. If a book were a life, Melville would now by all rights have been the man of the soundest and deepest well-being in all America. But a book is very far from being a life, and if the solution of artistic problems had a close relation to the solution of life problems, the personal history of the arts and of literature would be very different from what it is. It was exactly because his "real" problems were so terribly difficult of solution that Melville was driven to wrestle as earnestly as he did in *Moby Dick* with the ideal difficulties of form and expression. No doubt there was a period, after the book was behind him, when he did actually enjoy the transitory euphoria of achievement. Certainly there were at least a few days of such

euphoria after he had had from Hawthorne a letter of wonderful understanding about the book. His own answer to
Hawthorne's letter is exultant: "A sense of unspeakable security is in me this moment, on account of your having understood the book." "Unspeakable security"! the phrase itself
tells us how intense was Melville's pervasive feeling of insecurity; and once the exultation over Hawthorne's imaginative sympathy had passed, the phantoms it had momentarily
exorcised must have gathered about him more fearsomely
than ever. Only a few weeks later we hear, again from Mrs.
Morewood, of his leading so recluse a life as to make his city
friends think him slightly insane, and of his answering this
humorous charge with the remark that he himself had long ago
come to the same conclusion.

The phantoms that besieged him rose up from various
levels of experience, as usually happens; the most awesome of
them arose from the pit itself. But they were not all phantoms
from the deeps; some of them were simply the heavy, humdrum worries of practical living. For the better part of twenty
years Melville and his family had habitually lived on intimate terms with genteel indigence, and now, after they had
all been led by the success of the earliest books to expect
brighter things, the problem was as acute as ever. By temperament Melville was probably less equipped to deal with
such anxieties than most men, even most writers; but in fact
he had more of them to deal with than most. It was not only
that he had a growing family of his own; in the first eight
years of their marriage, two sons and two daughters were
born to him and Lizzie; but in addition to these responsibilities, he seems much of the time to have been obliged to make
a home for his mother and for two or three of his sisters. It
was simply not possible for an American writer at that time
to live on such a scale and to live without worry, however
popular his works might be; and already, in the year when
Moby Dick was published, Melville was several hundred dollars in debt to his publishers, as well as several thousand

dollars in debt to Judge Shaw. If even his popular books had
not brought him financial ease, it was hardly in the power of
the unpopular *Moby Dick* to do so; and *Pierre,* the next year,
destroyed for good his capacity to make a living as a writer.
There was something symbolic in the fire at the Harpers'
that, in 1853, destroyed the stock of Melville's books; and a
year or two later G. W. Curtis was only recording a general
impression in the literary world when he remarked to a
publisher that Melville had quite lost his prestige.

It was an all but mortal blow to a man who still wished,
more than anything else, to be a productive writer: he was
being commanded by circumstance to suppress that one talent which is death to hide. What he had longed for, as he said
in a letter to Hawthorne, was "the calm, the coolness, the
silent grass-growing mood in which a man *ought* always to
compose"; but he had had it, perhaps, only for a year or two
at the outset; and now it was out of the question. A presenti-
ment was on him, he had said, that he would at last be worn
out and perish, like an old nutmeg grater, grated to pieces by
constant attrition. Something of the sort came very near to
happening. Meanwhile, however, he had not allowed himself
to crumple helplessly under his practical difficulties; he had
made head against them with what weapons he had. Political
appointments were always a possible resource for American
writers at this period, and Melville had made repeated and
touching efforts to obtain one. He had felt really hopeful of
this, in 1852, when Hawthorne's friend, Franklin Pierce,
was elected to the presidency, so that Hawthorne himself,
rather oddly, could apply a certain pressure at the White
House. Other friends too—Dana, Judge Shaw, and others—
came to his support; there was a feeling among them that
Melville richly deserved a consulate like that at Honolulu.
Taken together, they must have had the air of a powerful
group of backers; but they accomplished nothing. Melville,
no doubt, had held himself too completely aloof from pol-
itics; he had put no man a penny in his debt, Whig or

Democrat; and then too there may have been, especially after *Pierre*, an ill-defined but damaging impression that he was not a man whose soundness and discretion could be counted on.

Nothing, at any rate in the 'fifties, came of his office-seeking. There was another great resource, however, at that time, for financially harried writers; this was the lecture platform, and now that the political door seemed shut in his face, Melville turned, with a distaste that one can easily imagine, to the drudgery of lecturing. Only the bitterest necessity could have driven him to it, but for two or three winters, in the late 'fifties, the most withdrawn even of American writers subjected himself to the ordeal of traveling on overheated trains and lecturing in underheated lecture halls, sometimes with a bad cold, for twenty or thirty dollars an evening, on such subjects as "Ancient Statuary" and "The South Seas." The experiment proved a humiliating unsuccess. Half consciously Melville wished it to be so, and his audiences could hardly have failed to feel this. They had turned out on winter evenings—in Ithaca, in Chillicothe, in Milwaukee—to have a look at the man who still had a certain notoriety, though a fading one, for having lived among the cannibals; they found only a middle-aged gentleman, with a brown beard, who spoke in a subdued tone and with a general lack of animation; and they were badly let down. Melville could hardly hope to compete with the great fieldpieces of the lecture platform, Bayard Taylor and Henry Ward Beecher and their like; and besides he was given to making, perhaps with a note of sharpness in his voice, such observations as that he prayed to have the Polynesians kept free from the demoralizing influences of Western civilization. In the third of these miserable winters Melville seems to have had only three engagements altogether; and with that he abandoned his heartbreaking attempt to become a showman.

His purely financial problems were to find a sort of solution as time went on, but in the few years that followed *Moby*

Dick he was continually beset by them—"dollars damn me," as he said—and moreover they were only the most tangible and practical of the strains to which he was subjected. It was bad enough to find that he could not make even a moderate living for himself and his family; it was much worse to discover that he could not hold his own as a writer in the minds of an audience that had begun by being so large. Nothing could have been more profoundly disheartening than to learn that, as he said, what he felt most moved to write was virtually banned because it would not pay; that he could go on forever writing *Typees* and "beggarly" *Redburns*, and keep his audience; but that one more *Mardi* or *Moby Dick* would be the death of him.

It is true that *Moby Dick* had not gone wholly unappreciated. If it had had no other recognition, there would have been Hawthorne's letter about it; and how full of insight that letter was we can guess from Melville's elated reply. The book had had, however, other kinds of recognition too; sensitive and eulogistic reviews in periodicals like *Harper's*, *Graham's*, and the *Literary World*, and two or three of the English periodicals. Popularly, nevertheless, it seems to have been a failure, and both in England and in this country there were reviews that, in their particular tone of contemptuous hostility, cannot have failed to give the sharpest kind of pain to a man who was, as he himself confessed in *Mardi*, "far more keenly alive to censure than to praise." It was one thing to be attacked, as he had been after *Typee*, *Omoo*, and *White-Jacket*, for his heterodox opinions about the missionaries or the Navy; it was another thing to be told, by the *Democratic Review*, that in spite of his "unbounded love of notoriety," he had "survived his reputation"; or to be told by the London *Athenæum* that *Moby Dick* was "so much trash belonging to the worst school of Bedlam literature."

Much harder things were in store for him, a year later, after *Pierre* appeared. He had actually believed, on finishing the book—or so, at least, he had expressed himself to his

English publisher—that *Pierre* was "much more calculated for popularity than anything you have yet published of mine." If this was what he literally thought, then he was getting alarmingly out of touch with ordinary reality. Not only was *Pierre* not calculated for popularity; it could hardly have been more effectively designed than it was to invoke on Melville's head a peculiarly harsh opprobrium. In the quarters where it was not speechlessly ignored, as it largely was, the book was subjected to a kind of drubbing that, in the 'fifties, an American writer could hardly hope to survive. Even the friendliest of the periodicals, even Evert Duyckinck's *Literary World*, felt itself forced to abandon the writer whom it had hitherto supported so generously, and to confess that, if the novel had any moral at all, it was a "most immoral" one. The other reviewers were less restrained. The *Southern Quarterly Review* expressed the fear that Herman Melville had gone "clean daft," and that the sooner he was put in ward the better. *Putnam's* talked about the "inexcusable insanity" of *Pierre*, and the *American Whig Review*, which had paid no attention to *Moby Dick*, found *Pierre* "affected in dialect, unnatural in conception, repulsive in plot, and inartistic in construction"; and as for Melville himself the same magazine expressed the view that his fancy was diseased and his morality vitiated.

"Bitter is it to be poor & bitter to be reviled," wrote Melville three or four years later, in a travel journal, after he had tasted literally of the acrid waters of the Dead Sea; and it is impossible not to imagine that, with his strongly neurotic capacity for suffering, he had undergone real anguish over the revilement of *Pierre*. Given, indeed, the insecurity of his emotional equilibrium, the curve that his literary career had described could hardly have been more unfortunate than it was; no other American writer—and very few writers anywhere—have undergone Melville's particular ordeal: excited, widespread, and rather exaggerated approval for his first books, and then an equally exaggerated and capricious indifference to his best work, followed by an explosion of abuse for the book that came next—and thereafter, on the whole, a dead silence. Other writers, like Hawthorne, have had to wait long for recognition; others have lost their audience, as James did, after a moderate early success; still others have been praised for their weakest work and chidden for their best. But, unless Byron's case is a kind of parallel, one searches one's memory in vain for a pattern like that of Melville. It is the heaviest count in our literary annals against the American mind. Not incomprehensible in its light is the bitterness Melville expressed, years later probably, in the little poem on Camoëns:

> What now avails the pageant verse,
> Trophies and arms with music borne?
> Base is the world; and some rehearse
> How noblest meet ignoble scorn.

After writing *Moby Dick* he must have been, to use another line from this poem, "exhausted by the exacting lay." Yet neither external pressures nor inward ones allowed him to indulge himself in a restorative idleness; and by the end of the year we hear of his being so deeply engaged on a new book as frequently not to leave his room, or even to eat a meal, until night had fallen. What had been, all in all, a healthy and high-spirited youth was now over, and Melville, midway on his journey, was about to lose the straight way and to enter the dark wood. It was not of course his practical or even his literary perplexities and frustrations that had basically brought him there; it was the accumulation of emotional strains that had begun in his earliest childhood, and that now, instead of setting him free, bore down upon him more crushingly than ever. They were all the more paralyzing because he could not have been clear-sightedly conscious of their true nature; they had to be combated in the dark or at least in a psychological twilight. Melville was lost in a personal and emotional entanglement of which we may never make out all the strands but the essential character of which is clear enough. He had somehow been drawn into a marriage that had proved no fulfillment of his deepest needs but a thwarting of them; it had not been followed by a genuine freedom from his mother but by an involvement with her perhaps closer than ever; it had pulled the smothering network of family relations and family responsibilities tighter than ever about his head; and it had cut him off from that easy, youthful, irresponsible, bachelor association with his own sex that was clearly a necessity to him.

It is evident from *Pierre* how violent and how confused the emotional issues were; how destructively divided Melville was—in his relations of feeling with his mother, his wife, and his brothers and sisters, and the memory of his father—between love and hate, between loyalty and vindictiveness, between a febrile attachment and a murderous resentment. Whatever its flaws and faults as a work of art, and regarded for the moment only as a document, *Pierre* is an extraordinary revelation of the sufferings of a noble nature, endowed with a capacity for high-minded conduct and devoted love, but erring to the brink of madness, and over it, in its incapacity to balance one good against another, and in the habit of exacting of every close human relationship an extremity of completeness that no such relationship can bear. Emotional absolutism is as truly Pierre's vice as it is Ahab's, though the one appears to be absolute in love and the other in hatred. They are equally mad, equally destructive, equally nihilistic in the end; and it is appalling to have to fix one's gaze on that psychoneurotic realm in which Pierre moves and acts; in which one begins by directing toward one's mother, one's remembered father, one's boy cousin, one's fiancée, and one's half sister, without much discrimination, a violence of attachment that is always incestuous in quality even when not literally so in fact; and in which one ends by turning murderously upon them all and destroying oneself and them: burning the father's picture to ashes, driving the mother to madness and death, shooting and killing the cousin, bringing death to the fiancée and the half sister, and at last gulping poison oneself.

Pierre is a work of art, however, not a mere document; and these horrors are dilated shadow-forms thrown upon the imaginative cave-wall by Melville's productive fancy; they are not biographical facts, even of the intangible order. They point to biographical facts, nevertheless, if we know how to interpret them; and they suggest to us that Hawthorne was indulging in no overstatement when he remarked about Melville, three or four years later, that "his writings, for a long while past, have indicated a morbid state of mind." This they had done, and biographically speaking the fact they chiefly suggest is that Melville felt himself emotionally trapped between his mother and his wife, and that his fantasies took the form of imagining an escape from them both through a relationship that would be as tabu in quality as brother-sister incest, even if it were not literally that. How deep his resentment was against both mother and wife we can make out not only in *Pierre* but in the sketch called "I and My Chimney," in which the wife is represented as a gorgon of domestic energy and tyranny who is determined to abolish the great chimney that is central and fundamental to her husband's existence, his essential and deepest self. Lizzie Melville herself once noted in the margin of this sketch that "all this about his wife applied to his mother—who was very vigorous and energetic about the farm, etc." It is natural and touching that Lizzie should have been able to believe this, but the truth is that wife and mother had been fused in Melville's mind into a single image of intrusive and oppressive hostility. Five years earlier, indeed, in the fall after *Moby Dick* was finished, Melville, in filling out the birth certificate of his son Stanwix, had put down his own name and his mother's, not his wife's, as parents of the new baby.

The inner stresses to which all these signals point were such as to destroy any man less endowed than Melville with a deep constitutional toughness; and they were intensified from another direction by the "irrational" but, on their own level, terribly real stresses of his relationship with Hawthorne. Irrational they certainly were, for there can be no doubt at all that Hawthorne entertained for Melville, both as a man and as a writer, a special and genuine regard: "he has a very high and noble nature," wrote the older man after seeing him in 1856, "and is better worth immortality than most of us." There were not many men of whom Hawthorne ever spoke in such terms, and he spoke thus in the privacy of his journal. His offence, in his relation to Melville, was that he could not play the superhuman role—of father, friend, elder brother, and all but God—that Melville, in his misery and egoism, would have had him play. "I shall leave the world, I feel, with more satisfaction for having come to know you," Melville had written. "Knowing you persuades me more than the Bible of our immortality." It was a tribute that can only have evoked very mixed and painful feelings in the bosom of the reticent Hawthorne.

In his own heart, doubtless, he was quite unconscious of having avoidably inspired any disappointment in his friend, though for a certain period he was embarrassed by his failure to get Melville a consular appointment. An estrangement, nevertheless, there ultimately was: after Hawthorne's return to America in 1860 the two men failed to meet, though Hawthorne lived four years longer, and they were separated by no greater distance than that between Concord and Pittsfield or New York. The little poem, "Monody," can only allude to Hawthorne—

> To have known him, to have loved him
> After loneness long;
> And then to be estranged in life,
> And neither in the wrong—

and even in 1852, a year after *Moby Dick,* and after a visit Melville paid to Hawthorne in Concord, there is a dryness and tiredness in the letter he wrote to the older man ("I greatly enjoyed my visit to you, and hope that you reaped some corresponding pleasure") that contrasts uncomfortably with the exultation of the letter he had written a year earlier. A curious, submerged token of Melville's bitterness may lie latent in the subject for a tale, the famous Agatha story, that had come to his ears during a stay on Nantucket, and that, on his visit to Concord, he had urged upon Hawthorne for his own use. The story of Agatha is the story of an adventurer who deserts the woman he has married, a sort of Yankee Patient Grissil living in a seacoast town; and who then, though he turns bigamist, revisits his lawful wife on two or three occasions as if driven back to her by some guilty compulsion. Surely there was a lurking and unconscious reproach in Melville's wishing to force upon Hawthorne's attention this tale of a woman deserted by the man from whom she had a right to expect nothing but complete loyalty.

A sense of having been somehow rejected, unreasonable and egoistic though it was, festered in Melville's consciousness. Years later, in the 'seventies, it found vent in still another guise in the long narrative poem *Clarel*. The central figure in this poem, Clarel, is a young American who has given up his studies for the ministry and is now traveling in the Holy Land, restlessly and ineffectually seeking both some answer to his spiritual problems and some fulfillment of his emotional needs. In a visit to the Pool of Siloam in Jerusalem he encounters a stranger, an older man, Vine, between whom and himself a bond of quick sympathy seems to establish itself. Vine, in his shyness, his reticence, his taciturnity, as well as in a curious soft charm of personal quality and a strain of suppressed mockery—Vine is Hawthorne to the life; and in the longing that Clarel feels for some completeness of mutual understanding between them, there is a memorial of Melville's ancient need.

A moment comes when Clarel feels that they are on the

brink of achieving that mutuality. The two of them have
joined a party of tourists who have set out from Jerusalem on
horseback to visit the Dead Sea and then the monastery of
Mar Saba. The party has reached the banks of the Jordan,
and there, wandering a little away from his fellow-tourists,
Clarel comes upon the older man lying at length beside the
stream in the midst of a cluster of willows. He throws himself
down beside Vine, and they enter into conversation; but what
is in Clarel's mind is no mere conversational topic:

> Prior advances unreturned
> Not here he recked of, while he yearned—
> Oh, now but for communion true
> And close; let go each alien theme;
> Give me thyself!

Vine, who seems wholly unconscious of his companion's
trouble for the moment, is uncharacteristically talkative, and
pursues his conversational track—a series of half-playful, half-
serious animadversions on the modern Arabs. They do not
successfully divert Clarel's thoughts:

> Divided mind knew Clarel here;
> The heart's desire did interfere.
> Thought he, How pleasant in another
> Such sallies, or in thee, if said
> After confidings that should wed
> Our souls in one:—Ah, call me *brother!*—
> So feminine his passionate mood
> Which, long as hungering unfed,
> All else rejected or withstood.

So strong is the impulse to confess these things that Clarel
does actually let fall "some inklings" of his mood; and at once
he is aware that a shadow has passed over Vine's manner. It is
as if the other man were rebuking him all but explicitly for
bringing both his doubts and his needs to one who has already had his share of pain: as if Vine were saying:

Lives none can help ye; that believe.
Art thou the first soul tried by doubt?
Shalt prove the last? Go, live it out.
But for thy fonder dream of love
In man toward man—the soul's caress—
The negatives of flesh should prove
Analogies of non-cordialness
In spirit.

It is a final, though unspoken, rebuke; and Clarel withdraws into himself, conscious that he neither can nor ought to expect more from Vine, and that indeed there is something amiss about such intense emotions in a man who is already, as Clarel is, engaged to be married:

Nay, dizzard, sick these feelings are;
How findest place within thy heart
For such solicitudes apart
From Ruth?—Self-taxings.

Ruth, at just this moment in the poem, is a shadow of Lizzie Melville; and perhaps it was on the visit to Concord, when Hawthorne, however gently, turned aside the Agatha story, that Melville had come to a final despairing acceptance of his friend's "non-cordialness." The two men met again, not in Pittsfield or Concord, but strangely and suitably enough in Liverpool, in the city beside the Mersey that had already signified so many dark and bitter things to Melville, and in which, for two or three years, so much of Hawthorne's own experience had been centered. He had gone to England in the summer of 1853 as American consul at Liverpool, and in the autumn of 1856 Melville arrived there on the first lap of his journey to Palestine. The Hawthornes were living not in the city itself but at Southport, a seaside place a few miles away, and here Melville visited them for a few days. On one of these, a fine, windy November day, the two friends went walking together along the desolate, sandy Lancashire coast, stopping once in a hollow among the sandhills to smoke cigars, while Melville, holding forth on Providence and futurity and "everything that lies beyond human ken," confessed to Hawthorne that he had "pretty much made up his mind to be annihilated." "It is strange," added Hawthorne in his journal, "how he persists—and has persisted ever since I knew him, and probably long before—in wandering to and fro over these deserts, as dismal and monotonous as the sandhills amid which we were sitting."

Two or three days later Hawthorne took Melville on an expedition to Chester, where they spent several hours. Late in the day they returned together to Liverpool, where Melville was to stay at a hotel, and there on a street corner, in the rainy evening, they parted. It was their real parting, one feels, though in the literal sense they met once or twice again, in Hawthorne's office, both then and on Melville's return from Palestine. By that time, however, all that they might ever have said to each other had been said, and the handclasp of good-bye on the rainy Liverpool corner must have betokened first and last things to them both.

The journey to Palestine had been undertaken at the urging of Melville's family, in despair over his health and perhaps also over the deepening strain of his mere presence among them. Largely no doubt for their sake Judge Shaw had come forward again with the money to make the trip possible. In the interval since *Moby Dick*, assailed as he had been by specters from within and without, Melville had passed through a prolonged emotional and nervous trial that, at a later period, would promptly have been described as a crack-up, and treated as such. There was no place for such a malady in the medical philosophy of the 'fifties, and Melville had had to weather his psychological Cape Horn as best he could, without much solace or support. It was not that Lizzie and the others, his mother, his sister Augusta, were not profoundly troubled by what they observed in him; it is evident that they were. "We all felt anxious about his health in the spring of 1853," Lizzie Melville later wrote; and there exists a letter of that same spring from Maria Melville to her brother Peter in which she expresses the fear that the strain of Herman's constant literary exertions is wearing him out.

The strain of Herman's constant exposure to Maria and her will was probably an even more disabling fact, but in any case the knowledge and the insight that his relatives, or anyone, could call upon was pathetically limited. They could raise, and it is said that they fearfully did raise, the simple dire question of "sanity" or "insanity." The dreary memory of Allan Melville's last days was doubtless with them, and there is a more or less authentic tradition that physicians were called in to examine Allan Melville's son and to pronounce on the soundness of his wits. Of course they could only rule that he was not mad and, with that, abandon the case as of no psychological importance.

Mad he was not, in the simple old-fashioned medical sense, but the germs of dementia were in him, and we can be sure that, like Pierre, Melville was visited during these black years by thoughts of his real or fancied hereditary liability to madness. Such thoughts would have formed but one, though perhaps the most ghastly, of the psychoneurotic miseries to which these years of sickness subjected him. Probably there were few that he was spared. Certainly he knew the insistent, sapping physical symptoms, the eyestrain, the neuralgic pains, the sciatica; and doubtless he knew the tortures of sleeplessness too and the ensuing dullness and languor of spirit. Nor were these by any means the worst; the writing Melville did during these years is our clue to that. Far worse than eyestrain or even insomnia would be the intangible miseries he suffered; the anguish of uncontrollable self-reproach and shapeless remorse, alternating with the anguish of weak hatred, helpless anger against others, and the loss of the last fragments of confidence in mankind; then, as a further turn of the wheel on which he was bound, the terror of nameless, formless dangers impending over him, of a vague encirclement by hostility and peril, and the sense of utter desertion, desolation, and forlornness; surely there were hours when the conviction of failure and shame all but overpowered him. It is as certain as such a truth can be that he heard during these hours the compulsive recurrent whisper of the temptation to suicide. In fantasy he drank poison with Pierre, or allowed himself to die of sheer hunger like Bartleby, or withdrew from the world like Benito Cereno to perish of remembering "the negro." Yet he was not mad; he did none of these things in fact; in the end he was healed of his hurt, and could bring himself to "laud the inhuman sea." He had escaped, though with little more than his life, from "the whale's black flukes and the white shark's fin."

Meanwhile, not even the purgatory of neurosis had very much impaired his productivity. Never again was he to perform such feats of speed and power as the composition of *White-Jacket* and *Moby Dick*, but even after the latter of these the twin demons of outward necessity and inward urgency were at his elbow, and within a few months he had written *Pierre*. When it was done, Melville collapsed at last, as one dimly makes out, with fatigue and despair, and during the year or more that followed he wrote only two tales, one of which was the wonderful "Bartleby," the tale in which he announced to those who could understand him that he would no longer willingly be misemployed. Even now, however, he could not agree that his real work was done, and as the months passed, reassembling his forces, he went on to write the long and powerful piece called "The Encantadas," and to follow this up with a short novel, *Israel Potter*, with "Benito Cereno," and with the other stories that went to make up the *Piazza Tales* or that, like "I and My Chimney," remained uncollected in his lifetime. Finally, in 1856, with what must have been a consciousness of moving down some inexorable stream toward its mouth and the sea, he began the dreariest, most unbelieving of all his books, *The Confidence Man: His Masquerade;* but, as if the dreariness were more than he could continue to contemplate, broke it off before he had brought it to any true conclusion—and renounced, as he did so, all further serious relations with the readers of his day.

Truncated as it was, *The Confidence Man* was published in the spring of the following year, but meanwhile, in the fall of 1856, Melville, as if to signalize by his physical departure the conscious end of his literary life, had yielded to the urgings of his worried relatives and set out for Europe and the Holy Land. What drove him forth on this journey was partly of course the old restless longing for movement and change, and the hope that these alone would somehow renew his sense of life; but beyond that there was something more special that sent him journeying to the East and to Palestine in particular. It was as if, having spent his youth voyaging westward, toward the spaces that lay beyond America, to the islands that had no history and were still pristine, he were under a compulsion now to reverse that movement and voyage eastward and backward, to retrace the Asiatic and the European currents to their headwaters, to immerse himself in scenes that, as he may well have felt, were *only* history, only memory, only the source and not the future. The nostalgia for the primitive had yielded in him to the nostalgia for the venerable and the moribund, and mingled with this was some still more special longing for the Biblical, the Hebraic, the Judaean past—the past of the patriarchs and the judges, the prophets and the kings. Few men's minds have been more richly stored than Melville's with the imagery of Biblical story, of the Old Testament record especially; it had been woven into the fabric of his imagination from earliest childhood, and he had constantly recurred to it; it was a permanent point of reference for his spirit, and he may dimly have hoped now that the mere resting of his eyes on the sacred places and the reverend objects—on Mount Zion and the Vale of Kedron, on Olivet and the Jordan, on the Tomb of Absalom and the Pool of Bethesda—would reawaken and reconfirm the old certainties that had so completely faded for him.

If he had hoped for any such result, the days in Jerusalem and nearby were a mockery of disappointment; what they actually did, as his journal makes evident, was much more to intensify his revulsion from, his weariness of, what he calls the "ghastly theology" of the Jewish prophets. How little solace, in that sense, the sights of the Holy Land brought to him is suggested by another note in the journal: "Is the desolation of the land the result of the fatal embrace of the Deity? Hapless are the favorites of Heaven." Yet if the stay in Palestine was fruitless of spiritual renewal there was, in this very desolation of the land, something peculiarly harmonious with the mood in which Melville found himself. What beguiled him now was not freshness, greenness, and gaiety, but emblems of ruin and decay. As he sailed among the Greek islands, they had looked worn and meager to him, "like life after enthusiasm is gone." The very color of Asia, as he first glimpsed it from the boat, had made him think of those Asiatic lions, lazy and torpid, that one sees in menageries. And now in Palestine he was, if not charmed, at least not repelled by the barrenness and blight that lay everywhere; by the gray, dilapidated city of Jerusalem, with the smell of burning rubbish always in the air; the naked ruins, unsoftened by moss or ivy as elsewhere; the plains covered with wiry, prickly bush; the barren mountains; and everywhere, as if the land itself were an unfleshed skeleton, stones, stones, stones; stony torrents and stony roads, stony vales and stony fields, stony eyes and stony hearts. Aridity, hardness, sterility—how willingly just now he lingered among their tokens!

It was not that he was incapable of responding to other impressions of travel. He had been fascinated in Constantinople by the grandeur of the site on the Bosporus, the splendor of the great mosques, and the squalor that, by way of picturesque contrast, lay on every hand. The port of Syra or Syros in the Aegean, where they touched twice, abounded in figures that might have stepped, fully and brightly costumed, out of an opera in a London theater. A visit to the Pyramids had moved him deeply, though the great monuments had oppressed him, too, with their massiveness and mystery. After he left the Holy Land he had visited Athens for a day or two, and had seen the ruins of the Parthenon, "like the North River breaking up." Later he had spent two months in Italy, sight-seeing almost as indefatigably as eight years earlier in England, but with a constant undercurrent of weariness and dejection. The pictures and sculptures in the galleries, in Naples, in Rome, in Florence, allured him almost endlessly, but the ground-tone of his mood is audible when, after a carriage drive from Naples to Posilipo, the promontory whose Greek name means "abating pain," he remarks in his journal: "At Posilipo found not the cessation which the name expresses." Or when, some weeks later in Venice, after a few days of seeing sights in company with a guide named Antonio, a ruined gentleman, he writes: "Floating about philosophizing with Antonio the Merry. Ah, it was Posilipo." So it doubtless was—but how briefly!

If he could have yielded to this weariness, Melville might imaginably have sunk down in some such sleepy and retired spot as the Armenian Convent in Venice, where the Lido would have been "a breakwater against the tumultuous ocean of life," or in some sequestered college at Oxford, the spot that interested him most in all England and that led him to remark: "In such a retreat old Burton sedately smiled at men." Any such weak escape as this from his personal duties was of course wholly out of the question, and Melville could never have done more than imagine it. There is nothing in his journal this time to suggest that he felt any spontaneous longing to return to Lizzie and the rest of his family, but there is nothing in his life to suggest that he ever seriously considered the possibility of not doing so. Late in the spring of 1857 he set his face homeward once more, and was soon back at Arrowhead. There now began for him the long period of almost complete silence and obscurity, in Pittsfield and later in New York, which stretched to the end of his life. Full as it was to be—of study, of reflection, of quiet work, even of renewed writing—there was something inescapably post-humous in this existence of more than thirty years, and no one was more aware of this than Melville himself. In a copy of Chapman's translation of the *Batrachomyomachia,* two or three years later, he underlined one elegiac, almost epitaphic line: "The work that I was born to do is done!" As it turned out, this was not the literal truth; he was still to do work that one might well say he had been "born" to do; but what he himself, in the next few years, was chiefly conscious of having before him was the work that personal self-respect and fidel-ity to others demanded of him.

Perilous Outpost of the Sane

THE SPECTACLE of Melville composing *Moby Dick* is the spectacle of an artist working at the very height of his creativeness and confidence, like a great athlete who has reached, and only just reached, his optimum in age, in physical vigor, in trained agility. The spectacle Melville presents immediately following *Moby Dick*, and for some years afterwards, is that of a great athlete who has somehow sustained an essential, if not very apparent, injury, and though he plays or performs now, in intermittent spurts, with a brilliance no ordinary man could achieve, is all too evidently shaken, confused, uncertain of his strokes, and liable to sudden, prostrating fatigue. What might have been true, if circumstances had permitted Melville a long recuperation after *Moby Dick*, it is impossible to say. Circumstances did not permit such a respite. Within a few weeks, tired as he must have been, he had plunged into the writing of *Pierre*, and it was not until five years later that he at last threw in the sponge, and confessed that his career as a writer for the general public had come to an end. What he was yet to write, when he returned to writing, was for himself and a small imaginable handful of friends and admirers.

There is an inescapable effect of anticlimax, as a result, in turning to the work that followed *Moby Dick*. Critically speaking, and from the point of view of poetic value, almost nothing Melville later did is comparable to his one very great book. Much that he later did has so real an interest, and has incited so much commentary, as to blur and becloud the fact that it is work not only on a lower level but on a level that is lower by several wide degrees. It is not simply secondary to *Moby Dick*; it is lesser work in a much more decided sense, related to that book not as *Paradise Regained* is related to *Paradise Lost* but as *Timon* is related to *Hamlet*, or *Bouvard et Pécuchet* to *Madame Bovary*. *Timon of Athens* and *Bouvard et Pécuchet* are clearly the work of very powerful minds, and the same remark would hold for almost everything in Melville's later period also; but Shakespeare's weaker plays and Flaubert's unfinished novel are the productions of minds that are working on half-characteristic materials or on the margin of their resources, and with some natural qualifications this is what strikes one as one reads Melville's later novels, tales, sketches, and poems. No one else could possibly have done such work as some of it is, but for Melville, for the author of *Moby Dick*, it is mostly by-work and sometimes it is botchery.

For the first four or five years it was all "written in dejection," and that accounts for much: great things have been written, needless to say, out of the midst of anguish and even despair, but rarely out of the midst of psychoneurotic fatigue. And there were more intangible, less easily statable reasons than this for what happened. One of these was the failure of Melville's audience: the unpreparedness of his readers, both here and abroad, to follow him into the intellectual and imaginative regions that were his true territory. At the apex of his powers, alone as he almost was, he had moved with wonderful ease and mastery in those regions; but even Melville could hardly be expected to do so indefinitely. His audience was not prepared to play its indispensable role, and the hall was rapidly emptying. Partly for this reason, partly for more inward ones, there was a derangement in his own relation to his work; the felicity of instinct that had guided him, in *Moby Dick,* straight to his ideal matter and his true manner, failed him when the book was finished, or visited him only capriciously; and he wandered, much of the time, among uncharacteristic subjects and not quite appropriate forms. What he could do now and then, even with these, was so extraordinary that one has little sense of loss when one fixes his attention exclusively on the piece or the passage in question. But in the setting of Melville's whole *œuvre* it is clear that one is dealing with relatively minor values.

Pierre itself, taken as a whole and considered on strictly literary grounds, is one of the most painfully ill-conditioned books ever to be produced by a first-rate mind. So extreme is its badness as an integral work of art that some faint-hearted readers might well wish to be excused from any prolonged discussion of it, a discussion such as its scale, if nothing else, seems to demand; yet this is out of the question. And it must be said at once that *Pierre's* badness is an active and positive, not a merely negative one; it is the badness of misdirected and even perverted powers, but not of deficiency or deadness.

It has of course, morally speaking, a great theme; a theme that, if stated abstractly enough, is an ancient one, as ancient at least as the *Antigone;* but defined more specifically is one that had a special importance for writers of the nineteenth century. It is the tragic, or sometimes the tragicomic, but in any case the ironic, ambiguity of idealistic absolutism; the spectacle of enthusiastic and utterly uncompromising virtue or highmindedness spreading havoc and misery about it instead of peace and well-being. At just the time that Melville was writing *Pierre,* Hawthorne was dealing with the theme in his own manner in *The Blithedale Romance,* where Hollingsworth is a kind of plebeian Pierre; and Melville's young idealist has at least close relatives also in Tur-

genev's Rudin and Tolstoy's Pierre Bezúkhov. Still closer
to him, in his nobleness and his blindness, is the great figure
of Brand in Ibsen's play:

> Know, that I am stern to crave,
> *All* or *Nothing* I will have.

It was the peculiar Hubris of the romantic, the nineteenth-
century mind, this determination to have, morally speaking,
All or Nothing; to insist on the rigorous alternative of Good
and Evil; to declare, as Kierkegaard did: "Either/or is the
pass which admits to the absolute. . . . Yes, either/or is the
key to heaven. . . . Both/and is the way to hell." To this
sort of passionate absolutism Melville himself was particularly prone, and it was, taken by itself, one of the noblest
traits in his nature: without it we would not have had what is
honorable in his life and intense in his work, and Pierre is the
embodiment of this whole side of him; the Pierre who cries:
"Guide me, gird me, guard me, this day, ye sovereign powers!
Bind me in bonds I cannot break; remove all sinister allurings from me; eternally this day deface in me the detested
and distorted images of all the convenient lies and duty-
subterfuges of the diving and ducking moralities of this
earth." Despite the feverish and absurd alliterations, there
is grandeur of feeling in such an outbreak, and Pierre, in
conception if not in concrete embodiment, is a kind of
Protestant Don Quixote to whom, on a certain level, one
cannot refuse a melancholy respect. It was characteristic of
Melville's complex vision, however, that he saw what was
harsh, egoistic, inhumane, and destructive in this ostensibly
virtuous enthusiasm, both in himself and in Pierre; and he
wrote the book partly to undergo an ideal expiation for his
own sins of virtue.

This is the transparent meaning of the famous, but often
misinterpreted, pamphlet, *"El,"* allegedly written by one
Plotinus Plinlimmon, which Pierre discovers in the coach
that is conveying him and Isabel to the city; the pamphlet

that sets forth, through the metaphorical contrast between "chronometrical" and "horological" time, the unbridgeable antithesis between absolute, heavenly Truth and relative, worldly, human truths; with its conclusion that "a virtuous expediency . . . seems the highest desirable or attainable earthly excellence for the mass of men, and is the only earthly excellence that their Creator intended for them." Many readers of *Pierre* have imagined that Melville's simple purpose in this whole passage was to deride the preachers of a low, expedient, comfortable morality of compromise and adjustment; but surely this was not at all his conscious intention. On the intellectual level, the level of deliberate reflection, "Chronometricals and Horologicals" means just what it says, and means it with something of the same seriousness with which Ibsen means the song of the Invisible Chorus in the last act of *Brand:*

> Dreamer, thine is not His spirit,
> Nought to him thy gifts are worth;
> Heaven thou never shalt inherit,
> Earth-born creature, live for Earth!

The whole drift of the action of *Pierre* is intended to demonstrate that the hero's tragic error lay in his not distinguishing early enough between absolute, ideal Good and the good that is possible, achievable, consistent with other goods, and therefore genuinely human. *"El"* exemplifies in another vein, and a far less poetic one, the insight that Melville had already embodied in the symbolism of the doubloon in *Moby Dick*. Both passages represent his most serious and mature wisdom, a wisdom that he doubtless bought at a painful cost.

It is one thing, however, to say that on the rational level Melville meant Plinlimmon's pamphlet to be taken at its face value, and another to say that he was wholly at one with himself in his acceptance of this moderate, Montaignesque morality. It was the kind of morality—reasonable, tolerant, humorous, yet serious and uncynical—in the spirit of which

he wished to school himself, and in the long run he succeeded; but at the time he wrote *Pierre* he was so far from
being at one with himself that he was in fact torn by the most
confused and conflicting impulses, and the book itself is the
expression, not of a state of ripe serenity, but of something
approaching inner chaos. The word is too strong, but it remains true that, emotionally speaking, the center of the book
is not Plinlimmon's mature sagacity but Pierre's intense and
anguished awareness of the dubiety, the shiftingness, the
mocking evasiveness, the "ambiguity" of all truths, all standards, all distinctions between Right and Wrong; and an approach to the suicidal conviction that Truth itself is a liar,
and Good only Evil in the making. What lay behind this was
the neurotic sense of the nightmarish unreality of all things,
physical and spiritual, but to say that this sense is neurotic
is not to say that the experience itself is unreal: in its
phantasmal way it is intensely real, and one of the things that
save *Pierre* from utter nullity is its rendering, not with full
dramatic success but at least lyrically, of the sometimes over-
powering vision of the Equivocal—of "the infinite cliffs and
gulfs of human mystery and misery."

What makes human behavior so radically equivocal, so
deeply ambiguous and mysterious as it is, not only to the
neurotic mind but "in itself," is, from one point of view, the
abysmal contrast between its conscious, rational, social surface and the wild irrationality of what lies out of sight below;
and it was a reward of Melville's sufferings, given the initial
power of his mind, that they enabled him to have glimpses,
such as few even of his great contemporaries had, into the
murky and chaotic regions of the unconscious. He had
pointed in those directions already in *Moby Dick*, and now
in *Pierre* he continued to fix his gaze thither and to report on
what he obscurely saw: "Deep, deep, and still deep and
deeper must we go, if we would find out the heart of a man;
descending into which is as descending a spiral stair in a
shaft, without any end, and where that endlessness is only

concealed by the spiralness of the stair, and the blackness of the shaft."

Nor is it only a question of incidental insights; the action itself, however confusedly and imperfectly, embodies Melville's instinctive feeling for the paradoxes of human conduct. The conscious and admitted motive that leads Pierre to befriend Isabel and to rescue her from her forlornness by pretending to marry her, is a pure, quixotic, self-abnegating desire to redress a great injustice and to demonstrate to the unbelieving world that at least one man can act in the light of transcendent Truth. His "real" motive, as he himself half discerns, is to establish a close and precarious intimacy with a woman who is not only strangely and darkly beautiful, and endowed with a physical magnetism of electric potency, but who bears a mysterious, alluring resemblance to Pierre's father. Perhaps she is really his half sister; perhaps not; but at all events Pierre as a child, before his father's premature death, had made his father the object of an idolatrous love that partook already of the incestuous, and then, when his father's death thwarted him, he had turned inevitably to his handsome, possessive mother, and demanded of her the fulfillment of his emotional needs. In all possible ways Mary Glendinning, deprived of a husband's love, had responded to Pierre's demand, and she and her son had behaved toward each other almost like romantic lovers. Such a love was not of course literally possible, and Pierre's overintense relations with his mother had only had the effect of frustrating him still further, and destroying his capacity for happy and normal relations with the opposite sex.

Consciously, to be sure, Pierre supposes himself to be deeply and genuinely in love with the charming, wholesome, and highly "suitable" Lucy Tartan; and Melville himself was probably not fully conscious of suggesting that this was not true. Pierre's actual behavior, however, is that of a man whose unconscious is lying in wait for the first plausible opportunity to desert. One side of his nature, the side that is still healthy, goes out to Lucy and her blonde purity; but the other side, the more deeply instinctual one, the one that has already been given its perverse direction, goes out to the erotically more enticing Isabel. Pierre's unconscious wish is to escape from Lucy and to preserve the incestuous bond with his father by uniting himself to this mysterious girl who, as he all too readily believes, is his father's illegitimate daughter, and who at any rate strongly resembles that parent. This is the wish on the basis of which Pierre acts; and if, in doing so, he destroys his mother's happiness, her sanity, and even her life, that too is a goal he has unconsciously aimed at; the obverse of his unhealthy attachment to his mother is a matricidal hatred. Such too is the obverse of his attachment to his father's memory, and he demonstrates this in the only manner available to him by burning his father's portrait in a frenzy of bitterness. What awaits Pierre now is only further and more intense frustration. The incestuous relationship with Isabel cannot move to any erotic consummation, and cut off at last from all avenues of emotional fulfillment, Pierre goes mad with accumulated hostility; he ends by destroying not only Isabel and Lucy but himself.

When its action is outlined in this way, it is evident that *Pierre* is the work of a man who has acquired a terrible knowledge of human motives, a terrible insight into all the concealed and unapparent regions of human nature, and the association there of the most passionate love with the most murderous hate. If Melville's constructive and expressive power, when he wrote *Pierre*, had been equal to this knowledge, the book would have been the great book it so signally fails to be. Even as it is, Melville's expressive power by no means wholly deserts him. Only once in the book does it break free from its bonds for more than a few moments at a time; only once does it carry him through a sustained passage of noble eloquence almost comparable to some of the great stretches in *Moby Dick;* but then it does so, and this is in the magnificent pages given over to Pierre's dream of the

Mount of Titans and the great image of the Enceladus rock. Here the strain and the unnaturalness that mar almost every other page of *Pierre* suddenly fall away; the fogs of mannerism and exaggeration lift, and we are launched on the broad, full rhythms of such prose as only a great master could write. The need to express again a Promethean defiance of fate has stretched full the sails of Melville's utterance.

Nowhere else in the novel is there any such prolonged triumph as this, but that does not mean that the murkiness of *Pierre* is not from time to time relieved by gleams of at least a fitful and flickering radiance. There are whole passages that waver back and forth between absurdity and genuine power: the communion of Pierre with his father's portrait, his strange second interview with Isabel while the soft ground-lightnings of the summer night play about them, the approach to the city at nightfall with the shutters of the inhospitable shops going up. There are small touches of imaginative truth, too, that convey an irresistible *frisson*: the sudden coolness of the knocker on the door of Lucy's cottage as Pierre touches it, the thrill that runs down the baluster from Mary Glendinning's grasp to her son's, the "scintillations" of the melody that Isabel evokes from her guitar. And there are the incomparable metaphors that appear in such passages as these:

> He felt that what he had always before considered the solid land of veritable reality, was now being audaciously encroached upon by bannered armies of hooded phantoms, disembarking in his soul, as from flotillas of spectre-boats.

> . . . thus sometimes stood Pierre before the portrait of his father, unconsciously throwing himself open to all those ineffable hints and ambiguities, and undefined half-suggestions, which now and then people the soul's atmosphere, as thickly as in a soft, steady snowstorm, the snowflakes people the air.

Now, from his height of composure, he firmly gazed

abroad upon the charred landscape within him; as the timber man of Canada, forced to fly from the conflagration of his forests, comes back again when the fires have waned, and unblinkingly eyes the immeasurable fields of fire-brands that here and there glow beneath the wide canopy of smoke.

An infixing stillness now thrust a long rivet through the night, and fast nailed it to that side of the world.

But in long night-watches at the antipodes, how heavily that ocean gloom lies in vast bales upon the deck. . . .

For Faith and philosophy are air, but events are brass. Amidst his gray philosophizings, Life breaks upon a man like a morning.

For in tremendous extremities human souls are like drowning men; well enough they know they are in peril; well enough they know the causes of that peril; nevertheless, the sea is the sea, and these drowning men do drown.

Images like these flare up in the surrounding vapor and gloom like signal lights, and remind us that we are dealing with the author of *Moby Dick*; but not even they are enough to keep *Pierre* from being four-fifths claptrap, and sickly claptrap to boot. The great theme is there, certainly, but it is not embodied in a great action, as that of *Brand* for example is. The great insights into the psychological subterranean are also there, and they *are* embodied in the action in a manner that makes exposition possible. The fact remains that the theme and the insights are incorporated in fictional symbols —an action, a group of personages, a scene—that quite fail to endow them with dramatic truth and power. There is a gap between the conception and the performance that is never bridged, and the result is fiasco. For this there were doubtless several "reasons" that can be made out, in addition to the general fact of Melville's illness and fatigue. Something was wrong psychologically with the distance between Melville and his material: he could not remove himself far enough from it to be its master rather than its victim. Family relations of this close, heated, confined, incestuous sort—was it possible for Herman Melville, embosomed in the midst of mother, wife, sisters, children, to contemplate these things with the passionate detachment, the distant nearness, that the labor of creation demands? The stuff of *Pierre* was the stuff of Melville's daily sufferings as he wrote it—his rock of Sisyphus, which he should not have attempted both to roll uphill and to describe.

Nor was he more fortunate in the form he was attempting than in his matter. He had evolved a great and highly idiosyncratic form in *Moby Dick*—as, in *Redburn* and *White-Jacket*, he had moved toward it—and now, as if he were not a master but a disciple and a tyro, he put aside all that he had learned in doing this, denied himself all his most personal resources, and undertook to express himself in a hybrid form that had come to him, quite mistakenly, from a hodgepodge of models. These included the old novel of sensibility, the Gothic romance, the novel of romantic sophistication, and even Elizabethan tragedy. The hands are Melville's hands, but the voice, too much of the time, is the voice of Mrs. Radcliffe or Susanna Rowson, of Charles R. Maturin or Disraeli. The plot of *Pierre*, quite regardless of its connection with Melville's own experience, is not a spontaneous and characteristic invention of his natural genius; it is an unholy amalgam of elements lifted out of novels like *The Power of Sympathy*, *The Monk*, and *Henrietta Temple*. The characters, at the same time that they bear a phantasmal relation to people in Melville's own life, are, in a literary sense, stock types out of the fiction and poetry of the romantic movement. Pierre himself is the Childe Harold or Lara of a hundred romantic poems and novels; Isabel glides straight out of "Monk" Lewis and the Balzac of *Séraphita*; Mrs. Glendinning is the haughty dowager or worldly matron of *The Italian* and *The Mysteries of Udolpho*; and the comic innkeeper, porters, and cabdrivers are late and degenerate descendants of Shakespeare's tinkers and constables. Second-hand, too, though they are undeniably used with a curious freshness and a sort of power, are the Gothic properties Melville borrowed from his predecessors, the Magic Portrait (the "chair portrait" of Pierre's father) and the Magic Instrument (the guitar that Isabel "plays" without touching its strings). And in its trifling way it is eloquent of Melville's inventive fatigue in writing *Pierre* that the very names of the characters should come out of other novels—the family name Glendinning, for example, from *The Monastery*—in a manner that suggests the strongest contrast with the names of Ahab, Stubb, and Tashtego.

All this is evidence of Melville's quite genuine taste, as a reader, for romantic, Gothic, and melodramatic fiction, but not of his wisdom in undertaking to write in a form that was as inexpressive for him as a foreign tongue. Hawthorne, for his part, had a great taste for the novels of Anthony Trollope, but his sense of his own capacities effectually kept him from attempting a *Barchester Towers*. And it was one effect of Melville's working in this unnatural vein that there should be so radical an obliquity as there is at the very center of the action of *Pierre*. Pierre is presented to us as an Enthusiast to Duty; well and good; we are wholly prepared to believe in his acting in an ideal, absolute, self-abnegating, intolerant, and even destructive manner. We are not prepared to believe in his acting like a madman. The merciless "All or Nothing" of Brand, in Ibsen's play, leads him to such acts of inhumanity as the refusal to allow his wife to preserve any memorials of their dead child; these pitiful tokens would be concessions to the weakness of the flesh, and Brand's cruelty is understandable in the light of his more-than-human morality. Pierre's behavior is really not understandable in the light of any morality, whether expedient or absolute. After he has heard Isabel's melodramatic tale, he makes not the slightest effort to corroborate it: he accepts it as gospel truth chiefly on the ground of his—and her—intuitive "surmisings," and of the resemblance he fancies he sees between Isabel and his father's portrait.

At the end, indeed, the moral firmness of the whole action is undermined when Pierre, Isabel, and Lucy, visiting a gallery of paintings in the city, come upon the portrait of a European youth to whose features Isabel's bear quite as striking a resemblance as to those of the elder Glendinning. The effect of this is to intensify our sense of the extreme irrationality of all human behavior, but not our sense of the folly of moral absolutism; and Melville is chargeable in the end with an abysmal lapse of moral seriousness and coherence. For meanwhile Pierre has behaved, not in fact like a Don Quixote, but like an Orlando Furioso. Without explanation or apology, he has flung his outrageous news in his mother's face; he has terrified Lucy with his staggering announcement, wildly delivered; he has insulted the Rev. Mr. Falsgrave; he has defied his cousin Glen in a preposterous scene at a party; and he has conducted himself generally like a psychopath. The wake of ruin he leaves behind him is inevitable. All this by no means keeps *Pierre* from having a genuine interest and value as a study of psychopathology; it does largely deprive it, however, of the ethical significance to which it lays claim.

Meanwhile, it is another consequence of Melville's working at an ill-conceived subject and in an uncongenial form that the prevailing texture of the prose in which *Pierre* is written should be so disastrously unequal as it is to the demands of the theme. There are passages of great power, as we have seen, but they are intermittent and unrepresentative, and in general the book is composed in a tone that mingles extravagance with flatness and bombast with namby-pambyness. At scarcely one of the cardinal points, in hardly one of the crucial scenes that ought to be deeply impressive, does the prose itself fail to destroy every illusion of truth and reality. This is the vein in which much of Isabel's tale is told to Pierre:

"Then the bewilderings of all the loneliness and forlornness of all my forlorn and lonely life; all these bewilderings and the whelmings of the bewilderings rolled over me; and I sat down without the house, but could not weep."

When Mrs. Glendinning, her dearest hopes destroyed by Pierre's announcement, soliloquizes in her grief, she can only express herself in rant like this:

"That such accursed vileness should proceed from me! Now will the tongued world say—See the vile boy of Mary Glendinning!—Deceitful! thick with guilt, where I thought it was all guilelessness and gentlest docility to me. It has not happened! It is not day! Were this thing so, I should go mad, and be shut up, and not walk here where every door is open to me."

At the very end, when Lucy's brother Fred comes upon her lifeless body in the prison cell where Pierre and Isabel also lie dead, he breaks into language like this:

"Yes! Yes!—Dead! Dead! Dead!—without one visible wound—her sweet plumage hides it.—Thou hellish carrion, this is thy hellish work! Thy juggler's rifle brought down this heavenly bird! Oh, my God, my God! Thou scalpest me with this sight!"

Meanwhile, it is not only in dramatic scenes that Melville's hand fails him; in reflective passages, too, though his language is far more likely to be adequate and even fine, it lapses sometimes into a vein of softly tinted effeminacy that suggests no one so much as Mrs. Sigourney:

Love is both Creator's and Saviour's gospel to mankind; a volume bound in rose-leaves, clasped with violets, and by the beaks of humming-birds printed with peach-juice on the leaves of lilies.

It would be charitable to attribute such mannerism to the

intention of parody; unhappily, the context makes such an interpretation impossible.

Conscious parody of fashionable fiction was certainly not Melville's purpose in writing *Pierre*, but in spite of this there is something in the violence, the overheatedness, the hysterical forcing of now one note, now another, in the novel, that inescapably suggests a doubleness in the mind of the man who wrote it, a bitter distaste of and disbelief in his own book in the very process of writing it, and a half-confessed intention to invoke ridicule and even contempt on the literary act itself. That is the tone in which, toward the end, Melville describes Pierre's weary labors on *his* manuscript; and it is no wonder that, in a book which sprang out of so resentful and resistant a state of spirit, one should feel that an effect of angry parody somehow dominates the whole. It is not an effect that, in its original conception, *Pierre* could have deserved to suggest.

The experience of writing *Pierre* had demonstrated to Melville himself how utterly uncharacteristic and inexpressive for him that conventional novelistic form was: he never returned to it. This was partly because he was too conscious of flagging vitality and depleted inventiveness to attempt so ambitious a piece of fiction again in the succeeding months, but it was also because he himself had become aware of the falsity of the form. It was a question now both of finding less unsuitable forms and of making what use he might of the low vitality and fitful inventiveness that were left to him. During the two or three years that follow, Melville has the air of consciously sparing himself; sparing himself by attempting only short and unexacting flights or by leaning heavily on some bookish source, some old volume of voyages or "remarkable adventures." For the first time, and if only because it takes less breath, he tries his hand at the short tale, or rather, as a rule, at that ill-defined and not very intense form in which the sketch seems always nerving itself to become the tale, or the tale seems always about to droop and revert to the sketch. Once only, in "Bartleby," does he achieve a clear and strong perfection of fictional form; elsewhere, only in parts of "The Encantadas" and a few scenes in *Israel Potter* does he make on us an impression of great and unencumbered power. Then, at the end of this short period, there comes a moment when Melville seems once more on the verge of a serious and sustained flight; of cutting the cables of the sketch or tale, throwing his bookish sources overboard, and launching himself again on an ambitious "allegorical" fiction of his own devising. To read the first two or three pages of *The Confidence Man*, in the whole setting of this development, is to have the most poignant sense that a great faculty is about to reassert and revindicate itself, and this without the least self-repetition. One reads on, however; the anticipatory moment passes; the illusion fades; and page by page the whole extent of Melville's creative enervation becomes oppressively plain. It is only too clear why he himself breaks off at last, as the light of the swinging lamp in the *Fidèle's* cabin wanes and then expires, with the weary and impatient sentence: "Something further may follow of this Masquerade."

It is true that he seems to have thought from time to time of going on with his protean Confidence Man, but the dying lamp in the cabin was an all but conscious symbol of his own dimming powers. A year later he told one of his brothers-in-law that he was not going to write any more "at present"; in reality it was more than thirty years before he again attempted a work of prose fiction. Meanwhile, in the years between *Pierre* and *The Confidence Man*, the work he did is never, or almost never, wholly lacking in interest and character, and sometimes it has the character of greatness. Superficially there is such a variety among these pieces as to give the effect of mere miscellaneousness, and in fact it is a symptom of Melville's fatigue that he should have so much the air as he does, in these years, of rummaging about uncertainly among the contents of his mind. Yet a little under the surface one detects a kind of homogeneity, a kind of continuity, in these ill-assorted fictions, long and short.

Thematically speaking they all, with one or two exceptions, revert to the two or three motives that were uppermost in Melville's mind during these years. There is the motive, for example, that is clustered about by the ideas of failure, bankruptcy, anticlimax, the miscarriage of hopes, and a wilful withdrawal from the life of men; there is the closely related motive of exile, desertion, forlornness, or sterility; and there is, sometimes interacting with these others, the motive of treachery, fraudulence, and falsity. The characters who embody these motives belong to a few recurrent types. Half of them may be said to be objects of compassion, half of them objects of horror, or of a contempt that borders on horror. Almost none of them are the objects of heroic regard. Among the figures of pathos one moves past a melancholy series of exiles (Israel Potter), victims (Benito Cereno, Hunilla, the dupes of the Confidence Man), and failures (Bartleby, Jimmy Rose, Merrymusk the woodsawyer, "my elderly uncle" in "The Happy Failure," Hautboy in "The Fiddler"); and nothing is more expressive of the wintriness that lies over most of these pieces than the frequency with which Melville, who was of course in his thirties when he wrote them, identifies himself with some aged or elderly man, jolly perhaps and bright-cheeked, but with his youth and his hopes left equally far in his wake. Meanwhile, over against his victims and his bankrupts, there are the monsters who persecute or tyrannize over them (Babo and the other blacks, Oberlus, the dark-complexioned man in "The Tartarus of Maids," the constables and their like in *Israel Potter*) and there are the frauds and the cheats—the thimble-riggers, to use one of Melville's characteristic words—who try to take them in (the Lightning-Rod Man, Mr. Scribe in "I and My Chimney," the Confidence Man in his various guises).

Victims or victimizers, they all move about in the midst of scenes or objects that express, sometimes with singular power, the bleakness of the moral world they inhabit. The landscape, when we are conscious of it, is desolation itself: the dismal, clinker-bound landscape of the solitary Encantadas; the leaden-gray sea, becalmed and clouded, that surrounds a desert island off the coast of Chile; a frozen landscape of New England hills and ravines in the dead of winter; a group of sheds and brick-kilns encamped upon a wild waste moor, around which the blank horizon coils like a rope. Everywhere one's eye falls upon images of ruin or negation: the windows of an attorney's office open only upon dead blank walls; in an old village house there is a garret festooned with cobwebs and overrun with caterpillars, ants, and half-torpid flies; the rooms of another house, an old city mansion, are hung with faded wallpaper; the ship that tries to make her way into the island harbor looks, in her grisly dilapidation, as if her keel had been laid and her ribs put together in Ezekiel's Valley of Dry Bones. A rotting woodpile on a wooded mountainside; the stump of a ruined tower, like that of a prostrate pine; a huge old chimney whose uppermost bricks are covered with blotches like those of the measles—such are a few of the emblems of decay and death that meet our gaze at every turn.

Yet it somewhat misrepresents both the tone and the intention of certain of these tales to dwell only on these deathful symbols. A lightness of manner is attempted in a few of them, and if it often rings rather hollowly, it sometimes, as in "I and My Chimney," is convincing enough. The inner drama they all reflect, even the weakest of them, is Melville's struggle, during these black years, to heal himself of the suicidal nihilism in which *Pierre* had closed, and to work his way back, or forward, to the doubleness of vision he had adumbrated in *Moby Dick*. The lusty crow of Trumpet the cock, in "Cock-a-Doodle-Doo!", is a metaphor, though a pretty perfunctory one, of courage and cheerfulness triumph-

ing over defeat and death. The elderly uncle, in "The Happy
Failure," after the first stunning shock of disappointment
over his invention, pulls himself together bravely, and "with
a strange, rapt earnestness" exclaims to his young nephew:
"Boy, I'm glad I've failed. I say, boy, failure has made a good
old man of me. It was horrible at first, but I'm glad I've
failed. Praise be to God for the failure!" The flashing, opales-
cent insect that works its way out of the apple-tree table, the
table that has been brought down from the garret of decay,
is an explicit allegory of life victorious over death. More
genuinely Melvillean than any of these, however, and more
authentic in every way, are the gigantic tortoises in "The
Encantadas," dragging themselves sluggishly over the vitreous rocks of those islands like the woebegone spirits of
wicked sea-captains; dark and melancholy as their upper
surface is, their underside is of a faint yellowish or golden
tinge, and this underside is as real as the other: "The tortoise
is both black and bright."

Few of the symbols in these tales are as firsthand or as
memorable as this, and few of the tales themselves are anything but thin, pale, insubstantial, and fatally easy to forget.
There is something tasteless in doing more than mention
such painfully concocted and convictionless pieces, artistically
speaking, as "Cock-a-Doodle-Doo!", "The Lightning-Rod
Man," "The Fiddler," "The Bell-Tower," and "Poor Man's
Pudding." Nothing could be more apparent than the want of
spontaneity in writing such as this: it is Melville whipping
himself on, without a moment's support from his deeper
nature, to be a disposable and pliant writer for *Harper's* and
Putnam's, to furnish the magazines with the literary staples
they will pay for, to enroll himself in the efficient ranks of
the Curtises, the Mitchells, and the Warners. He has the unhappy air, all the while, of supposing that there is a formula
for doing this if he can only lay his hand on it; that there is a
tone of genteel informality, of essayistic levity, out of Lamb
or Leigh Hunt, that will buoy up almost any matter on its

smooth surface, and that one needs no more, for the substance of a printable story, than the woes of a poor cottager, the visit of a lightning-rod salesman, or a trip to the circus with a middle-aged fiddler, once a child prodigy. The meaning Melville wishes to communicate in these sketches is, as we have just seen, intensely serious and deeply personal, but the fashionable little form is hopelessly inadequate to it.

The wonder is that he sometimes succeeds, as after all he does in "Rich Man's Crumbs" and "Temple First" ("The Two Temples"), in "I and My Chimney" and "The Tartarus of Maids," in communicating, despite the wilful airiness of the form, a real grimness or anger or extremity of feeling. "Rich Man's Crumbs," in its incongruous magazinish setting, has a startling ferocity of effect that suggests an essay of Elia suddenly turning Zolaesque before one's eyes; not since *Redburn* or *White-Jacket* had Melville struck quite that note of savagely pictorial indignation. In "Temple First" he made such pointed use of the image of a fine new church on Broadway that the editor of *Putnam's* felt obliged to reject the piece. Melville represents himself in it as imprisoned by chance high up in the steeple of this temple, solitary in his lofty removal from the fashionable congregation below him, and thus in "a fitter place for sincere devotions." There is no great power in this easy symbolism, to be sure, but the piece has the air of springing spontaneously from observed experience, and it precisely fills, without overfilling, its small frame. More prolix, too prolix, is "I and My Chimney," which like many of these tales betrays the pathetic attempt to cover pages; yet in spite of its redundance, the tone of surface good humor, with a suppressed understrain of deep resentment, is so naturally kept up, and the great spinal chimney, with its dark subterranean base, is so expressive a symbol of a man's essential self, that the sketch would always be worth preserving from oblivion.

The most curious of all these pieces, though its purely imaginative value is a minor one, is "The Tartarus of Maids," an allegorical sketch which, in the manner he two or three times recurred to, Melville wrote as a pendant to "The Paradise of Bachelors." This latter sketch, the most Lamb-esque of them all in its convivial setting of the Temple, is a mild and rather tame affair, a merely essayistic reminiscence of an agreeable evening spent in London at a bachelor dinner in Elm Court. "The Tartarus of Maids" is a very different matter: it does not so much recall Charles Lamb as fore-shadow "The Penal Colony." The imagery is not that of cosy bachelor quarters, good food, cigars, and wine, but a solitary New England paper mill on the banks of a strange-colored stream, the Blood River, which one reaches, on a bitter January day, by driving along a dusky pass called the Mad Maid's Bellows'-pipe until one comes to a great hopper-shaped hollow, the Devil's Dungeon. Here one enters the mill itself and finds a force of thin, pallid girls, all virgins, tending the machinery—the machinery that consists of such devices as a series of stalls before each of which a long, glittering scythe is upthrust, two great vats full of white stuff like the albumen of an egg, and, in a room stifling with a bloodlike heat, a great iron framework of rollers, wheels, and cylinders, over which, with measured and unceasing motion, passes the pulp that, in precisely nine minutes, neither more nor less, is transformed before our eyes into various grades and types of paper. What makes the whole spectacle specially terrible is "the metallic necessity, the un-budging fatality" that governs it.

It is certainly true that, on one level, the one closest to the surface, Melville was allegorizing here the mechanical inhu-manity of the factory system, as he himself had observed it on his own drives from Pittsfield over to the paper-mills at Dalton near by; indeed, he had already expressed in *Mardi* his horror of the industrial Moloch. But all this, serious though it is, is hardly more than a film on the surface of "The Tartarus"; immediately below it, the sexuality of the sym-bolism is so visible and so insistent that one wonders at the printableness of the sketch in *Harper's* in the sedate year 1855. It was the year, as it happens, when Melville's fourth and last child was born, and "The Tartarus of Maids" expresses his appalled contemplation of what seems to lie beyond human control in the whole inexorable process of human reproduction. The great iron framework in the paper mill of the Devil's Dungeon is a grimly powerful symbol of this. As for the virginal operatives, pinched and pale, they are of course enslaved to the reproductive machine not as if they were themselves the bearers of children but in some more indirect and enigmatic sense. All women, even spinsters, like one or two of Melville's sisters, he seems to say, are enslaved to that machine, if only in their bleak sterility. Male bachelorhood may be equally sterile, but it is at any rate a jolly and even a festive sterility; female spinsterhood is mere coldness, enslavement, and death. Emotionally again, for the moment, Melville is identifying himself with the feminine; and the devil in this Tartarus of virgins is the dark-complexioned mill-owner, a bachelor.

In its minor way the sketch is perfectly realized; nothing could be finer than the wintry New England landscape, all snow-covered hills and ice-bound ravines, that is its setting. A far more ambitious and superficially more impressive narrative than "The Tartarus of Maids" is of course "Benito Cereno," the longest and most celebrated of the *Piazza Tales*. Unduly celebrated, surely. For neither the conception nor the actual composition and texture of "Benito" are of anything like the brilliance that has been repeatedly attributed to them. The story is an artistic miscarriage, with moments of undeniable power. It was a mistaken impulse this time that led Melville to rewrite another man's narrative; for, as everyone knows, the material of "Benito Cereno" was lifted bodily from a chapter in the *Narrative of Voyages and Travels* of a Yankee ship-captain named Amasa Delano. What Melville could do with the substance of other men's books, at his best, was magical, as we have already seen; but he largely fails to do this with Captain Delano's undecorated tale. Liberties, to be sure, he rather freely takes with his original, but strictly speaking he takes too few, and takes these too half-heartedly; and nothing is more expressive of the low pitch at which "Benito" is written than the fact that with one incident in his original Melville takes no liberties whatever: the scene of the actual mutiny on the *San Dominick*, which might have been transformed into an episode of great and frightful power, Melville was too tired to rewrite at all, and except for a few trifling details, he leaves it all as he found it, in the drearily prosaic prose of a judicial deposition.

Much praise has been lavished on the art with which an atmosphere of sinister foreboding and malign uncertainty is evoked and maintained through all the earlier parts of the tale. It is hard to see why. There are a few fine touches in the very first paragraphs—the "flights of troubled gray fowl," for example, skimming fitfully over the smooth waters like swallows over a meadow before a storm—but even in these first pages the rhythms of the prose are slow, torpid, and stiff-limbed; and they remain so, with a few moments of relief, throughout. Nor is the famous "atmosphere" of "Benito" created swiftly, boldly, and hypnotically, as Melville at his highest pitch might have created it; on the contrary, it is "built up" tediously and wastefully through the accumulation of incident upon incident, detail upon detail, as if to overwhelm the dullest-witted and most resistant reader. Many of the details, too, are of poor imaginative quality: the hatchet-polishers on the poop are rather comic than genuinely sinister; the symbolism of the key hanging round Don Benito's neck is painfully crude; and it needed only a very commonplace and magazinish inventiveness to conceive the scene in which Benito is shaved by the wily Babo. The traces of contrivance, and fatigued contrivance too, are visible everywhere in the story, and the sprinkling of clichés on every page—"a joyless mien," "the leaden calm," "fiends in human form," "a dark deed"—is only a verbal clue to the absence of strong conviction with which Melville is here writing.

In all the intangible senses, moreover, the substance of "Benito Cereno" is weak and disappointing. A greater portentousness of moral meaning is constantly suggested than is ever actually present. Of moral meaning, indeed, there is singularly little. This is partly because the two or three leading personages are too simply conceived to be the bearers of any greatly significant burden. Captain Delano is moral simplicity in a form that borders upon weak-wittedness, as his perversely misdirected suspicions end by indicating; Babo is a monster out of Gothic fiction at its worst, not at its best; and as for Don Benito, with his husky whisper, his tottering step, and his constant attacks of faintness, he is not only hopelessly unheroic, as an image of persecuted goodness, but he is not even deeply pathetic: in his state of nerveless moral collapse he can only be the object of a half-reluctant compassion. The result would be an undermining of the moral structure of "Benito Cereno" even if the action itself were not so wanting in large significance as it is. It is certainly very credible that a shipload of African slaves should break out into mutiny, and massacre most of the white officers and crew; it is equally credible that the surviving captain should be intimidated and even persecuted by the mutineers, and that their ringleader should be cunning enough to impose upon a simple-minded ship-captain visiting the bedeviled vessel. As a parable of innocence in the toils of pure evil, however, all this is singularly unremarkable, and we are forced to feel that Don Benito has gone very little beyond the rudiments when, at the end, he enforces the lesson his terrible experiences have taught him: "To such degree may malign machinations and deceptions impose. So far may even the best man err, in judging the conduct of one with the recesses of whose condition he is not acquainted." To be sure!

Neither the story nor the images in the real Captain Delano's book had succeeded in rousing Melville from the lethargy into which he was falling: a year or two earlier, when he wrote the long piece called "The Encantadas," he had worked in a much happier and more characteristic vein. It is true that "The Encantadas" is only a loosely organized series of sketches, with no very intense unity among them, rather than a completely fused whole; that one or two of these sketches, the fourth and fifth, are hardly more than pedestrian; and that the eighth sketch, the story of the Chola widow, Hunilla, touching though its subject is, is written in a manner so forcedly and self-consciously pathetic that not even its substance redeems it from the lachrymose. It remains true that nowhere in Melville are there grander images of utter desolation than those evoked, in the first three sketches, of the uninhabited and uninhabitable islands, the Galápagos, solitary, rainless, strewn with volcanic ashes, and overhung by a swirl of gray, haggard mist. "Apples of Sodom, after touching, seem these isles"; and in these first three wonderful sketches Melville's deepest, most despairing sense of abandonment and sterility is expressed. There is a powerful and intended incongruity, later, in the rather wild humor of the seventh sketch, the story of the Dog-King of Charles's Isle, with its Mark Twainish note of the mock heroic; and the ninth sketch, "Hood's Isle and the Hermit Oberlus," is as dismally convincing, in its dramatization of pure deviltry, the delight in degradation for its own sake, as "Benito Cereno" is unconvincing. One touch in this sketch— the spectacle of the hermit Oberlus planting his potatoes, with gestures so malevolent that he seems rather to be dropping poison into wells than potatoes into soil—is worth all the heaped-up horrors of "Benito."

There is an extraordinary harmony of image and feeling, of matter and meaning, in the best passages of "The Encantadas": it is only because the piece as a whole is so loosely and unequally formed that it falls short, as it does, of the highest effect. A few months earlier Melville had written the solitary tale of this period in which the substance seems wholly adequate to the mold, the embodiment wholly adequate to the meaning. This is "Bartleby"—or, to use the fuller title it originally bore in *Putnam's*, "Bartleby, the Scrivener: A Story of Wall-Street." Very little that Melville elsewhere wrote succeeds in suggesting quite so much, with means so simple and even stark, as "Bartleby" does. In nothing else that he wrote did he achieve, by the accumulation of details in themselves commonplace, prosaic, and humdrum, a total effect of such strangeness and even madness as this. It reminds one of no other American story, certainly no other of Melville's time; if it reminds one of anything, it is of some tale by Gogol or Dostoevsky, "A Madman's Diary" perhaps or "The Double"; some tale of life in a Petersburg government bureau, with a pathetic understrapper in the leading role, that creates, in the midst of dinginess, an effect of wildness and terror. Is the setting of "Bartleby" a Wall Street law office or the cosmic madhouse?

It is of course both, and "Bartleby" has the quality, small though its scale is, of suggesting a whole group of meanings, no one of which exhausts its connotativeness. On one level doubtless it is a parable of the frustrated relations between the man of letters and the man of affairs, between the artist's world and the world of practice. Bartleby, who is rumored to have been a clerk in the Dead Letter Office, has already learned that communication between man and man is mostly impossible; and now, like a thwarted writer, he is reduced to the mechanical and uninspired drudgery of a scrivener, a mere copyist of dull documents that have no creative meaning whatever. Something of Melville's own plight is obviously reflected here, and when one remembers that Melville's brother Allan, for whom he entertained no strong affection, was a Wall Street lawyer, one can hardly miss the personal bearing of Bartleby's behavior: he very soon discovers that he would "prefer not to" engage in copying or indeed in any useful activity at all, and thus succeeds admirably in frustrating his employer. The sound practical solution to the embarrassment thus created would seem to be simple enough: let Bartleby take a month's wages in advance and clear out. But, alas, fruitless as the relation between Bartleby and his employer is bound to be, it is one that, like all human relations, cannot be dissolved. They are both, despite their lack of mutual understanding, "sons of Adam," and the practical man soon learns, with a terrified sense that the world of ordinary sanity is beginning to reel about him, that he is irrevocably responsible for a madman.

Is he himself, meanwhile, as sane as he has always supposed? He begins to doubt it; and as for his other clerks, Turkey and Nippers, competent though they both are, they too are only half sane, sane each of them during only half the day. There is a core of the irreducibly irrational in human existence itself, and poor meek Bartleby is being a kind of philosopher, though a wrongheaded one, when he answers his employer's plea ("Say now, that in a day or two you will begin to be a little reasonable") by responding mildly: "At present I would prefer not to be a little reasonable." What he would prefer is quietly to withdraw from the business of living and retreat farther and farther into his own gentle indifference and apathy: there is a level on which "Bartleby" can be described as a wonderfully intuitive study in what would now be called schizophrenia, and in Melville himself there were certainly the germs of schizophrenic detachment. This is far, however, from being the deepest meaning of the tale. What Bartleby essentially dramatizes is not the pathos of dementia praecox but the bitter metaphysical pathos of the human situation itself; the cosmic irony of the truth that men are at once immitigably interdependent and immitigably forlorn. "Immediately then," says the narrator, alluding to Bartleby, "the thought came sweeping across me, what miserable friendlessness and loneliness are here revealed! His poverty is great; but his solitude, how horrible!" If poor Bartleby is a lunatic, it is not because other men are somehow merely sane; it is because he has accepted his forlornness as a final fact and forgotten the fact of dependence. To forget it is an act of suicide, and Bartleby very fittingly expires of physical and moral inanition, in the shadow of his prison wall.

It was not only in "Benito Cereno" that Melville in these years sought to whip up his flagging inventiveness by drawing on the substance of a printed book. The short novel, *Israel Potter*, which appeared in several installments in *Putnam's*, owed its subject and much of its substance to a little volume called *Life and Adventures of Israel R. Potter*, printed at Providence in 1824, which had fallen into his hands a few years earlier. It had caught his fancy at once, apparently, and he had formed the intention of making something of his own out of it; in the journal he kept while he was in England in 1849, he remarks, after buying a map of eighteenth-century London: "I want to use it in case I serve up the Revolutionary narrative of the beggar." Now, four or five years later, the thought of Israel Potter's story came back to him, doubtless with more poignancy than ever, and he served it up with a good deal of garnish of his own. It is easy enough to see what touched Melville's imagination in this firsthand little narrative, capably ghost-written, of a New England country boy, a rebel and a Revolutionary soldier, who had been successively a prisoner of the British, the leader of a mutiny, a fugitive from justice, the object of repeated pursuit, and then, after the end of the Revolutionary struggle, for long years an exile from his native land, living in an alien world, in poverty and oblivion. The real Israel Potter's fate, in short, as Melville puts it, was one "whose crowning qualities were its remoteness from relief and its depth of obscurity." No wonder the story came back to him now.

It was so natural for him to feel an imaginative kinship with the old Revolutionary exile that *Israel Potter* might conceivably have been a superb book. In fact, however, it is hardly more than a heap of sketches, some of them brilliant ones, for a masterpiece that never got composed. The use of another man's book, in this case as in "Benito Cereno," was a literary deadfall for Melville: the splendid transmutative power he had exhibited in *Moby Dick* was no longer in him, and the result here is that he follows his source either too closely or not closely enough. *Israel Potter* could have been a masterpiece only if Melville had treated the *Life and Adventures* as a mere hint for an otherwise free and unimpeded improvisation of his own; or, less probably, if he had stuck closely to the facts of Israel's life and endowed them, step by step, with an intensity and a richness of meaning that only he could give them. What he actually did was neither: what he did was to vacillate between faithfulness and freedom, following the original narrative conscientiously up to a certain point, then taking off for a series of episodes mostly of his own invention, and finally, in the last five chapters, returning wearily to his source and bringing the book to a hurried and perfunctory close. Naturally the product is not a narrative with any profound unity or serious inner coherence of its own.

It is disappointing that this should be true, for some of the separate episodes are Melville, if not by any means at his best, then certainly at his second best. When Squire Woodcock, the American sympathizer, hides Israel away in a secret chamber over his fireplace, a chamber that in the Middle Ages had been used by Templars as a sort of coffin-cell for penitents, and Israel escapes only after three days and nights, the symbolism of burial and resurrection is suggested with a curious homeliness of force. Later, when he labors in his sunken pit at the brickyard, Israel undergoes a similar experience of descent and re-emergence. The death-like dismalness of the brickyard itself is boldly drawn, but neither this nor the other incident has its full and deep symbolic effect because neither of them is prepared by, or itself prepares, any other significant action. Israel himself has hardly been characterized at all: he is, and remains, an almost featureless *recipient* of experience, a narrative convenience, not a character; and nothing that happens to him, as a result, takes on the fullness of meaning one looks for.

He learns as little from people as he does from circumstance. The only personal relationship into which he enters more than casually is the masculine comradeship that he strikes up with Paul Jones—or rather, since Israel is mainly passive here too, the affection that Paul Jones conceives for him. The figure of Jones, it must be said, is imagined with much of Melville's old energy: he strides into the book and out of it with a swagger of controlled ferocity that reminds one of the writer who conceived Ahab. A "disinherited Indian chief in European clothes," with a tattooed arm, a savage, self-possessed eye, and a look like that of an unflickering torch, this "Coriolanus of the sea," this "cross between the gentleman and the wolf," is both the largest and the most complex character in Melville's work between *Moby Dick* and *Clarel.* He falls short of the stature of Ahab or Mortmain, nevertheless, because he remains the actor in a mere episode; when he disappears from sight, his work is done, and nothing that follows is affected by his having appeared. Certainly Israel himself is unaffected by it: unlike Ishmael and Queequeg, Paul Jones and Israel cross each other's path without seriously touching each other's spirit, and the friendship is a fine accident, not a bond. It is the surest clue to the radical aimlessness and disunity of the book.

The Confidence Man is a still greater disappointment: it might so easily, one feels, have been a prodigious work. Even if perfectly realized, *Israel Potter* could hardly have been more than a strongly affecting parable of persecution and exile bravely undergone and patiently endured: so long as the original substance remained recognizable at all, the novel would have been condemned to a minor quality. *The Confidence Man,* on the other hand, if it had realized the whole intention behind it, might have been a vaster, more animated, and of course more modern *Ship of Fools*, or even an American *Gulliver*. There was a real breadth and largeness in Melville's *ideal* purpose, the comic exposure of a long procession of frauds and shams, national frauds and contemporary shams, and particularly the quackeries of a false humanitarianism, an insensate optimism. This, in fact, was the greatest of all subjects for satire in Melville's time and place, as bigotry and traditionalism had been the greatest of subjects in Rabelais'. Not only did the American world abound in large and small impostors of this stripe, but minds of great power had succumbed to the prevalent delusions, and Melville was not gunning, in theory at least, for small game. There was a real felicity, too, in the scene he conceived for his allegory; a Western scene, a river scene; a steamboat descending the Mississippi from St. Louis to New Orleans, crowded with a miscellaneity of passengers, discharging some and taking on others at river towns like Cape Girardeau or Cairo, and throwing them together in the risky promiscuity of frontier travel, or of human existence itself.

Conceptually and rather abstractly, there is a genuine ingenuity in a dozen details of *The Confidence Man*. It is April Fool's Day when the boat steams away from St. Louis, and the boat itself is carefully misnamed the *Fidèle*. The persons who embark on it—the Confidence Man in his various masks, his dupes, and his challengers—are, in intention, the Chaucerian pilgrims of this faithless pilgrimage, as representative of their world as the Pardoner and the Man of Law are of theirs; the agent of a Widow and Orphan Asylum among the Seminoles, a backwoods Methodist preacher, the agent of a certain Black Rapids Coal Company, a herb-doctor in a snuff-colored surtout, a Missourian in a coonskin cap and rawhide leggings, and other such. The agent of the orphan asylum has also invented a Protean easy-chair, so bejointed and behinged, so elastic and springy, that the most restless body and the most tormented conscience can somehow find rest in it.

This same personage has conceived the grand idea of a World's Charity, a sort of global Community Chest, the aim of which would be to organize all the charity in the world and quicken it with the Wall Street spirit. The herb-doctor dispenses, among other nostrums, the Samaritan Pain Dissuader, a pure vegetable extract warranted to remove the acutest pain in less than ten minutes; and in the men's cabin, late at night, there appears a rather sinister small boy who is peddling a curious patent lock for travelers and some little papers he calls Counterfeit Detectors.

There is a lively foretaste, in these touches, of Colonel Sellers's Infallible Imperial Oriental Optic Liniment and Salvation for Sore Eyes, as there is a foretaste of more than one touch in *Antic Hay* or *Brave New World*. In themselves these things distil a pleasant enough poison of comic acerbity, but the satirical force of *The Confidence Man*, such as it is, does not depend wholly on them: it breaks through, from time to time, in other, more purely dramatic forms. It breaks through, for example, in the herb-doctor's allegation that his herbs are nature's own and that "nature is health; for health is good, and nature cannot work ill"—a cheerful metaphysic that is repudiated by the bearish Missouri bachelor; he wants to know whether deadly nightshade is not a natural "yarb" too, and who it was if not nature who froze his teamster to death on the prairie. These are questions that the optimistic herb-doctor prefers not to consider seriously. The Confidence Man who follows him, the agent of the Philosophical Intelligence Office, professes to believe that boys (and of course men) are virtuous by nature, and is shocked when the same bachelor cries out: "Don't talk of boys; enough of your boys; a plague of your boys; chilblains on your boys!"—and continues, in a speech that quivers with a genuine ferocity of misanthropy, to announce that from now on he wants neither men nor boys to work for him, but only machines. This backwoods Swift is now convinced of the moral superiority of corn-huskers to boys.

An obsessive sense of the lurking treacheries in both nature and man is at the heart of this uncomforted book, and at least once it expresses itself with something like real eloquence. This is in the despairing speech of the country merchant as he sits over a glass of wine across from the man in a tasseled traveling cap, who has just told him the gloomy story of a broken marriage:

> "Ah," he cried, pushing his glass from him, "Ah, wine is good, and confidence is good; but can wine or confidence percolate down through all the stony strata of hard considerations, and drop warmly and ruddily into the cold cave of truth? Truth will *not* be comforted. Led by dear charity, lured by sweet hope, fond fancy essays this feat; but in vain; mere dreams and ideals, they explode in your hand, leaving naught but the scorching behind!"

In a culture in which boundless confidence was alleged to be reposable in nature, in other men, and in oneself, there was need of a book that should remind its readers of older and less flattering truths; and *The Confidence Man* might have been that book. In fact it is not; in fact it is little more than a tantalizing scenario for a book that never came into being. When he wrote *The Confidence Man* Melville's purely plastic power, his fictive and dramatic power, was at too low an ebb for him to give a rich imaginative embodiment to the things he wished to say; and *The Confidence Man* is not a great allegorical satire because it is not a living narrative. The setting Melville hit upon was the perfect one for such a book, but the setting is named or indicated rather than fully rendered. One is alleged to be on a steamboat descending the greatest of American rivers, but sensuously, pictorially, kinaesthetically, one has little or no sense of being on such a boat or such a river: the river does not flow and the steamboat does not move ahead, and one ends by feeling that one might equally well be riding on a train of cars or even sitting in the lobby of a hotel. There is an infinitely stronger sense of flow and movement in two pages of *Life on the Mississippi* than in all the forty-five chapters of Melville's book: the magical power of sensuous embodiment that had rendered the sea with such grandeur in *Moby Dick* had now failed him, all but wholly.

So, too, had the power of imagining a large or even a lively action: narratively speaking *The Confidence Man* is meager and monotonous. A work like *Candide,* which expresses somewhat similar thoughts, is still viable because, as a tale, it moves; moves swiftly, gaily, and variously; Melville's book is all but motionless. It is a series of conversations rather than an action, and though there is now and then a certain life in these conversations, on the whole they keep recurring to the same theme too compulsively, with too few variations, to be anything but unendurably repetitious. Who, moreover, are the speakers in these unending dialogues? Who are the pilgrims in this pilgrimage, this progress? There is a certain variety among them, and a few of them—the man with the gimlet eye, the Missouri bachelor, the ex-convict from the Tombs—have a jerky, marionettish, rather ghastly semblance of vitality. They have no more than that, and for the most part the others have not even so much: the herb-doctor is hardly distinguishable from the cosmopolitan, or the man in the violet vest from the man in the gray coat and the white tie. Great emphasis, indeed, is laid upon their costumes, in a curiously Melvillean way; and in a work of which the theme is falsity, there are good artistic reasons for this. Costumes are hardly enough, however, to bring a group of personages, even allegorical types, into full dramatic existence; and one has hardly finished the last page of *The Confidence Man* when the human figures in it begin to lose such outlines as they have had, and to drift irrevocably out of one's vision into a remote blur of indistinctness.

There is more than that amiss with the book; more that is much less tangible. *The Confidence Man* is one of the most *infidel* books ever written by an American; one of the most completely nihilistic, morally and metaphysically. It was not until a later era, the era of Mark Twain and Henry Adams, that other books comparable to it, in bleakness of rejection, were written. By the time he came to write it, Melville had quite forgotten, or lost his belief in, his own injunction to remember that "the tortoise is both black and bright." *The Confidence Man* might have been a work of great and bitter intensity, nevertheless, if, in the first place, Melville had not forgotten that blackness itself, unless it is to lose all its painterly value as blackness, needs some small area of light as a set-off; that, even in *Timon of Athens*, there is a Flavius. There is no Flavius in this book, and the result is a fatal want of moral chiaroscuro. Yet the real failure of *The Confidence Man* lies not so much in its monotone of blackness, as in the fact that, for the most part, that blackness is only a deep and dreary shade of gray. The actual effect of the book imaginatively is, after all, not terror but tameness; what in fact it expresses, except at rare moments, is not a passion of bitterness but a dull despondency of mistrust and disbelief. The Confidence Man is simply not, in any of his masks, a humbug of heroic proportions; his swindles are simply not swindles on a grand scale; they are the trifling and almost harmless dodges of a small-time thimble-rigger. What had happened to Melville that he could not imagine chicaneries more imposing than these?

The answer can only be that, in losing for the moment his last shred of confidence in both nature and man, he had lost his sense of the tragic. What was left was hardly more than psychoneurotic suspiciousness. This had not been true when he wrote *Moby Dick:* he had been capable, at that time, of imagining and embodying human error in association with human greatness, as he had been capable, in the figure of Fedallah, of dramatizing the principle of pure evil. He had had the capacity, too, to perceive in nature both the diabolic and the deific. He had had, in short, a vision of tragic grandeur. He had lost it by the time he came to write *The Confidence Man;* an obsession with littleness and falsity had taken its place; the question now was whether, and how, he could regain the vision he had lost.

Trophies of Peace

THE STATE OF SPIRIT in which *The Confidence Man* had been written was one that neither Melville nor any man who was not merely a patient could have persevered in: the light that symbolically expired at the end of that book was one without which continued existence would have been intolerable. He was still in his mid-thirties when he wrote it; he was to live for another thirty-five years, and that fact alone is eloquent of the slow, uncertain, irregular, and always precarious, but nevertheless effectual process of healing that took place in the years that just followed. What he attained, it is true, was a kind of infirm well-being at the best, an anxious and delicate stability of spirit that, at least until the very end, could be endangered by any strong pressure from without or from within. Twenty years after the period of *The Confidence Man*, at the time Melville was seeing his long poem *Clarel* through the press, his wife was so alarmed by the signs of his agitation that she could write: "If ever this dreadful *incubus* of a *book* (I call it so because it has undermined all our happiness) gets off Herman's shoulders I do hope he may be in better mental health—but at present I have reason to feel the gravest concern & anxiety about it—to put it in mild phrase."

This troubled spring of 1876 was pretty certainly not the

only period during those many years when Melville found himself threatened again by the whale's black flukes and the white shark's fin: he was never utterly free from peril, and he knew it. The great afflatus of spiritual power he had experienced when he wrote *Moby Dick* never recurred to him: his strongest hours now were feeble by the side of that. Yet the wonder is that he knew such hours at all, and there is no doubt that he did. The journey to the Holy Land, disappointing as it was on a certain level, had somehow proved to be a curative one; it was as if, after all, like Clarel and his companions, Melville had seen a fogbow form itself, noiselessly and iridescently, over the brackish waters of the Dead Sea. It had hovered there for only a moment or two, and then paled away and vanished. But he was never to lose the remembrance of it wholly.

It is true he had told Hawthorne at Southport that he had pretty much made up his mind to be annihilated; that he had all but renounced the hope of personal immortality. He never did entirely renounce it, but meanwhile the very attempt at renunciation had borne unexpected fruit: a renewed sense had come to him of the raw, primary value of life itself, mortal life, sentient life, however void of things he had once supposed essential to happy existence. He had doubted this value as sweepingly as a man can doubt it, short of self-annihilation, but now he had put the extremest doubts behind him, probably, once for all. "Life is, of all we know, God's best," he says in one of his Civil War poems, and at about the same time he writes, in a superficially jocose vein, to one of his brothers-in-law: "I once, like other spoonies, cherished a loose sort of notion that I did not care to live very long. But I will frankly own that I have now no serious, no insuperable objections to a respectable longevity. I don't like the idea of being left out night after night in a cold churchyard." He liked, in spite of everything, the idea of living, and there was a great preservative virtue in the mere preference.

It had been a bitterly difficult decision—a *schwer gefasste*

Entschluss—for he had had to confront the austere fact that living, for him, would inescapably mean a large forgoing. It would mean a forgoing of many things he had wished for, and of some things he had wished for with all the intensity of his nature. He had wanted fame; he had wanted friendship; he had wanted religious certainty. He could have none of these things, not at least at a pitch that answered to the vehemence of his need of them, and he was not disposed by temperament to be content with lower pitches. How much he had longed for fame it takes no rare intuition to discern: one's sense of it, however, is sometimes confirmed in small ways. One of the books Melville read with most interest in these years was a book called *The Genius of Solitude*, by a now forgotten writer, William R. Alger. In a passage in which this writer speaks of the wretchedness of most men of genius, Melville underlined this sentence: "It is not aspiration but ambition that is the mother of misery in man"—and appended in the margin his own initials. He must have felt that, in the terms in which he had conceived it, his work had failed. At another time he marked the last sentence of Arnold's essay on Heine: "That is what I say; there is so much power, so many seem able to run well, so many give promise of running well;—so few reach the goal, so few are chosen. *Many are called, few chosen*."

He himself, as he almost certainly felt, was not one of the few; there was a goal—of achievement, of recognition, of fulfilment—that he had not reached and would not now reach; and it was deeply characteristic of Melville not to wish to soften the contours of this hard truth. If he could not have fame on his own exacting terms, he would not have it on any terms: what he *would* have was its contrary, obscurity; and the cultivation of obscurity, the giving it a positive personal value, became one of the leading motives of his later life. In this, to be sure, he was by no means consistent with himself; his publishing four volumes of poems is a clue to that; he wanted obscurity, too, so to say, on his own terms. But this only means that the opposing forces in his nature continued their very unequal contest to the end.

As it was with the longing for fame, so it was with the longing for friendship. Perhaps he renounced this with even greater difficulty and with more frequent lapses of consistency. He had turned fifty or thereabouts when he wrote *Clarel*, and one of the central strands in that poem is the unappeased, perhaps unappeasable, but never quite abandoned reaching out for the perfect mutuality of an ideal friendship. It eludes Clarel himself with much the same mocking pertinacity with which religious faith eludes him, and yet he can scarcely bring himself to believe that his passionate need is a merely delusive one:

> Can be a bond
> (Thought he) as David sings in strain
> That dirges beauteous Jonathan,
> Passing the love of woman fond?
> And may experience but dull
> The longing for it? Can time teach?
> Shall all these billows win the lull
> And shallow on life's hardened beach?

There was terror for Melville in the thought that this might be true; in the thought that Toby Greene and Jack Chase and Hawthorne had been phantoms conjured up by his own need of them quite as truly as they had been independent beings, and that, even as phantoms, they would now have no successors. Yet, even before he had made the Palestine journey, this was the reality that experience had seemed to enforce upon him, and as time passed he not only came to terms with it, but, as he had done with the wish for fame, countered it with his passionate cultivation of solitude. Isolation he could endure; he could even take an austere satisfaction in it; what he could no longer endure was the "shallow" of ordinary sociability. In the end he came to accept the painful wisdom, which he found Schopenhauer expressing, that "no man can be in *perfect accord* with any one but himself," and that "genuine, profound peace of mind . . . is to be attained only in solitude." The torment of unreciprocated ardors was at any rate spared him.

On a still deeper lever Melville had been frustrated in his longing for some ultimate revelation of absolute spiritual truth. His need for religious certitude waged a long and always indecisive contest with his habit of doubting and questioning, his Montaignism, his unwillingness to accept truth from without, in another man's coin. Two souls dwelt in his bosom, as they familiarly did in Faust's, and one was as difficult to subdue intellectually as the other was eager for entire self-surrender. A kind of truce was eventually reached between them; the long contest ended in a spiritual armistice that was as near to true peace as a man of Melville's stamp could hope to come. One finds the evidence of it in the writing he did, inconspicuously and almost privately, during his middle and later years. Meanwhile, he himself had furnished the perfect phrase for the inner character of these years when he remarked, in *Moby Dick*, that after the doubts of adolescence and the disbelief that follows them, one comes to rest at last in "manhood's pondering repose of If."

Outwardly, during these decades, Melville's life was almost as devoid of incident as life in a not very strict monastery. It was by no means, however, free from adversity. He had returned from the journey to Palestine in somewhat restored health and spirits—to one of his nephews, a few months later, he appeared to be "in a fine flow of humor"—but he had come back to find the old, insistent practical problems as far from solution as ever, and the next three or four years were to be the most grinding he had known or would know. He had now pretty much abandoned the hope of supporting his family and himself as a professional writer. When the editors of the new *Atlantic Monthly* appealed to him for contributions, he replied that he would be very happy to send them something, but he added that he could not name the day when he would have anything ready, and in fact nothing ever came of the overture.

The dismal experiment of lecturing now followed, with the ill success we have seen, and when it was behind him Melville began again to climb the uphill path of the office-seeker. Early in the spring of 1861, just after Lincoln's inauguration, he betook himself to Washington with letters in his pocket to the new President and to Charles Sumner. Sumner received him cordially, and Melville was still adventurous enough socially to attend a levee at the White House one evening and to shake hands, among scores of others, with the President, whom he found both younger-looking and better-looking than he had expected. For some reason he believed that he had a kind of hope of obtaining the consulship in Florence, but while he was waiting in the anterooms of Washington, word came of Judge Shaw's death in Boston; it was necessary for him to return to New England at once, and this new attempt to get an appointment proved as fruitless as the others had done. The death of his father-in-law was doubtless a deep bereavement to Melville, and the whole period a mournful one, though it had a brighter aspect, in the worldly sense, in the fact that Lizzie received a substantial legacy in her father's will.

Very quickly on the heels of these events came the outbreak of the Civil War. Unexpectedly perhaps, even to himself, the final breaking of the storm, after so many lowering and thunderous years, burst upon Melville with a mingled effect of shock and exhilaration: apathetic he decidedly was not, and he remained anything but aloof or indifferent during the four violent years that followed. Doubtless he himself was surprised to find that his feelings were so much closer to those of his countrymen than he could have supposed before Sumter. Yet so it was. Complex and many-faceted they certainly were, as they were bound to be, but on the merely political level he found himself writing, like any good Northerner, that "Secession, like Slavery, is against Destiny," and that the implied end of secession was "the erecting in our advanced century of an Anglo-American empire based upon the systematic degradation of man."

He was to have many other thoughts before the whole struggle had receded into history, but meanwhile the poems he wrote during the war suggest how eagerly he had scanned the newspapers for word from the various fronts, how anxiously he had studied the bulletin boards when he was in the city, with what intensity of feeling he had watched the regiments of young volunteers march away to the South. Amid the pastoral quietness of Arrowhead and the Berkshires there was hardly a detonation of the great battles—Antietam, Shiloh, Lookout Mountain, the Wilderness—that did not reach his ear; and the human figures that now filled his imagination were those of the common soldiers, Northern and Southern, and their admirable leaders, Grant, McClellan ("unprosperously heroical"), Sheridan, Stonewall Jackson ("the Roman heart"), "dark Breckenridge," Lee. The war had gone far to restore to Melville his sense of human largeness.

Perhaps it was partly some restiveness of discontent with the quietude of life in Pittsfield, while events like these were taking place, that led him, the third year of the war, the year of Chancellorsville and Gettysburg, to sell Arrowhead at last to his brother Allan and move back once more to New York. Doubtless there were deeper motives too for this return to his native city, to "mast-hemm'd Manhattan," to the neighborhood of the docks and the harbor, and the nearness of the open sea. Doubtless he had wearied again of his inland life and was turning, as if by instinct, to at least the proximity of ocean. In the fall of 1863, at all events, he and Lizzie and the children took their departure from Arrowhead, and established themselves in the house at 104 East Twenty-sixth Street that was to be his home until his death.

Three years later his long, unromantic quest for government employment at last had its reward, somewhat patronizingly, and Melville was appointed a District Inspector of the Customs in New York. Then began for him the life that, in unprotesting and conscientious obscurity, he was to carry on for almost twenty years, a life as prosaic, as incongruous with his real life, as, after all, Chaucer's had doubtless been when he served as controller of customs in the port of London. It consisted of a daily walk back and forth from Twenty-sixth Street across town to some pier on the North River—in the later years, to piers far uptown—and there busying himself, from nine to four, at a salary of four dollars a day, boarding and inspecting incoming vessels, weighing and gauging their merchandise, inspecting the baggage of arriving passengers, and reporting to his superior officers any violation of the revenue laws that might come to his attention. It was not only a humdrum but a far from uncorrupted environment in which Melville found himself; he had hardly entered upon his duties when the great age of boodle and bribery got under way, and the pressure to participate in the low venality all round him was no doubt a steady and even an hourly one. Naturally he resisted it, quietly and inflexibly, and when, in 1877, two hundred employes of the Customs were dropped after an investigation, Melville's record was so unassailable that he was spared. His job had been in danger, nevertheless, as every man's was in that shabby era; it was in danger again in the middle 'eighties, but by this time Melville himself had ceased to be dependent on it. At the end of 1885, a man now in his middle sixties, he resigned the inspectorship voluntarily, and withdrew to his study and his books in Twenty-sixth Street.

When he told young Lemuel Shaw, just after his return from Palestine, that he was not going to write any more "at present," Melville may very well have doubted privately whether the will to write would ever visit him again. Certainly he had ceased to expect, or even to wish, to communicate with the large body of readers he had once had. Certainly he could no longer have expressed himself with any profundity of conviction in forms so available as those of the novel or the tale. But in spite of the rebuffs he had suffered, the expressive impulse itself, the plastic impulse, was still too strong in him to be denied; and it may have been within a few months after his return that he began to experiment with verse. Or rather to continue the experiment, for already in *Mardi* he had scattered through the narrative more than a score of incidental poems. They had all been of a singular badness, however, and it was not until *Moby Dick* and the fine hymn that Father Mapple reads out in his chapel ("The ribs and terrors in the whale") that Melville had given evidence of any natural command over verse. In the year or two before the war he appears to have devoted himself to his new interest steadily enough to have, at the end, a small manuscript volume of poems for Lizzie to circulate among publishers during his absence from home—for in the summer of 1860 he had made a voyage round the Horn to San Francisco. Nothing came of this new literary venture at the time, but the manuscript probably consisted of the poems based on his European and Near Eastern wanderings which he later included in *Timoleon* as "Fruit of Travel Long Ago."

The failure of these poems to find a publisher had not disheartened Melville enough to silence him, and the excitement produced in him by the Civil War found vent in a whole new group of poems, for the most part better ones, for which he did find a publisher; in 1866 Harper's brought out *Battle-Pieces and Aspects of the War*. The book was hardly noticed at all, but notice appears to have meant little to Melville now, and in the late 'sixties and early 'seventies, with what leisure he could find from his duties on the piers, he patiently composed the very long and extraordinary narrative poem, *Clarel: A Poem and Pilgrimage in the Holy Land*, which the generosity of Peter Gansevoort enabled him to have published by Putnam's in 1876. Nor did *Clarel*, ambitious though it was, exhaust Melville's poetic vein. In the last three or four years of his life he published privately, and in very small editions, two more volumes, *John Marr and Other Sailors* and *Timoleon,* and even after his death there were found among his papers two further sheaves of miscellaneous poems with the titles, "Weeds and Wildings" and "At the Hostelry."

For thirty years, in short, verse of some sort was the only form of expression Melville had any wish to turn to: the result could hardly fail to be a body of work that, however uninviting on the surface, would have a highly personal quality and a very particular interest. And in fact, though it has gone largely unread and very little criticized, Melville's work as a poet has far too marked and masculine a character to be neglected or forgotten. Except for Whitman, the best of whose work was done when the Civil War was over, Melville strikes one now as much the most interesting writer who was publishing verse in this country during those arid decades of the decline. It is true that poetry was a kind of afterthought for Melville, that he is primarily a prose writer, like Hardy or Meredith, and that when he writes verse one feels at once it is a prose writer who is at work. In a serious sense, indeed, his verse strikes one as more prosaic than much of his prose. This was not the result of inattention, however, but of a more or less conscious design: if Melville's poems have a strongly prosaic quality, this is their distinction, not their defect.

In the lean decades in which he was writing there seem to have been two directions in which American poetry could profitably move. One of these was the direction that Poe and Whitman had pointed toward, and that Lanier was now taking: an enhanced musicality, a more incantatory diction, an approach to the indirections and the allusiveness of symbolism. The other, which Emerson had hinted at, and which Emily Dickinson was privately taking, was the direction of colloquialism, the antipoetic, the gnomic and "metaphysical." One sees both tendencies in Melville, especially in *Bat-*

tle-Pieces, where poems like "The Conflict of Convictions," "A Canticle," and the well-known "Sheridan at Cedar Creek," have both the melodic line and the "indefiniteness" of language that suggest the more strictly symbolist impulse. But it was the other direction, the direction away from the "poetic," that became most characteristic of him. It is understandable that it should have been so. Romantic as his mind in its deepest reaches was, it had always had, like most powerful minds, the other bias too, the bias toward "facts," toward materiality, toward the unromantic impermeability of things. As time went on Melville became steadily more discontented, not with the essential metaphysics of romantic idealism, but with all that was visionary, enthusiastic, and illusory in the romantic habit of mind, especially in its decay. Like Hardy, at very much the same time, he wanted to see things, and struggled to see them, not in the light of his hopes and wishes but in that of the unideal Actual. He might have said, with Hardy, that he wanted to do justice to "the mournful many-sidedness of things." So that, even when he makes use, as he does in a poem called "The Æolian Harp," of a symbol that had been a favorite one with romantic poets, he uses it not to a romantic but to an actualistic end. "Listen," he says of an Æolian harp hanging in the window of a seaside inn:

> Listen: less a strain ideal
> Than Ariel's rendering of the Real.

His poems deal by preference with what are called unromantic subjects, or at any rate with the unromantic aspects of such subjects as they treat: we shall see a little later what these are. Meanwhile, the form and texture of his verse is highly expressive of the toughness of its substance. Even metrically, for the most part, it is so: it was hardly a disadvantage that Melville's ear was so uncertain as it was, both in prose and verse; capable of great feats of harmony and rhythm, and capable too of cacophonies that suggest the tone-deaf. There were states of special and intense feeling, during the Civil War, that moved him to utterance of genuine musicality, as we have just seen; but even then, and certainly later, what prevailed was not the lyrical or the melodic—not the logœdic measures he used with such skill in "A Canticle" —but a slow, weighty, tight, and rather toneless line that stubbornly refuses to give the ear an inappropriate pleasure. It came to be his characteristic line, and ungainly though it is, it is singularly appropriate to the nature of Melville's matter, as this stanza from a poem on the battle between the *Monitor* and the *Merrimac* suggests:

> Yet this was battle, and intense—
> Beyond the strife of fleets heroic;
> Deadlier, closer, calm 'mid storm;
> No passion; all went by on crank,
> Pivot, and screw,
> And calculations of caloric.

It is the metrics of an age of ironclads, and Melville's characteristic language too is highly suitable to the density of his substance. His impulse here was to put behind him the effete conventions of English romantic diction, its expansiveness, its orotundity, its remoteness from speech, in the interests of a vocabulary that should either be actively antipoetic or at any rate have a fresh expressiveness if only by virtue of its extreme rarity, oddity, or even ugliness. Quite inconsistently with this, it is true, Melville sprinkles his pages with the stalest of stale poetic archaisms, with withered leaves like *wight, elf, fain, deem, wend,* and *ween;* and there are far too many rhymes like *prime, clime,* and *sublime.* His strength lay elsewhere of course. It lay partly, for example, in the use of a powerfully prosaic vocabulary of terms that suggest business, industry, the law, and even mathematics; terms that, when they appear, have an extraordinary effect of blunt factuality or unromantic precision. One comes upon words like *escheat, underwriters, operatives, quotas, geometric, le-*

galized, and *functionally*. In a stanza of the fine poem, "March into Virginia," a purely legal term appears to excellent effect:

> Who here forecasteth the event?
> What heart but spurns at precedent
> And warnings of the wise,
> Contemned foreclosures of surprise?

Even bolder is the use, in "After the Pleasure Party," of two familiar but "unpoetic" words from arithmetic:

> What Cosmic jest or Anarch blunder
> The human integral clove asunder
> And shied the fractions through life's gate?

In lines like these Melville comes very close to some of the metaphysicals of the seventeenth century, and his language at such times, like Emily Dickinson's, has an unmistakable flavor of Donne's or Marvell's. Diction of this sort, however, is somewhat less pervasive than diction that suggests another tradition, the tradition of the Elizabethan playwrights and, in Melville's own century, of Browning—and indeed Carlyle. He had, like them, a love of the expressively rare and strange, even the grotesque, in language, and he looks forward here, as in other respects, to poets of our own time. The special quality of his verse, as of his prose at its best, depends very importantly on these rare, archaic, or dialectical terms or terms that he himself, with conscious oddity, invents. They are never poetic in the Wordsworthian or Tennysonian sense, but they are sometimes admirable in their pictorial or tactile precision, as the dialectical word is in this line from "The Berg": "Seals, dozing sleek on sliddery ledges." Melville likes such strongly physical, uneuphonious words, and he likes words of his own coinage, or recoinage, especially when a certain grotesqueness in their make-up redeems a line from tameness. He abounds in curious adjectives in -*y* or -*ful*— *roofy, Juny, fally, flushful, hintful, fraudful, charmful*—and in nouns rather forcibly derived from verbs—*scrutineer*, *transcender, remindings, mufflement, disenslavers*, and the noun in this line, again from the poem on the iceberg: "Impingers rue thee and go down." In his verse, as in his prose, he is not very inventive of verbs, but he is much given to odd participles based on nouns—*vowelled, foliaged, glenned, journaled, heathenized*—and in *Clarel* there is a striking line in which the night skies over the Arabian waste are described as "Bee'd thick with stars in swarms how bright." Only rarely does Melville devise an active verb from a familiar noun, as he does in another line from *Clarel;* he is speaking of the grass on the uplands near Bethlehem:

> Lower it crept as they went on—
> Grew in advance, and rugged the ground.

Language such as this is everywhere in Melville's poems, but these poems are not, after all, wholly dependent on nonce-words and rare locutions for their verbal intensity. Again and again, on the contrary, Melville exhibits his native mastery over language by his use of a familiar or not unfamiliar word in a manner that suddenly confers on it a linguistic *mana*. Sometimes the word is a single adjective or verbal adjective unexpectedly used:

> The moody broadsides, brooding deep.

> Each bloomed and died an unabated Boy.

> (*Weird John Brown*).

Sometimes it is a familiar enough verb:

> (What like a bullet can undeceive!)

> Nirvana! absorb us in your skies,
> Annul us into thee.

> And disillusion opens all the shore.

In other lines it is not easy to distinguish between the potency of single words and that of the metaphor:

With golden mottoes in the mouth.

Hunt then the flying herds of themes!

Ha ha, the rust on the Iron Dome!

When Asia scarfed in silks came on
Against the Greek and Marathon.

The spider in the laurel spins,
The weed exiles the flower.

There is a certain suggestion, in these last few lines, as there is elsewhere in Melville's poems, of the lapidary manner of Landor, as there is also of the manner of the French Parnassians, especially Gautier, though Melville could hardly have known those poets at first hand.

Quite as far from the conventionally poetic as his language is Melville's highly idiosyncratic imagery. One has to make a simple distinction here between the purely pictorial imagery, the imagery given by the subjects themselves, and the true metaphors. The pictorial imagery of *Battle-Pieces*, for example, is of course the imagery of war, and here it is not too much to say that Melville is the first poet in English to realize the meaning of modern technological warfare, and to render it, grimly and unromantically, in his work. He is the Brady of Civil War verse, in a sense in which none of the others, not even Whitman, was. Melville's war poetry is not mainly that of fitfully flaming bivouac-fires or mystical vigils kept on the field at night. It is the harsher poetry of mathematics and machinery, of what he calls "plain mechanic power"; the poetry of the military engineer and technician, of gunboats and torpedoes and ironclads, of grape and canister, of earthworks and rifle-pits and batteries, of wagons mired in the mud and shrapnel screaming through the air. Melville discerned that the day of the dragoon and the grenadier, as well as of "the carved and castled navies," was past and gone, and that the day of the military railroad and the torpedo-boat had come to stay. Though this is only one of

its dimensions, *Battle-Pieces* derives much of its force from
Melville's conscious intention to place war

> Where War belongs—
> Among the trades and artisans.

This, at any rate, was his conception of modern war as an
activity. It was very far from being his only feeling about the
Civil War as a crisis in American history. On this plane, his
response to the catastrophe was extremely complex; anger,
pity, revulsion, the love of heroism, the hope of reconciliation
—all these, and more, were elements in it. But his deepest,
most instinctive apprehension of the war was none of these,
but as the metaphors tell one, a radical and ambiguous emotion of mingled horror and elatedness, of terrified jubila-
tion. It was the appalled consciousness of looking on at some
wild but splendid convulsion in the natural world; some sudden and shocking eruption, upon the smiling scene, of
elemental forces of destruction and re-creation. *Battle-Pieces*
is dominated by the imagery of stars, meteors, comets,
eclipses, and Northern Lights; of winds and storms, thunder
and lightning, frost and ice; of earthquakes, cataracts, rushing rivers, the sea, and the primordial deeps. The language
of comets, storms, and thunder, it is true, suggests itself even
to the ordinary patriotic bard and to the war correspondent
himself, and sometimes Melville's naturalistic metaphors
("the hurricane from the battery") are banal enough.

Mere adherence to convention, however, will not account
for the intense force of the elemental imagery in the best
poems of *Battle-Pieces*. What lies behind them is something
more profound and personal than that. This is certainly true,
in "The Portent," of John Brown's "streaming beard" seen
as "the meteor of the war"; it is true, in "Aurora Borealis,"
of the "steely play" of the Northern Lights that sink and fade
with the coming of peace; it is true, in "Apathy and Enthusiasm," of the "thunder-cracks of massy ice In intensity of
frost"; and it holds, in a poem like "A Canticle," for the

strange, cloudy, confused, but exciting imagery of precipice, gorge, cataract, and thunder, or in a greater poem, "The Conflict of Convictions," for the complex imagery of returning comets, wreck-strewn sands, the miner in the cave, and "Derision" stirring "the deep abyss," laying bare the "slimed foundations" of the gulf. In the poem "Misgivings" the metaphor of the tempest is used with magnificent freshness to suggest the tensions of the months just before the war and the outbreak of violence for which they were preparing:

> With shouts the torrents down the gorges go,
> And storms are formed behind the storm we feel:
> The hemlock shakes in the rafter, the oak in the
> driving keel.

There was a mingling of dismay and exhilaration in all this, and *Battle-Pieces* makes it clear that the war had roused Melville, for the time at least, from the mood of disbelief and apathy into which he had fallen in the 'fifties, and given him an invigorating sense of participation in the emotions of his countrymen generally. The long poem, *Clarel*, is much more a product, from this purely historical point of view, of the mood of reaction, letdown, and anxiety into which, like other writers, Melville fell in the rather squalid years that followed the war. The poem has a great interest on that level, but its interest is by no means limited to the historical. In general *Clarel* is an extraordinary work, a very full and rich expression of Melville's later intellectual life, and one regrets that its uninviting form and its extreme length—it is perhaps twice as long as *Paradise Lost*—seem destined permanently to keep it from being much read.

Yet it belongs to a literary type that is rare in American literature even now, and we can hardly afford to undervalue it. It is not a poem of romantic and picturesque wanderings in the style of *Childe Harold* (though it too is a "pilgrimage"), but a novel of ideas in verse; it harks back to a long poem like *The Excursion*, and in some of its qualities it looks forward to a work of our own time like *The Magic Mountain*. As with such works, its narrative line is, as it ought to be, of the most tenuous: what counts is not the action—there is the least possible of that—but the drama of thought and argument that, however indecisively, is enacted among a group of strongly characterized and contrasted people, thrown together by the chances of travel. It is deeply characteristic of Melville of course that the personages of *Clarel* should be, however joggingly, on the move. Clarel himself, a young divinity student tormented by doubts, a "pilgrim-infidel," has arrived at Jerusalem on his travels. In the midst of the holy places he strikes up a variety of casual acquaint-anceships, and falls in love with a young Jewish girl, Ruth, whose father, an immigrant to Palestine from America, is killed by hostile Arab raiders. In the period of mourning that follows, Clarel is forbidden by Jewish custom to see anything of the girl, and in his grief and restlessness he sets out with a group of companions on horseback on a pilgrimage that takes them to the Jordan, the Dead Sea, the Greek monastery of Mar Saba in the mountains, then Bethlehem, and at length Jerusalem again. On his return to the city Clarel finds that Ruth has died of grief in his absence, and his own future seems more uncertain than ever.

The poem ends with an inconclusiveness so conscious that it cannot be regarded as an artless defect. Meanwhile, however, Melville has thrown obstacles in the way of even the best-disposed and most receptive reader. The chief of these is the form and much of the language of the poem. The metrical dryness and tightness that, again and again, are in keeping with the emotion in Melville's short poems are of intermittent felicity here. *Clarel* is written throughout, except for some incidental lyrics, in Melville's version of the irregularly rhyming octosyllabics that Scott and Byron had used in such poems as *Marmion* and *The Bride of Abydos*. These were not very good models for Melville, who neither had nor needed to have the empty, indefatigable fluency of such writers; and much of the time his tetrameters are painfully clogged and gnarled even for a poem of which the movement is quite properly a prosaic one. They force him back constantly on ugly ellipses ("At glimpse of face of countryman") and grotesque inversions ("Up with him sat he all that night"); and since Melville was uncertainly resourceful with rhymes, the form betrayed him into the repeated use of dull combinations like *elf* and *self*, *erst* and *versed*, *wight* and *light*. The pages of the poem are strewn with archaisms of the wrong kind—*lone* and *parle* and *hap* and *eld*—and the strongly prosaic manner is in repeated danger of tumbling into Wordsworthian platitude ("Much he admired the impressive view").

Yet it would be easy to exaggerate and throw out of focus the purely stylistic crudities of *Clarel*. At the worst they are far from fatal blemishes in a poem of which the interest is so great as this poem's is. To the reader with a vigorous enough taste to accept these clumsier mannerisms the form and language of *Clarel* will in other ways seem admirably suited to its intention. Even the octosyllabics, when they break free from their clogs, as they repeatedly do, will end by striking him as after all the right measure for a poem that aims at a middle tone between poetry and prose. They move with less stateliness, with a more pedestrian gait, than any blank verse could do, yet they lend themselves at need to other kinds of expressiveness: to a novelistic nicety of touch in characterization, to a strong and often a grim rendering of scene, and again and again to a bitter eloquence in speech. A verse style that can adapt itself to purposes so various as these, and adapt itself energetically, is hardly a failure; and the fact is that, when he wrote *Clarel*, Melville's linguistic and compositional powers were passing through a kind of autumnal rejuvenescence.

It is easy to cite passages in which he stumbles, but these should be countered by passages in which, even in the most delicate verbal sense, the sharpness of his eye and the precision of his language combine to produce an effect of the happiest exactness. They do, for example, in the lines that describe a train of Moslem pilgrims in the desert, who

> Spread the worn prayer-cloth on the sand,
> Turning them toward the Mecca stone,
> Their shadows ominously thrown
> Oblique against the mummy land.

Or take the passage in which Vine's special quality of almost virginal unworldliness is sketched:

> Pure as the rain
> Which diamondeth with lucid grain
> The white swan in the April hours. . . .

Or the lines at the end of the fine canto, "The High Desert," in which "each wrinkled Arab Bethlehemite," gazing down on the travelers from an adjoining ledge as they climb toward Mar Saba, is said to resemble a kite

> On Sidon perched, which doth enfold,
> Slowly exact, the noiseless wing. . . .

Visual and emotional truthfulness could hardly be more complete than it is in passages like these, and in general the sense of place, the feeling for scene, is masterly in *Clarel:* it counts here very much as it does in some novels, *The Magic Mountain* for example, that are like it in other ways. The look and tone of Jerusalem, of the Dead Sea, of the stark Palestinian landscape generally, had sunk deep into Melville's memory, as tenacious of such things as that of some great painter; and now, after the lapse of more than a decade, he renders them with superb boldness and breadth. Details are seen at times with a *trompe-l'œil* exactitude, but they are all subordinated and held in place by one paramount, overarching impression, the unspeakably desolate impression of aridity. The physical scene against which the action of *Clarel* takes place is a scene of intolerable and apparently hopeless drought, like that of the most famous poem in our own time, and of course to a very comparable symbolic effect.

Jerusalem itself, the city of David, is now "a stony metropolis of stones," parched, dusty, gray, and ruinous, crumbling slowly into a heap of melancholy detritus like some merely geological site: the literal Mount Zion, like the faith it symbolizes, is subsiding, grain of sand by grain of sand, back into the submerged sea-bed of the spirit. All round it are flint-strewn plains, arid valleys, stony uplands, and the calcined masses of the Judaean mountains. One approaches the Dead Sea through a valley like "Pluto's park," enlivened with stunted and twisted shrubs, and floored with a nitrous mud. One comes upon the Sea itself to find it rimmed round by beaches where "all is charred or crunched or riven." The surface of its waters is as vitreous as the leagues of ice that lie about the pole. What wonder if, as the travelers later move upward toward the heights of Mar Saba, one of them should leave behind him, on a ledge they have lingered at, a cairn of dry stones as a monument to all this barrenness?

The travelers themselves and indeed the characters altogether are on the whole a remarkable assemblage of distinct and freshly noticed people. The best of them have just the quality the personages of *The Confidence Man* so largely fail to have, the quality of reconciling poetic representativeness with a real sharpness of outline as individuals. Unlike the characters in *Pierre*, moreover, they owe, most of them, little or nothing to literary convention and a great deal to Melville's own looking about him: they are "types" that had mostly not got into fiction before, but that were going to appear more frequently in the future. Not all of them, by any means, emerge into high relief or are intended to do so. Clarel himself, a kind of *Sorgeskind* like Hans Castorp, is too blank a character, too passionless a pilgrim, to exist with anything but a neutral sort of vitality. Ruth and even her mother are dimly seen and vaguely felt, like most of Melville's women, and they are promptly left behind. The amateur geologist, Margoth, with his irreverent hammer and his notion that there should be a railway from Mount Olivet to the sea, with a station at Gethsemane—Margoth is the clown of this prevailingly somber drama, and he has a real comic value as such. Yet only that; as an embodiment of the scientific spirit of the age, the single one in the poem, Margoth is too angry a caricature to carry any serious imaginative conviction. As well might Melville have embodied the religious spirit in some coarse backwoods revivalist.

The forestage is occupied not by these people, not even by Clarel himself, but by five finely conceived and fully realized characters. The shy and taciturn Vine, toward whom Clarel is emotionally drawn, is, as we have already seen, a fictive presentment of Hawthorne, with his peculiar charm and his peculiar disappointingness: there is no account of Hawthorne that outdoes this one in lambency of truthfulness. Where, on the other hand, Melville had encountered his darkly pessimistic Swede, Mortmain, the disillusioned revolutionary, one does not know. He suggests that other disenchanted enthusiast, the Solitary in *The Excursion*, but there were men after '48, just as there were after '89, whose thwarted hopes had soured in their spirits and converted them into unrelieved Nay-sayers. Mortmain is a recognizable man of his century, and indeed an ancestor of men in our own generation: there was naturally more than a little of him in Melville himself, and when, standing on the shore of the Dead Sea, he leans over, scoops up a handful of its briny water, and madly tries it, he is enacting a small, bitter ritual that could not be more Melvillean. There is also something of Melville himself in the much-traveled American, Rolfe, with his sunburned features, his fine forehead, his air in the saddle of being an Osage scout or a gaucho of Paraguay, "a messmate of the elements." With a genial heart and an austere mind, Rolfe is much given to study and thought, but he is "no scholastic partisan," and his chief role in the poem is to question all one-sided partisanships, all oversimplified and over-confident affirmations. His many-sidedness, in fact, is so determined, so unrelenting, that it ends by seeming to Clarel somehow hollow; and there is self-criticism as well as self-portraiture in the figure.

The fullest and most brilliant characterizations of all, however, are those of the two most antithetical persons in the poem, the English parson, Derwent, and the ex-Confederate soldier, Ungar. These two men embody very nearly the extremest poles in the intellectual life of that era; the extremest poles, moreover, that Melville himself could encompass with any sort of imaginative sympathy. For there is such sympathy even in the portrait of Derwent; no character in all of *Clarel* is more completely rounded out than he. There are few personages in American fiction indeed more fully *treated* than this Broad Church parson, optimistic, liberal, humane, apparently incapable of serious doubts and unwilling to dwell on the dark realities; a man whose clerical coat sits upon him and whose cloth cape floats about him as lightly as his opinions. He represents much that repelled Melville in his contemporaries; much more on one level than Ungar does, the descendant of Maryland Catholics on one side and of an Indian woman on the other, with his copperish high-boned cheeks, his long black hair like a Cherokee's, and his slouched reserve of strength and grace in the saddle. He is something such a young Southerner as James was later to "do" in Basil Ransome of *The Bostonians*, but Ungar is far harsher than Basil Ransome, more sweeping in his misanthropy, savager in his jeremiads against the canting cruelty of Anglo-Saxon industrialism and the "civic barbarism" toward which, as he sees it, the "harlot on horseback," Democracy, is driving America.

He expresses himself with such quivering eloquence that one is bound to read much of Melville's own darkest feelings into his speeches. They are certainly there. Yet no more than any one of the other characters is Ungar a simple, unambiguous spokesman for Melville's attitudes, as he takes pains in an undertone to hint. The great purpose Ungar serves, and serves admirably, is to furnish a vent for Melville's blackest apprehensions for the future and his gloomiest doubts about mankind. Yet the very intemperance of Ungar's misanthropy is intended to suggest how unphilosophic a state of mind it voices, and Clarel himself reflects that, if man be in fact what the young soldier says he is, if "the ever-upbubbling wickedness" be the whole truth about him, the natural question that follows is: "What's left us but the senses' sway?" Meanwhile, one misses much of the intellectual tragicomedy of *Clarel*, much of its deceptively quiet play of irony, if one fails to observe how the cheery Derwent, who begins by striking one as a merely fatuous Yea-sayer, grows in grace as the poem proceeds, developing lights and shades of personal quality one had not suspected, inspiring a more and more genuine liking in the very Melvillean Rolfe, and giving expression in his modest and kindly manner to insights that Melville elsewhere expresses as his own. One must attend to both Ungar and Derwent, as well as to some of the others, if one wishes to distinguish all the intonations of Melville's own voice.

These are the great foreground figures of *Clarel*, but they by no means divide the whole human scene among themselves. On the contrary, the desolation of the natural scene and of the inner spiritual world is matched and countered by the animation and almost the crowdedness of the social landscape. Nowhere else, not even in *Moby Dick*, does Melville fill the stage more populously, though without confusion, or succeed more brilliantly in giving vitality to secondary and even to incidental figures: to such figures as that of the saintly and simple-witted visionary, Nehemiah, or the luxury-loving Greek merchant from Salonika, or the silent and stately Druse guide, Djalea, on his beautiful Arabian mount. The least omissible of all the minor figures, however, is the series, now so much to be foreseen, of comely youths; youths whom Clarel or the whole group of them encounter briefly, and who embody in their various ways the two life-tendencies between which Clarel is torn. There are the youths who, like the Syrian monk on the Mount of Temptation and Brother Salvaterra, the young Tuscan monk in Bethlehem, are the representatives of a passionately ascetic spirituality; and there are those who, like the Greek merchant's lighthearted son-in-law, Glaucon, and the charming young commercial traveler from Lyons, are the representatives of a carefree and pleasure-loving worldliness. The beauty of holiness and the *gai saber*—must one choose between them? Impossible to answer simply, but it is worth remarking that, after meeting the young Lyonese in Bethlehem, Clarel has his one moment of relief from paralyzing doubt, his one moment of hopeful and even buoyant resolution.

The moment does not last long: a few hours later, after nightfall, the pilgrims have regained Jerusalem; Clarel comes upon a group of men in the Jewish cemetery burying Ruth and her mother by lantern-light, and in the bitter grief that descends on him, all the old doubts and vacillations return. Meanwhile, the real purpose of this versified novel has been to body forth, in a hundred visual and dramatic ways, the spiritual ordeal of an age in which, for many men, religious faith had ceased to be possible on the old grounds without ceasing to be desperately necessary. "That vast eclipse . . . we undergo"—this is the real setting of *Clarel*, and no American work of the imagination contains a fuller or more sensitive record of that spiritually darkened time, as it was for certain minds. From a rigorously philosophic point of view, the dialectical play in *Clarel* is by no means always impressive: Melville's mind was not in that sense a rigorous one, and the issues between religion and science, dogma and freedom, idealism and "this naturalistic knell," are not always presented in a manner that any longer imposes itself on the reflective intelligence. That, however, is only partly relevant to a judgment of the poem: its real interest, as one need not say, is an imaginative one. It abounds in clues, nevertheless, to the "philosophy" that, unsystematic and intuitive as of course it was, became the spiritual home of Melville's declining years. What this was we ought to attempt to say, but meanwhile we must glance at the volumes of verse that followed *Clarel* after the lapse of more than a decade.

The physical setting of *Clarel*, as we have seen, is the landscape of Palestine; the land, not the sea, is the setting for this drama of faith and doubt. A certain dwindling of intellectual boldness is betokened by that very fact, and yet the sense of the sea is recurrently present in *Clarel* after all. It makes itself felt in a series of powerful images of the ocean and of ships; one turns to the later volume, *John Marr and Other Sailors*, and encounters such imagery on every page. Naturally enough, given the title and the substance of the little collection; but in any case there can be few poets anywhere, since Camoëns, more genuinely seagoing than Melville is in this volume. *John Marr* smells of salt air and seaweed, it reverberates with the uproar of storms at sea, as very little poetry in English or perhaps any modern language does. For most poets to whom the sea has been a profound symbol—for Heine, for Whitman, for Rimbaud—it has been the sea mainly as a landsman would know it and feel it, the sea as envisaged from the shore or in fancy, a symbol of freedom, of liberation, of infinitude. Melville is a rare case of a serious poet who has also been a sailor before the mast, and the sea exists in his verse with a kind of cruel, bitter, but still salubrious reality with which it exists in few of the others.

It appears mainly as a symbol of destructiveness and terror; it is still the sharkish sea of *Moby Dick*. The sea-creature that appears most characteristically is in fact the shark; the shark that already, in *Battle-Pieces*, "glides white through the phosphorous sea," and that reappears here as the ferocious Maldive Shark, with its saw-pit of a mouth and its charnel of a maw. Even the seafowl which appear, and there are several of them—gannets and petrels, the white goney, the man-of-war hawk—are birds of ill omen for the most part. The most sinister of them are the haglets or shearwaters that appear in

the fine narrative poem, "The Haglets." Inscrutably following with "untiring wing and lidless eye" the flagship that is
sailing proudly home from a great victory over the Spanish
fleet, these birds portend the ironic disaster that overtakes
the vessel:

> The hungry seas they hound the hull,
> The sharks they dog the haglets' flight;
> With one consent the winds, the waves
> In hunt with fins and wings unite,
> While drear the harps in cordage sound
> Remindful wails for old Armadas drowned.

The Admiral's ship is driven on a lee shore by a tempest
when the vessel's compass is deflected by the heat of the captured Spanish swords: the very tokens of victory have become
the means to destruction. And the dominant symbol in *John
Marr* is indeed the symbol of wreck and disaster: a deserted,
dismasted, drifting, waterlogged vessel in "The Æolian
Harp"; in "Far Off-Shore" a deserted raft flying its now
ineffectual signal; a martial ship, in "The Berg," that strikes
an iceberg and goes down without jarring the least spur or
pinnacle of the great cold mass. The dead indifference of the
iceberg stands of course for the feelingless unconcern of the
natural world generally, but there is restoration and a new
health in the transcendence of this hurtful knowledge. Such,
at least, is the last note struck in the volume, in the final little
poem of the group called "Pebbles":

> Healed of my hurt, I laud the inhuman Sea—
> Yea, bless the Angels Four that there convene;
> For healed I am even by their pitiless breath
> Distilled in wholesome dew named rosmarine.

Many of the poems in the last collection Melville printed,
Timoleon, seem weaker, tamer, and more conventional than
those in either *Battle-Pieces* or *John Marr*. This may be because some of them were pretty certainly written years

earlier, in the late 'fifties, when he was only beginning seriously to experiment with verse and had not arrived at any strongly featured manner of his own. One whole group of them were based on the impressions that had come to him in Europe and the Near East at the time of his Palestine journey, and as one would expect, their imagery is that of sightseeing, almost that of the guidebook. They abound in palaces, villas, and gardens, in statues and paintings, in temples, cathedrals, and pyramids. Only occasionally does this imagery of the *sehenswürdig* really glow with a metaphorical luminousness, but it does so, at the least, in "Pisa's Leaning Tower" (with its metaphor of suicide), in the extraordinary Venetian poem, "In a Bye-Canal," and in the familiar little exercise in the style of Landor, "The Ravaged Villa." For the rest, *Timoleon* would be memorable if only for the now well-known and certainly remarkable poem, "After the Pleasure Party," with its renewed use, after *Battle-Pieces*, of large astronomical images—"starred Cassiopeia in Golden Chair" —and of other elemental images, such as prairie fires and geysers, which are symbols here of sexual desire.

The poems that Melville left in manuscript were mostly, as it appears, the work of his very last days. The larger number of them are quiet to the point of colorlessness, though there are a few fine exceptions to this, but what is most noteworthy about the sheaf called "Weeds and Wildings" and the other miscellaneous poems is the almost complete transformation of mood, after *Battle-Pieces* and *John Marr*, which they embody. Quite gone is the elemental imagery of the one and the disastrous nautical imagery of the other; in their place appears the homely imagery of countrified retirement and quiet domestic simplicity. Nothing could be more eloquent of the unprotesting tranquillity that Melville achieved at the end of his life than this low-pitched poetry of weeds and wild flowers, of red clover, hardhack, and sweetbriar, and of a bird life as far as may be from that of *John Marr*; of robins, bluebirds, owls, meadowlarks, and hummingbirds.

The prose dedication to "Weeds and Wildings" makes it clear that the red clover is being consciously used as a metaphor of humility, of the commonly and broadly human—almost as the grass is in Whitman—because it is "accessible and familiar to everyone" and "no one can monopolize its charm." Nor is it only the clover that expresses this; so, too, do most of the symbols in these poems. The tasseled corn of the Western prairies appears, in a poem called "Trophies of Peace," as an emblem of unwarlike, undistinguished, unhistoried, tranquil human living; and when, in a very late poem, "The Lake," Melville seeks to express his sense of the primordial rhythms of death and rebirth, of decay and renewal, he does it through the image of a small New England lake in the midst of pines, from the banks of which one has glimpses, on the uplands beyond, of barns and orchards and cornfields, basking in the autumn sunlight. It is an extraordinarily peaceful and pastoral coda to a body of work that had been predominantly stormy.

In the moral and intellectual sense, that is the deep interest Melville's poems have: from *Battle-Pieces* to "Weeds and Wildings" one follows the progress of a great redintegration, a great though never a perfect recovery of wholeness and well-being. There had been a point at which Melville's universe had all but disintegrated about him and reverted to chaos and night; he was thinking of this when he said to Hawthorne at Southport that he was now prepared for annihilation. Hawthorne had been struck by the spiritual desolation at which his friend had arrived, but he had been struck too by the honesty and courage with which Melville continued to struggle for either a settled belief or a stoic disbelief, and he would have honored, if he had lived to see it, the patience with which Melville worked his way back to some intuition of order and meaning.

He had risen in *Moby Dick* to a tragic and mythic conception of the world and man's place in it; to a conception of the deific principle in nature and the heroic principle in human nature, engaged, both of them, in continuous struggle with the diabolic and the egoistic principles, but retaining their ultimate validity even in apparent loss and defeat. From the height of this conception he had fallen, almost at once, into the abysses of moral nihilism out of which *Pierre* was written; he had succumbed in "Bartleby" to a suicidal acceptance of the immitigable irrationality of all existence; and in *The Confidence Man* he had reached a dead end in the repudiation of all heroism in man and all beneficence in nature. Impossible to move farther in that direction; it was a choice, at that point, between moral self-destruction and toilsome recuperation.

It was of course the latter alternative that Melville chose. When one says "recuperation," however, one does not mean that Melville ever regained the visionary power of *Moby Dick,* any more than he regained the plastic power he had there revealed. The moral and metaphysical insights in all his later work seem, at the best, relatively dim, hesitant, and secondary beside the mythopoeic boldness and grandeur of his greatest book, just as the poetic force of that work seems weaker. Yet the insights one finds there were the harvest of prolonged and serious meditation, however lacking this was in one kind of rigor, and they define for us one of the great possibilities for the mind of Melville's time. What chiefly strikes one in reflecting on them is that, after *The Confidence Man*, Melville gradually recaptured, though on a less lofty level, the doubleness of vision he had adumbrated in the emblem of the Doubloon. He had been the victim, in his malady, of what Hans Castorp calls "counter-positions"—the victim of one-sided and monistic exaggerations; and then he had relearned the truth that "the position of the *Homo Dei*," as Mann says, is in the center, "between recklessness and reason." He had learned again that man must be "the master of counter-positions," must exercise sway over contrarieties, and find the path to true understanding through a transcend-

ence of opposites. This is what the young Syrian monk in
Clarel hears the "whisper intermittent" say to him on the
Mount of Temptation:

> "Content thee: in conclusion caught
> Thou'lt find how thought's extremes agree—
> The forethought clinched by afterthought,
> The firstling by finality."

Already indeed, in *Battle-Pieces*, in the fine poem called
"The Conflict of Convictions," Melville had given this intuition an even more gnomic expression:

> YEA AND NAY—
> EACH HATH HIS SAY;
> BUT GOD HE KEEPS THE MIDDLE WAY.

He himself, it is true, did not always have the courage of
his deepest perceptions: on one level he disappoints us badly
by shrinking from them. He had always been conscious of a
conflict between the mind and the faculty of nonrational insight, between the Understanding and the Reason, as Coleridge would say, or as Melville himself habitually put it, the
"head" and the "heart." Long ago, in a letter to Hawthorne,
he had remarked: "I stand for the heart"; but he had also implied that there need be no ultimate conflict between the
two; and in *Moby Dick* he had intimated a genuine balance
between the heart and the discursive reason. Now, however,
he had lapsed into a thoroughgoing and not always unsenti-
mental irrationalism. One of the few things in *Clarel* about
which there is no uncertainty is the complete and unqualified
rejection of science—"Science the feud can only aggravate"—
and, beyond that, there is a passage in which Rolfe seems to
call into question the serious value of intellectual enlightenment generally. On this ground there is no doubt that Derwent is speaking for Melville when he says to Clarel:

> "My fellow-creature, do you know
> That what most satisfies the head

> Least solaces the heart? Less light
> Than warmth needs earthly wight."

One might imagine that this was but one more of Derwent's cheerful evasions of reality if the whole tenor of the poem were not with him, and if the Epilogue did not make all plain:

> Then keep thy heart, though yet but ill-resigned—
> Clarel, thy heart, the issues there but mind. . . .

There is no denying or mitigating the distrust of the intellect and its works that runs through most of *Clarel*, and no gainsaying that it meant a failure of imagination. Melville was later to recover some of his earlier duality of vision here, and on every other ground, even in *Clarel*, he was faithful to his own intuition of the rightness of the Middle Way. As a result, the view of things he arrived at in these years can only be described in paradoxes. It was an unillusioned humanism, a hopefulness within distrust, a skeptical theism, a spiritualism strongly biased toward the realistic. Duality, in any event, was its essential character, and it is tempting to call it a New Manicheanism.

For Melville, as for the Manicheans, there is nothing illusory in the fact of Evil. Both in the physical and in the moral senses, evil is a final reality, and cannot be conjured away. "Evil is no accident," he says in a prose sketch called "Rammon." "Like good it is an irremovable element." But the good is an irremovable element too; like evil it is a final reality, and what experience seems chiefly to demonstrate to a reflective man is the continuous, complex, mysterious interplay and interaction between these two ultimate principles; there is a paradox at the very heart of life:

> Evil and good they braided play
> Into one cord.

Thus Rolfe in *Clarel*, and thus Melville himself, explicitly or by implication, in everything he now wrote. It is true that in all but his very last writings he reveals a bias toward the contemplation of evil, but that was partly an effect of temperament and partly of a desire to furnish what he once called, in a letter, "a counterpoise to the exorbitant hopefulness, juvenile and shallow, that makes such a bluster in these days." That there is an ultimate principle of good he no longer doubted.

He refused of course to turn his eyes away from the spectacle of moral evil. He refused, as he had always done, to subscribe to the optimistic view of man's nature, the view that man is inherently virtuous and that only "institutions" have corrupted him. He would not be guilty of the folly and the pride of those who chanted the nineteenth-century hymn to man:

> Lodged in power, enlarged in all,
> Man achieves his last exemption—
> Hopes no heaven, but fears no fall,
> King in time, nor needs redemption.

The Calvinism in which Melville had been nurtured had never lost its sway over him on these grounds, and now he certainly shared Ungar's doubt whether any incantation would quite stanch "the ever-upbubbling wickedness." That doubt made him look forward to the future, even in progressive and democratic America, with deep apprehension. Yet only a moment or two after Ungar has thrown out the bitter phrase just quoted, Clarel looks off toward the horizon from the hillside where they are standing, and sees there "one beckoning star." Melville's own final conception of the nature of man was far less purely gloomy, far more "dualistic" than Ungar's:

> Such counter natures in mankind—
> Mole, bird, not more unlike we find:
> Instincts adverse, nor less how true
> Each to itself.

In the years since *The Confidence Man* he had won his way back to a sense of moral light and shade, of the vital contrarieties in the human scene, the eternal intermingling of the heroic and the little, the innocent and the depraved, the noble and the base. He himself would not have left the whole matter just as Derwent does, but it was an aspect of his own thought that he put into the good parson's language: "Man has two sides: keep on the bright."

It was the same radical polarity that he saw in physical nature. Ferocity, malignity, bloodthirstiness—the jackal, the tiger, the scorpion, the shark—he continued until nearly the end to hold that these were as real an expression of the life of nature as what Bryant had fatuously called "Nature's everlasting smile." Yet the meaning of *Moby Dick* had been that beneficence and malignity, destructiveness and creativeness, are somehow mysteriously interinvolved in the natural world, and that it is a tragic error to deny it. In *Clarel*, which abounds in the feeling of nature's cruelty, he comes back to the same theme:

> At variance in their revery move
> The spleen of nature and her love:
> At variance, yet entangled too—
> Like wrestlers.

There is an aspect of nature in which she seems bent only on destruction and death, but there is another aspect, and it is no less real, in which her intention seems rather that of renewal, restoration, and a fresh life. Toward the end of *Clarel* the people of Jerusalem are celebrating the festival of Easter, "the hallelujah after pain," "that Best, the outcome of the Worst," and we are asked not to reproach them for this,

> Since Nature times the same delight,
> And rises with the Emerging One;
> Her passion-week, her winter mood
> She slips, with crape from off the Rood.

There are emblems in nature of hope as well as of despair; in the Epilogue to *Clarel* it is "the crocus budding through the snow"; and in "The Lake" it is the eternal cycle of the seasons, of cold and warmth, of winter and summer:

> Since light and shade are equal set,
> And all revolves, nor more ye know;
> Ah, why should tears the pale cheek fret
> For aught that waneth here below.
> Let go, let go!

What is affirmative in Melville's later thought and work is a Yea-saying of the most reserved and melancholy sort, yet it justifies his own remark in a letter that he was neither an optimist nor a pessimist. The serene trust of a confident religious belief he never achieved, and if he returned in these years to the conception of some transcendent, and not merely immanent, deity, which he was willing to call God, it was a God that he found in none of the creeds that were available to him. It was a God of the most impersonal, inscrutable, and even fearful sort:

> Behind all this still works some power
> Unknowable, thou'lt yet adore.
> *That* steers the world, not man.

It is Mortmain who utters these words, but Melville himself had little doubt of the existence of such a power, and he was hesitantly willing to believe that the crocus budding through the snow or "a swimmer rising from the deep" was a symbolic assurance of immortality:

> Emerge thou mayst from the last whelming sea,
> And prove that death but routs life into victory.

When Melville resigned in the mid-'eighties from his post in the Customs, less than six years of life remained to him. Those years have all the quality of a broadly tranquillizing exodos to a drama that has been riven by trouble and conflict. They were not crowned with honors, as the old age of some of his contemporaries was, but there is something extraordinarily suitable and satisfying to the imagination in the picture they present of touchily guarded solitude and rather grim obscurity. The touchiness and the grimness redeem the tranquillity from mere placidness, and Melville in these years suggests, as he would have liked to do, some almost nameless old man-of-war's man who, after a long life dutifully spent in the maintop amid tempests and sea-fights, has belayed his last halyard and slipped into obscure moorings ashore. There is something a little uncanny about him, to tell the truth, as there is about the old seaman, Daniel Orme, in a sketch of his own, who is rumored to have been in early life a buccaneer. The gossips might well have regarded Melville, as they did Orme, as a *man forbid*, and doubtless there was a quiet leonine droop about the angles of his own mouth that said to approachers: "Hands off." Daniel Orme, at any rate, is found at the end sitting alone and dead against an obsolete battery of rusty guns on a height overlooking the great harbor to whose shore he had moored. With his eyes still open, he faces the outlet to the ocean, his glance fixed on the hazy waters and the dim-seen sails coming and going or at anchor nearer by. It was the posture in which, in every sense but the literal one, Melville himself would finally be found.

Meanwhile, his retirement from official duties was not a withdrawal into mere inaction and death. On the contrary, it was a liberation from the clogs of a routine that had grown increasingly tedious, and it was followed by a short but not unprosperous period of leisured study, reading, and even writing of his own. He had certainly looked forward to liberation on this account. "I have lately come into possession of unobstructed leisure," he wrote to one admirer, "but only just as, in the course of nature, my vigor sensibly declines. What little of it is left I husband for certain matters as yet incomplete, and which indeed may never be completed." Those "matters" must have included the preparation of *John Marr* and *Timoleon* for private publication, the writing of still more poems, and the quite unexpected return to prose fiction with such pieces as "Rammon," which indeed never *was* completed, and *Billy Budd*, which was. These were the affairs that chiefly occupied Melville now, in this not un-vigorous late autumn, as he sat at his large mahogany desk in the rather austerely furnished study in Twenty-sixth Street, with its bleak northward exposure, its cretonne-covered black iron bed, and a wide table in the alcove piled with papers. When he was not at work on his own manuscripts, he was reading—reading the books he had accumulated for so many years and continued to accumulate.

His bookishness, in short, was unabated to the last. But this did not mean, as it would have done with any other man, an eagerness for literary society and literary talk. His need of such things had dwindled almost to the vanishing point. It is true that, in the early eighties, the founders of the Authors' Club, Charles DeKay, Stedman, Brander Matthews, and others, invited him to become a member, and that he at first accepted their invitation. But he very soon repented of this impulse, and wrote to say that he had become too much of a hermit after all and could no longer stand large gatherings. Brander Matthews remembered, even so, that "the shy and elusive Herman Melville" did occasionally drop in at meet-ings of the Club; but these visits doubtless grew rarer and rarer toward the end. It was an eremitism of his own choosing that he practised, and visitors from distant parts were wisely deterred by their friends from intruding on Melville's pri-vacy.

He was difficult to approach, but he was not utterly unap-proachable. Young Arthur Stedman, son of the banker-poet and an admirer of Melville's work, found access to him—the two families lived not far apart—when he went to ask for a portrait to be used in an anthology. Although he was given the impression that such matters were of negligible impor-tance, he was treated with pleasant courtesy. An old man-of-war's man named Peter Toft later claimed to have struck up an acquaintanceship with Melville and to have drawn him into much delightful talk, though he confessed that the elderly author had had to be handled carefully. The one subject he would not be lured into discussing was that of his own writings. "You know more about them than I do," he said to Toft. "I have forgotten them." And to another person who asked to borrow some of his books he replied that he did not happen to own a single copy of them. What he had written meant too much to Melville to be the subject of easy conversation now.

Retired though his life was from formal society, he was by no means literally secluded. A small boy who worked in a bookshop on Nassau Street later remembered an elderly gentleman in a low-crowned hat and a dark blue suit who came into the shop one day and entered into conversation with the proprietor about ships and the sea. His knowledge of such things seemed wide and various, and when he was asked his name, he could only answer that it was Herman Melville. Later, the same small boy was sent from time to time with parcels of books to the house in Twenty-sixth Street, and was not to forget the generous tips that were given him there. A British visitor of the Stedmans', probably Ernest Rhys, refrained from intruding on Melville, but he recalled the glimpses he had had of the old man's grave, preoccupied face. For the rest, Melville was physically active, and almost daily his erect figure was to be seen as he walked with a rapid stride and an almost sprightly gait, dressed in dark blue and carrying a stick, through the streets of the city and particularly in Central Park.

His companion on some of these walks was his small granddaughter, Eleanor, the child of his daughter Frances, who had married and was living in East Orange. The little girl was evidently a favorite of Melville's, and indeed it was a token of the calm he had arrived at that his relations with his grandchildren were happier than those with his own children had ever been. These latter had been darkened and embittered from an early period, for the years when his own four children were small were the years of his greatest misery. All that, however, had now passed, and there was nothing but easy friendliness between the old man and the small girl as they walked about Central Park together on a bright spring afternoon. When the child's gaiety found vent in running down the rocky hillocks, her grandfather, following her more slowly, would call: "Look out, or the 'cop' may catch you!" And though others alleged that he could not be brought to talk about his famous escapades, it was not so with Eleanor, who used to climb on his knee as he sat in an armchair at home, and listen to his wild tales of cannibals and tropic isles.

Except for the child, the only person now who had any reality for him as a companion was his wife. Duyckinck had died in the late 'seventies. Five years later, while Melville was still at work on the piers, his favorite brother, Tom, who had been a ship-captain, had also died. No one really close to him remained except Lizzie, and far apart as they had always been on one plane, they had probably always been close on another; certainly that was true in these mild later years. Nothing but the tenderest concern for him breathes through Lizzie's quiet family letters—"I always try (though I can't succeed to my sorrow) to smooth the fancied rough edges to him wherever I can"—and no one could mistake the depth of affection that expresses itself in the "Clover Dedication" to "Weeds and Wildings" that, in the very last months of his life, remembering their wedding day forty-four years earlier, Melville wrote for his wife. It was of Lizzie, too, he was thinking in the last little poem of the *Timoleon* volume, "The Return of the Sire de Nesle," a poem of homecoming after years of roving that have only proved how terrible is the earth:

> But thou, my stay, thy lasting love
> One lonely good, let this but be!
> Weary to view the wide world's swarm,
> But blest to fold but thee.

The last months of his life were occupied in putting "Weeds and Wildings" together and in finishing, as he did in April 1891, the manuscript of *Billy Budd*. He had not been well during the preceding winter; he had developed a bad cough, and on one bitterly cold January day he had insisted on going for a walk as usual, and on walking, despite his frailness, three-quarters of a mile. The following night he suffered some sort of stroke or heart attack which his physician thought might eventuate fatally. He recovered, however, and Lizzie spoke of him, the next May, as "tolerably well"; but he seems never really to have regained his old vigor, and on September 28th he died quietly in his bed. Tenaciously as he had guarded his obscurity in these autumnal years, he would have been gratified to know that his death went all but unregarded by the world.

There are not many final works that have so much the air as *Billy Budd, Foretopman* has of being a Nunc Dimittis. Everyone has felt this benedictory quality in it. Everyone has felt it to be the work of a man on the last verge of mortal existence who wishes to take his departure with a word of acceptance and reconciliation on his lips.

It was begun, according to Melville's own notes, a little less than three years before his death—begun as a shortish tale, "Baby Budd, Sailor"—and it must have been present to his mind during almost all the time that followed. Discontented with what may have seemed to him the meagerness of the shorter tale, he revised and amplified it to more than twice its original proportions, slowing down its movement but enriching its inner interest, and a few months before he died dismissed it as finished at last. Doubtless he would have had it privately published, as he did the poems, if his health had made this possible.

If there is a great deal of the Nunc Dimittis in the essential feeling of *Billy Budd*, there is a great deal of the Backward Glance in its subject. After so long an interval during which he had lingered over other themes, Melville's mind was turning back more and more in these late years to the sea and to sailors, to thoughts of his own days on a man-of-war and of the men he had known there: happy thoughts of Jack Chase, for example, and grimmer thoughts of the man, whoever he was, whom he represents in *White-Jacket* as the knavish master-at-arms, Bland. *Billy Budd* is dedicated to the memory of Jack Chase, "that great heart," and the character of Claggart is a kind of redoing of the figure of the master-at-arms on the *Neversink*. For the action of his tale, moreover, Melville had turned back to an event that had occurred more than forty years earlier, while he himself was in the South Seas, and that had a curiously personal and poignant association in his own memory. This was the famous case of the brig *Somers*, the American naval vessel on which, in 1842, a young midshipman, Philip Spencer, with a boatswain's mate and a common seaman, had been charged with mutiny and, after being haled before a drumhead court, had been hanged at the yard-arm. A cousin of Melville's, Guert Gansevoort, a few years older than he, the executive officer of the *Somers*, had presided over the court that found young Spencer guilty, and many of the sympathizers with the unfortunate (or reprehensible) midshipman—Fenimore Cooper, among others—regarded Lieutenant Gansevoort as little less to blame for a shocking piece of injustice, as they felt it was, than the commander of the vessel himself. Whether they were right or not, Guert Gansevoort appears to have brooded remorsefully over the incident during the rest of his life; to have been embittered and even broken by it. The case of the brig *Somers* had come home to Melville in an intimate and probably a painful way.

Now, almost half a century after the hanging of Philip Spencer, and more than two decades after Guert Gansevoort's death, Melville's imagination, doubtless reawakened by a magazine article on the old affair, was suddenly stirred to an awareness of what a tale like that of the *Somers* could be

made to signify. For reasons that are easy enough to understand, he placed the action of his story, not on an American
brig in the 'forties, but on a British seventy-four at the end
of the eighteenth century, a short time after the famous
Mutiny at the Nore. All these, however, are matters of the
surface; they have a genuine interest, but they say little about
the real feeling of *Billy Budd*. This feeling is very deep and
very affecting; it triumphs even over the stiff-jointed prose,
the torpidity of the movement, the excess of commentary, and
Melville's failure to quicken any of the scenes with a full
dramatic life. In spite of these blemishes of form and manner, the persons in *Billy Budd* and the moral drama they en-
act have too much largeness, as well as too much subtlety, in
their poetic representativeness, not to leave a permanent
stamp on the imagination.

For the tale of the Handsome Sailor and his unhappy end
has an archetypal depth and scope that no reader can quite
mistake; it is Melville's version of a primordial fable, the
fable of the Fall of Man, the loss of Paradise. There are
vibrations in it of the Book of Genesis, of the *Works and
Days*, of Milton; there are other vibrations that are pure Melville. Billy himself, at any rate, is on one level Primal Man;
he is Adam; indeed, it is said of him that, in the nude, he
"might have posed for a statue of young Adam before the
fall." His physical beauty, certainly, is such as the First Man's
would necessarily be; but so, too, and of course more vitally,
is the purity of his innocence, his incapacity so much as to
imagine evil, his utter freedom from all malice and envy, and
his helplessness in the presence of the wrong. His goodness,
moveover, is not mere blank innocence; it is an active and
disarming *good nature* also, and it draws upon him the spontaneous affection of his mates. But there is a complete absence
from it of any intellectual element whatever; the illiterate
and mindless Billy is "radically" a barbarian. And perfect as
Billy is in the innocence of his heart, he is touched nevertheless by the primordial imperfection of humanity. His stutter

is a symbol of this, and there is a mysterious justice in the fact that this stutter is his undoing.

If Billy is the Adam of this naval Eden, Claggart is of course its Satan. Malign as he is, Claggart, like the great Enemy in *Paradise Lost,* has a certain nobility of form and type. In physical presence, with his tall figure, his shapely forehead, and his curling black hair, he is quite without meanness, and it is only his strangely protuberant chin and his unwholesome pallor of complexion that hint at the depravity of his being. That depravity is inherent and terrible, but it does not express itself in what are called vices or small sins. As a naval officer, Claggart is a model of dutifulness and patriotism, and intellectually he is a man of marked superiority. He is dominated, indeed, by his intellectuality; dominated by it, at any rate, in his *means,* for his aims are mad; with all his "rationality," he is completely exempt, at heart, from the law of reason. Instinctively he hates the good; hates Billy precisely because he is innocent and guileless. In the deepest sense Claggart is a rebel and a traitor, like his great exemplar; a rebel against the law of reason and a traitor to the image of man. There is a Guy Fawkes, as Melville says, prowling in the hid chambers of his nature, and it is wholly suitable that the charge he brings against an innocent man should be the charge of mutiny. It is true that Billy has been guiltless of what he is accused of; guiltless of rebellion and disobedience; but was not that the sin to which Satan tempted the first of men? and is it not fitting that Claggart should now impute it to Billy? There is a strong suggestion of the old serpent in the master-at-arms, and when, after his death, Billy and Captain Vere attempt to raise his body to a sitting posture, "it was like handling a dead snake."

Now that he has struck dead an officer of the Navy, Billy is indeed objectively guilty, under the Mutiny Act, of a crime of exactly the same heinousness as that with which he was falsely charged. It may be that, as the officer of marines protests, Budd *intended* neither mutiny nor homicide; Adam did not *intend* disobedience either, and, as Captain Vere observes, "Budd's intent or non-intent is nothing to the purpose." The Mutiny Act, like war, of which it is the offspring, "looks but to the frontage," and Captain Vere, as the embodiment of naval authority, the Jehovah of the drama, has no choice but to administer, dutifully and grimly, the harsh terms of that Act. In order to do so, he must suppress not only the heart within him but his private conscience: it is the "imperial" conscience, formulated in the Naval Code, under which he officially proceeds. This means adjudging to death a youth toward whom he is drawn emotionally as a father to a son. Imaginably, Billy might *be* his son, for Billy is a foundling and one in whom noble descent is as evident as in a blood horse; and the aristocratic Captain Vere, a bachelor, "was old enough to have been Billy's father." The sacrifice of Billy by Captain Vere is a re-enactment of the sacrifice of Isaac by Abraham, though it is a completed one; and Vere does not turn aside from his duty, anguishing though it is. Billy is hanged at the yard-arm, and Vere, a few months later, mortally wounded by a shot from the *Athéiste*, dies with Billy's name on his lips.

Such is this rewriting of the first three chapters of Genesis, this late-nineteenth-century *Paradise Lost. Billy Budd* owes much of its subliminal effect on the imagination to the fact that it repeats, with variations, that primordial pattern. Yet quite as real as the repetition, and at least as vital, are the variations. There is no Eve in this Eden, for one thing, but far more importantly, the tale does not have, after all, the unequivocal spiritual and moral simplicity of the Christian legend or of any of its theological formulations. It abounds in what Melville himself calls ambiguities; it suggests no unambiguous dogma. There is a strain of irony in it that has no parallel in Genesis or in Milton; it is made explicit in a manuscript sentence that Melville later struck out: "Here ends a story not unwarranted by what sometimes happens in this incomprehensible world of ours—Innocence and infamy, spiritual depravity and fair repute." Unlike the world of theology, Melville's world is insuperably incomprehensible, and he makes no claim to comprehending it.

The drama of the Fall of Man is a drama in which divine and absolute justice is countered by infernal evil in a contest for the immortal soul of God's creature, Man, and in which Man, yielding to the temptation of the evil spirit, turns rebel against God's will, disobeys it, and involves himself and all his posterity in the guilt of Original Sin. Billy, on the contrary, is no rebel against divine justice, and he is not guilty, even symbolically, of disobeying some transcendent will. He is an unwitting, impulsive offender against the Mutiny Act, the child of war, itself an evil and infecting with evil everything that relates to it. Captain Vere makes no mistake about that. To the protest of the officer of marines that Billy intended no mutiny, he replies: "Surely not, my good man. And before a court less arbitrary and more merciful than a martial one that plea would largely extenuate. At the Last Assizes it shall acquit." If there is a divine justice, Billy is innocent in its eyes; he goes to his death as a penalty for breaking a law that has no absolute sanction whatever. His impediment in speech is a symbol of his irreducible imperfection as a man; it is not a symbol of total depravity, and Vere's real feeling about Billy breaks out when, gazing at Claggart's dead body, he cries: "Struck dead by an angel of God."

There is a far more enigmatic intertangling of good and evil in this universe of Melville's final vision than in the universe of theology or of dogmatic ethics: evil and good, as Rolfe had said, do indeed play, braided, into one cord. Billy may be as blameless as Oedipus of any conscious evil intention, yet a malign fate, working upon his inevitable limitations as a human being, brings it about that he commits in fact a capital crime. Meanwhile, Claggart's iniquity, terrible though it is, is not the absolute and transcendent wickedness of the principle of Evil itself, the Evil of the Father of Lies. It is, as Melville insists, "a depravity according to nature," born with him and innate, not the product of training; but it embodies some mysterious principle in human experience that "by no means involves Calvin's dogma as to total mankind." It takes chiefly the form of an instinctive hatred of the innocent and the good, but a hatred so spontaneous and so insane that it suggests a dreadful perversion of love. Claggart's glance, indeed, sometimes follows "belted Billy," moving about the deck, "with a settled meditative and melancholy expression," his eyes strangely suffused with tears. At such moments the diabolic master-at-arms looks like the man of sorrows. "Yes, and sometimes the melancholy expression would have in it a touch of soft yearning, as if Claggart could even have loved Billy but for fate and ban."

It is his miserable destiny, however, to be incapable of loving the good, indeed to be incapable of love itself, and there is no greater misery. For there is a solid reality in this incomprehensible universe, this universe of equivocations and contrarieties; it is the reality of "the heart within you." To mind "the issues there" is to know that, even in the dark midst of evil and hate, goodness exists, and that its essential reality is that of love. Neither goodness nor love can flourish in a nature "dominated by intellectuality," as Claggart's is, and certainly not in a nature like that of the ship's surgeon, with his materialistic, scientific rationalism. They attain their fairest form, perhaps, in a nature as pristine and even primitive as Billy's is, but they are not irrevocably at war with the life of the mind, and indeed they attain their highest form in association with it. Captain Vere is a man with "a marked leaning towards everything intellectual," a passion for books and learning, and a habit of abstracted meditation. Yet he is an image of the high virtue in which the sternest sense of severe and painful duty is united to a capacity for the purest and tenderest love, the love of father for son. And it was in the full imaginative realization of that love, given and received, that Melville brought his work as a writer to its serene conclusion.

After the drumhead court has pronounced its just and inexorable sentence, Captain Vere and Billy have a final interview alone together in the stateroom where Billy is confined. What occurred there was never known, says Melville, but he adds that "the austere devotee of military duty, letting himself melt back into what remains primeval in our formalized humanity, may in the end have caught Billy to his heart even as Abraham may have caught young Isaac. . . . But there is no telling the sacrament . . . wherever . . . two of great Nature's nobler order embrace." Whatever took place in the stateroom between the ideal father and the ideal son, its effect was indeed sacramental, an effect of the purest unction and the most complete reconcilement. When, during the night that follows, the chaplain of the vessel comes upon Billy lying asleep on the upper gundeck, he gazes down on the sleeping countenance and feels that even he, "the minister of Christ," has "no consolation to proffer which could result in a peace transcending that which he beheld." Ishmael, in the end, after so long a banishment, had been taken back to his father's heart. Billy's final words, as he stands the next morning with the noose about his neck, are an expression of rapturous surrender: "God bless Captain Vere!"

Bibliographical Note

WORKS

The only complete collected edition of Melville is still the Standard Edition, 16 vols. (London, 1922-24). A second collected edition, now in course of publication, includes at the present date the following volumes: *Collected Poems*, edited by Howard P. Vincent; *The Piazza Tales*, edited by Egbert S. Oliver; and *Pierre*, edited by Henry A. Murray. Special editions of *Moby Dick* are those by Willard Thorp (1947) and Newton Arvin (1948). There is a corrected version of *Melville's Billy Budd*, edited by F. Barron Freeman (1948). Of travel journals there are three: *Journal of a Visit to London and the Continent*, edited by Eleanor Melville Metcalf (1948); *Journal up the Straits*, edited by Raymond Weaver (1935); and the "Journal of Melville's Voyage in a Clipper Ship," *New England Quarterly*, II (1929), 120-25. A group of letters, inaccurately transcribed, was edited by Meade Minnegerode and published as *Some Personal Letters of Herman Melville and a Bibliography* (1922); corrected versions of most of these letters will be found in *Herman Melville: Representative Selections*, by Willard Thorp (1938). Other letters will be found in *Family Correspondence of Herman Melville*, edited by V. H. Paltsits

(1929); "Some Melville Letters," *Nation and Athenæum*, XXIX (1921), 712-13; John H. Birss, "A Mere Sale to Effect," *New Colophon*, I (1948), 239-55; and S. E. Morison, "Melville's 'Agatha' Letter to Hawthorne," *New England Quarterly*, II (1929), 296-307.

BIOGRAPHY

The first full-length biography of Melville, that by Raymond M. Weaver, *Herman Melville: Mariner and Mystic* (1921), is still valuable; it is supplemented, both in factual detail and in many interpretive insights, by Lewis Mumford's admirable book, *Herman Melville* (1929). The only other full-length biography is Jean Simon's painstaking volume, a doctoral *thèse*, *Herman Melville: Marin, Métaphysicien, et Poète* (Paris, 1939). One period of Melville's career is very fully treated, with the emphasis on ascertainable fact, in *Melville in the South Seas*, by C. R. Anderson (1939). Treatments of special aspects of Melville's life will be found in the following articles: William Charvat, "Melville's Income," *American Literature*, XV (1943), 251-61; Merrell R. Davis, "Melville's Midwestern Lecture Tour, 1859," *Philological Quarterly*, XX (1941), 46-57; William H. Gilman, "Melville's Liverpool Trip," *Modern Language Notes*, LXI (1946), 543-47; Wilson L. Heflin, "Melville's Third Whaler," *Modern Language Notes*, LXIV (1949), 241-45; Ida Leeson, "The Mutiny on the *Lucy Ann*," *Philological Quarterly*, XIX (1940), 370-79; Jay Leyda, "The Army of the Potomac Entertains a Poet," *Twice a Year* (1948), 259-72; Luther S. Mansfield, "Glimpses of Herman Melville's Life in Pittsfield," *American Literature*, IX (1937), 26-48; Merton M. Sealts, "Herman Melville's 'I and My Chimney,'" *American Literature*, XIII (1941), 142-54; Willard Thorp, "Herman Melville's Silent Years," *University Review*, III (1937), 254-62.

WHALES AND WHALING

Among the books on whales and whaling that Melville certainly read were the *Narrative of the Most Extraordinary and Distressing Shipwreck of the Whale-Ship Essex,* by Owen Chase (1821), the *Journal of a Voyage to the Northern Whale Fishery,* by William Scoresby, Jr. (1823), *The History of the Sperm Whale,* by Thomas Beale (1839), *Etchings of a Whaling Cruise,* by J. Ross Browne (1846), and *The Whale and His Captors,* by Henry T. Cheever (1850). He all but certainly read J. N. Reynolds's article, "Mocha Dick: or the White Whale of the Pacific," in the *Knickerbocker Magazine* (May 1839). The best recent books on American whaling are *The American Whaleman,* by Elmo Paul Hohman (1928), and *Lowered Boats,* by Rhea Foster Dulles (1933). There is also an excellent chapter on the subject in *The Maritime History of Massachusetts,* by Samuel Eliot Morison (1921).

CRITICISM

The introduction to *Herman Melville: Representative Selections,* by Willard Thorp, is interesting both biographically and critically. D. H. Lawrence's chapters in *Studies in Classic American Literature* (1923) are unsurpassed in their own apocalyptic vein. A similar manner is attempted in *Call Me Ishmael,* by Charles Olson (1947), and there are important biographical materials in Olson's book. K. H. Sundermann's *Herman Melvilles Gedankengut* (Berlin, 1937), another dissertation, is more relentlessly systematic than the subject will bear, but despite this it is not without valuable particular insights. William Ellery Sedgwick's *Herman Melville: The Tragedy of Mind* (1944) is a study of Melville's thought rather than of his literary characteristics, but as such it is serious and suggestive. More purely literary are the excellent chapters on Melville in F. O. Matthiessen's *American Renais-*

sance (1941). Other essays, interesting either in the strictly critical or in the scholarly sense, are: W. H. Auden, "The Christian Tragic Hero," *New York Times Book Review*, Dec. 16, 1945; Van Wyck Brooks, "Notes on Herman Melville," *Emerson and Others* (1927); Merrell R. Davis, "The Flower Symbolism in *Mardi*," *Modern Language Quarterly*, II (1941), 625-38; Wilson L. Heflin, "The Source of Ahab's Lordship Over the Level Loadstone," *American Literature*, XX (1948), 323-27; Robert Penn Warren, "Melville the Poet," *Kenyon Review*, VIII (1946), 208-23; E. L. G. Watson, "Melville's *Pierre*," *New England Quarterly*, III (1930), 195-234; R. E. Watters, "Melville's Sociality," *American Literature*, XVII (1945), 33-49. More perceptive than most criticism in prose is Mr. W. H. Auden's poem, "Herman Melville," in *Another Time*.

Index

Index